EFFECTIVE EXECUTIVE'S

The Seven Core Skills Required to Turn Excel into a Business Power Tool

GUIDE TO EXCEL 2002

EFFECTIVE EXECUTIVE'S GUIDE TO EXCEL 2002

The Seven Core Skills Required to Turn Excel into a Business Power Tool

David B. Maguiness
Stephen L. Nelson

REDMOND TECHNOLOGY PRESS

Effective Executive's Guide to Excel 2002:
The Seven Core Skills Required to Turn Excel into a Business Power Tool

Published by
Redmond Technology Press
8581 154th Avenue NE
Redmond, WA 98052
www.redtechpress.com

Library of Congress Catalog Card No: applied for

ISBN 1-931150-08-7
Printed and bound in the United States of America.

9 8 7 6 5 4 3 2 1

Distributed by
Independent Publishers Group
814 N. Franklin St.
Chicago, IL 60610
www.ipgbook.com

In the preparation of this book, both the author and the publisher have made every effort to provide current, correct, and comprehensible information. Nevertheless, inadvertent errors can occur and software and the principles and regulations concerning business often change. Furthermore, the application and impact of principles, rules, and laws can vary widely from case to case because of the unique facts involved. For these reasons, the author and publisher specifically disclaim any liability or loss that is incurred as a consequence of the use and application, directly or indirectly, of any information presented in this book. If legal or other expert assistance is needed, the services of a professional should be sought.

To Sue, Beth and Britt—Thanks for cheerfully letting me disappear for the days it took to do my part of this book, SLN.

To Karen, Kyle, and Ty—DBM.

Acknowledgments

Special thanks to our project editor, Paula Thurman, our proofer, Fred Lanigan, and our desktop publisher, Minh-Tam S. Le—SLN

Many thanks to the entire Redmond Technology Press team who helped make this book possible—DBM

Contents at a Glance

Contents

INTRODUCTION

Welcome to the *Effective Executive's Guide to Excel 2002,* the essential Microsoft Excel reference for executives, managers, and professionals. *Effective Executive's Guide to Excel 2002* was created to address the specific needs of professionals who use Excel to accomplish common business tasks. If you need to learn Excel quickly, or polish your skills for Excel, this book can help you achieve these goals.

Is This Book for You?

Effective Executive's Guide to Excel 2002 addresses topics of interest to executives new to Excel or unfamiliar with Excel. If you need to learn how to use Excel features, such as creating, saving, and reopening worksheets; sharing and sending worksheets in a network environment or on the Internet; and want to investigate the Small Business Financial Manager, then this book is for you. *Effective Executive's Guide to Excel 2002* can get you quickly up to speed on all these tasks and more.

If you are a financial analyst or accounting professional, however, you may find the *MBA's Guide to Excel 2002* more appropriate for your needs. The *MBA's Guide to Excel 2002* includes the same chapters as this book and adds information of interest to those in the finance and accounting fields, such as thorough coverage of financial functions, statistical functions, and templates for common business analysis, including break-even analysis, cash flow statements, depreciation schedules, forecasting sales, and so forth. The *MBA's Guide to Excel 2002* also includes a CD-ROM of the worksheets described in the chapters.

What Do You Need to Use This Book?

To use this book effectively, we assume you are a knowledgeable and informed executive who has experience using the Microsoft Windows operating system and Windows applications. You should know how to use a mouse and how to choose commands from menus and use tools on toolbars. You should also understand basic mathematical operations. We also assume from time to time you may need additional details that are included as appropriate.

What's in This Book?

This book contains the following skill-building steps:

Skill 1: Excel Basics

Skill 1 teaches you Excel basics, such as starting and stopping the program, creating worksheets by entering labels and values, using functions and creating formulas, and editing and formatting your worksheets.

Skill 2: Charting

Skill 2 explains how to create and customize charts based on the data in your worksheets.

Skill 3: Databases

Skill 3 introduces you to Excel's database capabilities and how you can put them to work for you.

Skill 4: Business Modeling

Skill 4 describes how to use data tables, Goal Seek and Scenario Manager for what-if analysis and how to use Solver for optimization modeling.

Skill 5: Share Workbooks

Skill 5 is of interest to executives who share workbooks through their organization's network, e-mail, and the Internet. You also learn how to use data from a source other than Excel, thereby saving you time and effort.

Skill 6: PivotTables and PivotCharts

Skill 6 introduces you to Excel's PivotTable feature and shows you how to view the data in your worksheet from other important perspectives.

Skill 7: Small Business Financial Manager

Skill 7 discusses the Small Business Finance Manager included with Microsoft Office to extract data from your accounting system and then perform financial analysis.

A glossary is also included with common Excel terms.

Conventions Used in This Book

We follow Microsoft convention and refer to an Excel file as a *workbook,* which contains one or more *worksheets.* We also include Notes, Tips, and Warnings, which draw attention to small bits of useful information. In particular, pay close attention to Warnings as they help you avoid potential problems.

Skill 1

EXCEL BASICS

Featuring:

- Workbook Basics
- Using Formulas and Functions
- Editing Workbook Data
- Formatting Workbooks
- Printing Workbooks

This chapter provides a primer on Excel—which means you may not need to read this chapter if you possess a lot of experience using Excel. If your Excel skills could use a little polishing, however, or if you've never used Excel, read this chapter to learn how Excel works.

NOTE *With the information provided by this chapter and the next one, you could handily pass the Microsoft Office User Specialist (MOUS) certification at the proficient user level and perhaps even the expert user level. You might not be interested in receiving this certification yourself, but it is useful to understand just what knowledge is required to receive this certification. MOUS certification may be relevant for hiring and training decisions you make.*

Workbook Basics

If you're new to Excel, you'll benefit most from a quick tour of Excel, including how you start Excel, work with its windows, and create and save a workbook. That's what we'll do here.

NOTE *This discussion assumes you're comfortable working with Microsoft Windows. You should know, for example, how to start and stop programs, choose commands, and work with dialog boxes.*

Starting Excel

You can start Excel either by starting the program directly or by opening an existing Excel workbook. To start Excel directly, click the Start button, choose Programs, and then choose Microsoft Excel. When you do this, Excel starts and opens a blank workbook.

To open an Excel workbook—which indirectly starts Excel—double-click an Excel workbook file (which has an icon with a green x and, if you're viewing file extensions, has the extension .XLS) in the My Computer or Windows Explorer window. If you've recently used the file, you can also open it from the Documents menu by clicking the Start button, choosing Documents, and choosing the Excel file you want to open. When you do this, Excel starts and opens the workbook you selected.

Working with the Excel Windows

The Excel program looks and works very much like other Microsoft application programs and especially Microsoft Office programs.

Reviewing Excel's Geography

When you start Excel, the Excel program displays the Excel application window, or program window. Inside this application window, Excel typically displays one or more document windows, or workbook windows. Figure 1-1 shows how your screen looks after you start Excel and includes some callouts to point out features of the Excel program window that may be new to you.

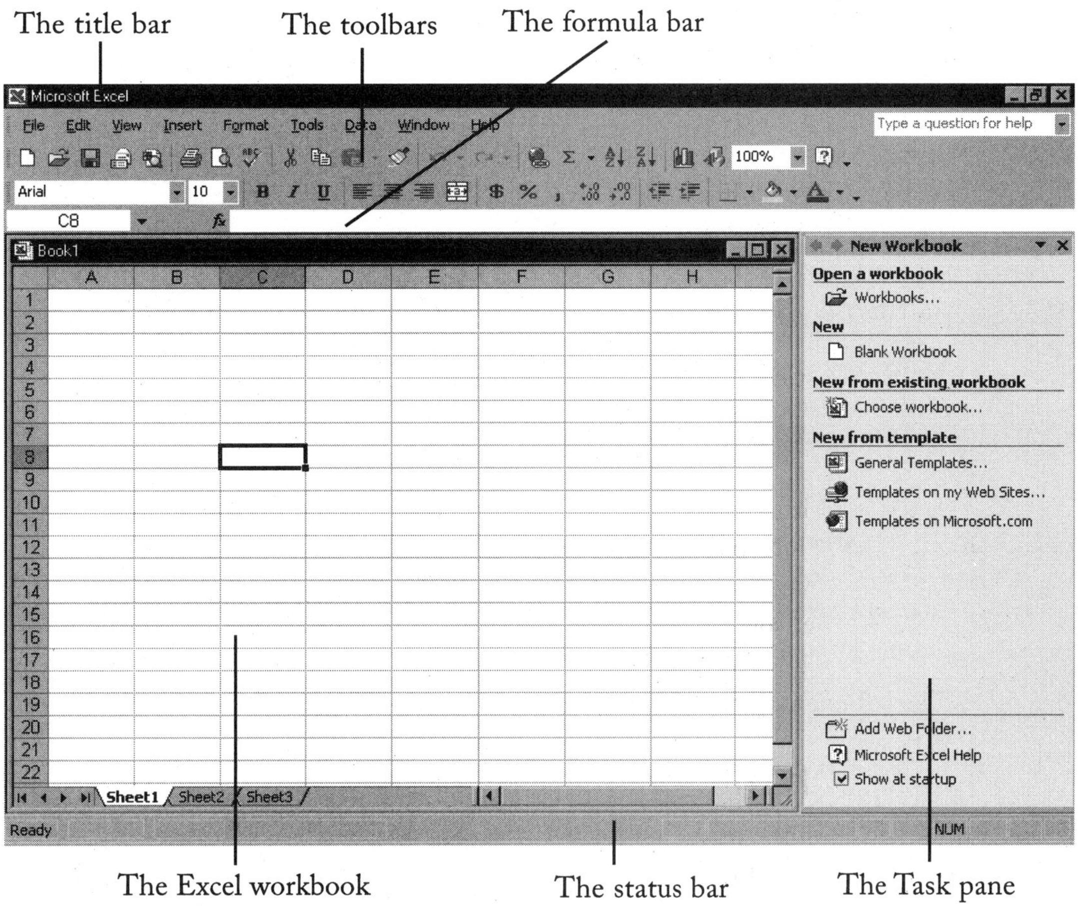

Figure 1-1 The Excel program with an Excel workbook.

The program window is the rectangle in which the Excel program displays its information. The Microsoft Excel title bar and menu bar appear at the top of the program window. The toolbar or toolbars, located just below the menu bar, provide a series of buttons that allow for faster selection of frequently used menu commands.

NOTE *Excel can personalize the menus and toolbars to show only the commands or buttons you most frequently use. If you have Excel set up to do this, and don't see a command you're looking for on a menu, click the double arrows at the bottom of the menu. Likewise, if you don't see a toolbar button on a toolbar, click the double arrows at the end of the toolbar.*

The formula bar displays the data you enter in your worksheet. At the bottom of the application window, the status bar displays a variety of messages, such as "Ready." The Excel workbook document appears in the area between the formula bar and the status bar.

The window on the right side of the workbook window is the Task pane. The Task pane provides you easy access to Workbook, Clipboard, and Search capabilities. You select one of these functions by clicking the Other Task Panes button in the upper right corner of the Task pane. If you want to close the Task pane, click the Close button in the upper right corner. From Excel's menu bar, choose View, choose Toolbars, and then choose Task Pane to redisplay the Task pane.

When you start Excel, it automatically opens an empty workbook file called Book1 that contains three pages, or worksheets. These pages are indicated by the tabs Sheet1, Sheet2, and Sheet3 at the bottom of the window.

NOTE *If you start Excel by opening an existing workbook, Excel displays that workbook in a window. It doesn't open an empty new workbook.*

In a worksheet, the letters of the alphabet identify each of the 256 columns. Excel uses double letters for columns 27 through 256.

The left edge of the document window identifies each row in your worksheet using numbers. An Excel worksheet can have up to 65,536 rows.

The intersection of a column and row is called a *cell.* Each cell has an address, called a *reference,* consisting of the column letter and row number. For example, the cell in the top left corner of the worksheet is cell A1.

A dark outline called the *cell selector* identifies the active cell. Figure 1-1 shows the cell selector in cell C8. The reference of the active cell also appears on the left side of the formula bar in the Name box. If you type a number and press the Enter key, Excel places the number in the active cell.

Moving Around a Workbook

With three (or more) sheets, 256 columns, and 65,536 rows, an Excel workbook is so large that only a small area is visible on screen at one time. Not surprisingly, Excel provides several ways for you to view different portions of the workbook displayed in the program window:

- With the mouse, you can use the vertical and horizontal scroll bars along the right and bottom edges of the document window to move through your worksheet. Just click inside the scroll bars to move one screen at a time. Click the scroll bar arrows to move one row or column.

- With the mouse, click a sheet tab to move to that worksheet in the workbook.
- The standard navigation keys, Page Up and Page Down, move through your worksheet one screen at a time. When you hold down the Ctrl key and press Page Up or Page Down, you move to the next or previous worksheet.
- The arrow keys move up and down, right and left one cell at a time. You can also move to the right one cell by pressing the Tab key; you can move to the left one cell by holding down the Shift key while pressing the Tab key.
- To move directly to a specific cell, enter that cell's name in the Name box and press the Enter key. (The Name box is located at the left end of the formula bar.) You can also choose the Edit menu's Go To command. When you choose this command, Excel displays the Go To dialog box. You can enter a cell reference in its Reference text box and then click OK to move to the cell.

Finding Help When You Need It

Excel, like other Microsoft Office programs, provides an animated character called the Office Assistant to answer any questions you may have. If you see the Office Assistant on your screen, click it to ask it a question. If you don't see the Office Assistant, choose the Help menu's Show The Office Assistant command. The Office Assistant displays a balloon you can use to enter your question, as shown in Figure 1-2. Just type your question, and click Search. The Office Assistant displays a list of topics related to your search. Click a topic to display the Microsoft Excel Help window with details on the topic you chose.

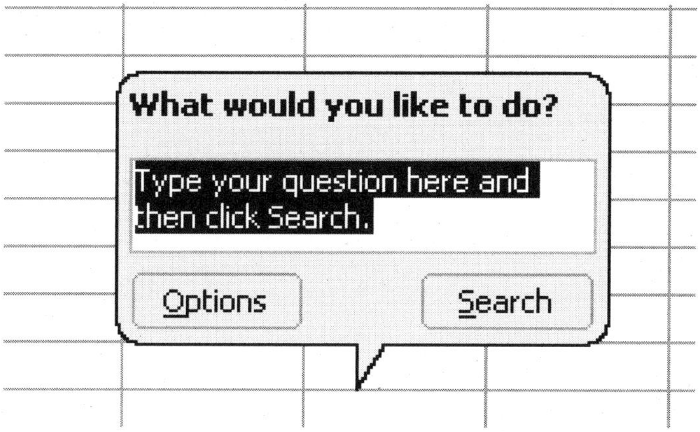

Figure 1-2 Asking the Office Assistant a question.

If the Help window doesn't answer your question, click its Show button. This displays the Contents, Answer Wizard, and Index tabs, as shown in Figure 1-3. Use the Contents tab to navigate through the help file the way you would navigate through a book by using its table of contents. Use the Answer Wizard tab to ask a question in a manner similar to the way in which you ask the Office Assistant a question. Use the Index tab to look up a keyword or phrase the way you would look up a word in a book's index.

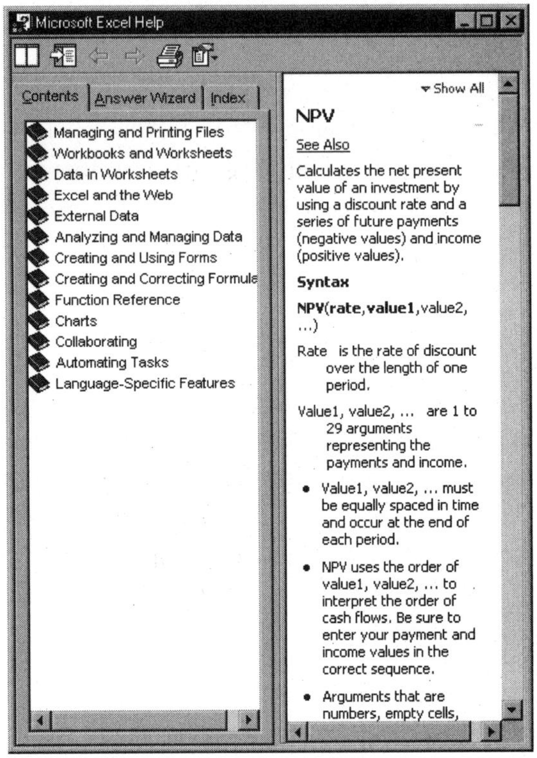

Figure 1-3 The Excel Help window.

Creating a Simple Workbook

To use Excel, you simply enter labels, values, and formulas in the cells of your worksheets. To construct a simple budgeting worksheet, for example, you would enter a handful of labels, values, and formulas.

NOTE *We're postponing a discussion of formulas for a few pages. Formulas and a related topic, functions, are described in detail in the chapter section "Using Formulas and Functions."*

Entering Labels

Labels are simply any information entered in a worksheet that you don't want to manipulate arithmetically. They often identify the values that are subject to calculation, so you normally enter them as the first stage in setting up a worksheet. Usually, labels are pieces of text, such as the expense categories in a budgeting worksheet or the employee names in a payroll worksheet. However, they can also be numbers that won't be used arithmetically, such as telephone numbers or part or project ID numbers.

To enter a label, follow these steps:

1. **Move the cell selector to the desired location.**

   You can do this by clicking the cell, using the navigation keys to move the cell selector, or using the Name box.

2. **Type the label.**

   As you do, Excel displays what you type in the formula bar. It also adds the Enter button (the one that looks like a check mark) and the Cancel button (the one that looks like an X) to the formula bar.

3. **Set the label in the cell.**

   You can do this by pressing the Enter key, clicking the Enter button on the formula bar, or moving to another cell.

Figure 1-4 shows a simple workbook fragment with just a handful of labels. Notice that Excel aligns text to the left edge of each cell and allows long labels to spill over into adjacent cells if they are unoccupied.

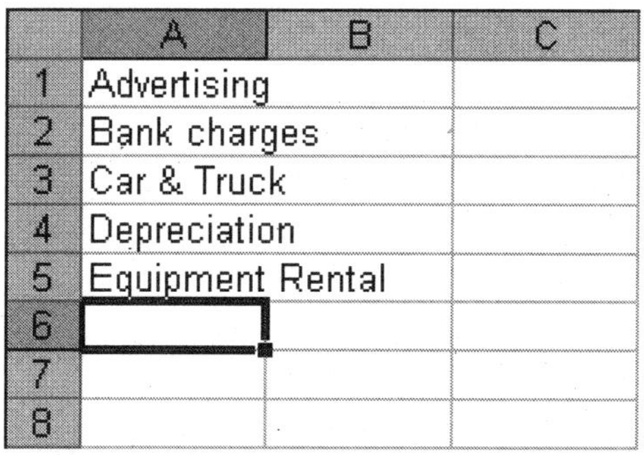

Figure 1-4 A worksheet with labels entered.

Entering Values

Values are numbers you want to add, subtract, multiply, divide, or otherwise manipulate in formulas. In a budgeting worksheet, for example, you would enter the budgeted amounts as values. Figure 1-5 shows the values, or amounts, entered beside each of the worksheet labels.

	A	B	C
1	Advertising		500
2	Bank charges		50
3	Car & Truck		500
4	Depreciation		2000
5	Equipment Rental		250
6			
7			
8			

Figure 1-5 A budgeting worksheet with labels and values.

To enter values, use the ten number keys either on the main keyboard or on the numeric keypad. To use the numeric keypad, the Num Lock key must be selected. Use the period key to show decimal places and the hyphen key to identify negative values.

To enter values, use the same three-step process you use to enter labels. For example, to enter the value 500 shown in cell C1, follow these steps:

1. **Move the cell selector to the desired cell.**

   In Figure 1-5, for example, you move the cell selector to C1 to enter the first value. You might do this by clicking.

2. **Type the value.**

   As you do, Excel displays the number in the formula bar. It also adds the Enter and Cancel buttons to the formula bar.

3. **Set the value in the cell.**

   As with setting a label, you can do this by pressing the Enter key, clicking the Enter button on the formula bar, or moving to another cell.

To enter the rest of the values shown in Figure 1-5, repeat the steps above for each value.

If a value is too large to fit into a single cell, Excel either increases the cell width or displays the cell contents using scientific notation. The number 123456789, for example, may appear as something like 1.2E+08 or 1.235E+08, depending on the width of the cell. Likewise, the number .0000001 may appear as something like 1E-07.

NOTE *Excel doesn't discard the extra digits if they don't fit in the cell. If you select the cell, you can see all the digits in the formula bar. Excel doesn't include characters such as dollar signs, percentage symbols, or commas as a part of a value (you can tell this by looking at the formula bar), but Excel does use these characters when it displays values in the worksheet. One exception to this rule concerns extremely large or extremely small values. Excel uses only the first 15 digits of a value. If you enter a value that uses more than 15 digits, Excel rewrites the value using only 15 digits. If the value uses more than 20 digits, Excel rewrites the value using scientific notation. If the value uses more than 15 digits but less than 20 digits, Excel replaces the sixteenth digit through the twentieth digit (counting from left to right) with zeros and then drops the zeros if they aren't significant. For example, the value 12345678901234567890 is rewritten to 12345678901234500000. And the value .12345678901234567890 is rewritten to .123456789012345.*

Correcting Typing Mistakes

Excel cells work like the text boxes you see elsewhere in Windows. This means that it's easy to correct any typing mistakes you make. If you make typing mistakes before setting a label or value in a cell, for example, you can use the Backspace key to erase characters to the left of the insertion point (the cursor) and then retype the correct data. You can also reposition the insertion point in the formula bar with the arrow keys and erase characters to the right with the Delete key. If you don't want to enter the data shown on the formula bar in the active cell, click the Cancel button or press the Esc key.

If you make a mistake but don't realize it until you set the label or value in the cell, move the cell selector to the cell with the erroneous content. To replace the cell's contents entirely, enter a new label or value. To edit the cell's contents, either click the formula bar or double-click the cell. Use the Backspace key to erase characters to the left of the insertion point and then retype the correct data (or reposition the insertion point with the arrow keys, erase characters to the right with the Delete key, and then retype the correct data). When the formula bar or editable text box over the cell shows the correct label or value, set it in the active cell by moving the cell selector to another cell, pressing the Enter key, or clicking Enter in the formula bar.

Saving and Opening Workbooks

To save the work you do with Excel, you save the workbooks you create. To later reuse a workbook, you open it. Neither task is difficult if you've worked with Windows a bit.

Saving Your Work for the First Time

When you first save a workbook, you must give it a name and tell Excel where to store it. If you've worked with other Windows programs, you'll find the procedure quite familiar. To save a workbook for the first time, follow these steps:

1. Choose the File menu's Save As command.

Excel displays the dialog box shown in Figure 1-6.

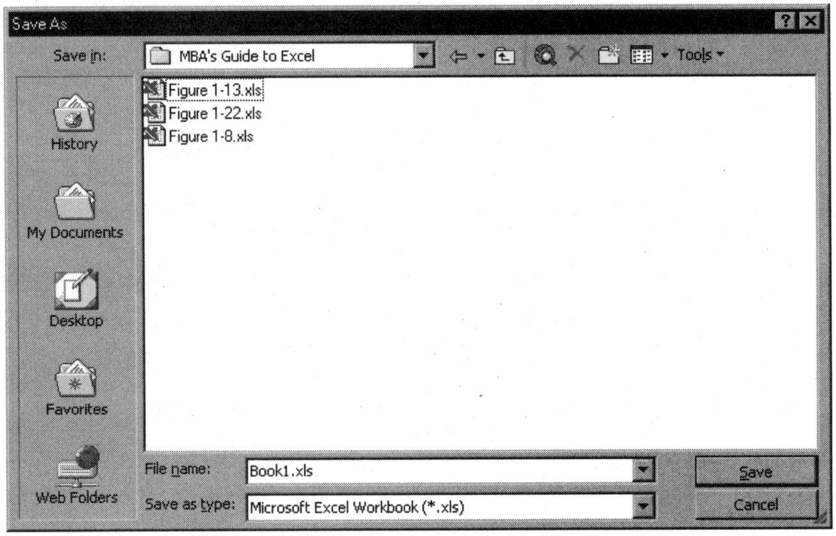

Figure 1-6 The Save As dialog box.

2. Choose a folder location for the new workbook.

To save the file in a common location for documents, click one of the icons on the left side of the Save As dialog box. For example, to save the file to the Windows desktop, click the Desktop icon. If you have Windows 95 or 98, click the My Documents icon to save the file to the default storage location for Office documents. (If you have Windows NT, click the Personal icon.) To save the file to a location other than one designated by an icon (such as a network drive), use the Save In drop-down list box and the large list box below to select the drive and folder location.

TIP *Use the Up One Level toolbar button to move up from a subfolder to its parent folder.*

3. **Name the workbook.**

   Enter a name for the file in the File Name text box. You don't need to add a file extension—Excel automatically does this for you. Excel allows you to enter very long filenames if you want, but if you do use long names, make sure that the first few characters clearly identify the workbook so it is easy to find later on.

4. **Select a file format from the Save As Type drop-down list box.**

   If you're the only one who will be using the file, accept the default format, Microsoft Excel Workbook. If you'll be sharing the file with other people, select the format they'll be using or select a format that both you and any other user can read, such as a tab-delimited or comma-delimited file.

NOTE *Selecting such a file type other than the Excel workbook format may result in the loss of formatting and functionality.*

5. **Click Save.**

   Excel saves the file in the specified location and format using whatever name you choose.

TIP *If you click the Tools button in the Save As dialog box and choose General Options, you can enter a password required to open or modify the file.*

Resaving Your Work

To save a file again and replace the previous file, click the Save toolbar button or choose the File menu's Save command. To save a file under a different name, in a different location, or in a different format, and retain the previous file, choose the File menu's Save As command. Use the Save As dialog box to specify a new name, location, or format.

Opening Workbooks

To open a workbook, follow these steps:

1. **Click the Open toolbar button.**

   Excel displays the Open dialog box shown in Figure 1-7.

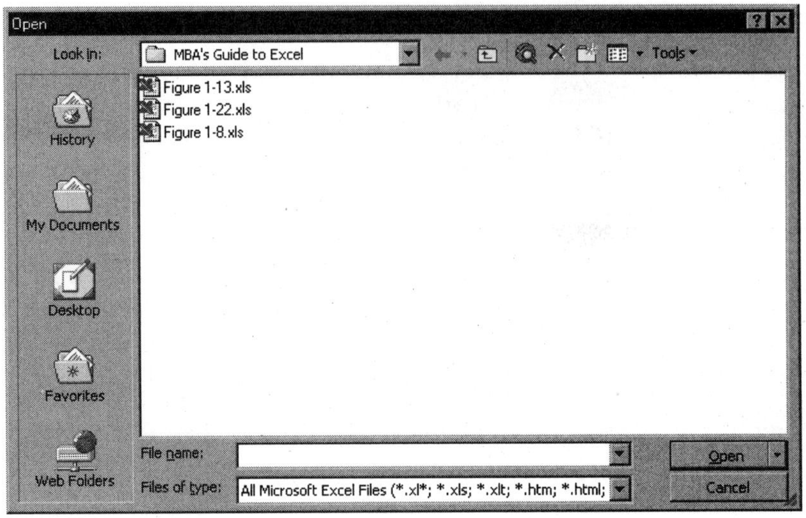

Figure 1-7 The Open dialog box.

2. **Open the folder storing the file.**

   Use the icons along the left side, the Save In drop-down list box, and the list box of folders and files to locate the file.

3. **Select the workbook.**

   After you find the workbook you want to open, select it by clicking it.

4. **Click Open.**

   Excel retrieves the file from the specified location and displays it in another document window inside the Excel program window.

TIP *Excel allows you to open multiple workbooks, displaying each in its own document window, or workbook window. To move to another document window, or workbook window, choose the workbook from the Window menu.*

Using File Properties

If you choose the File menu's Properties command, Excel displays a dialog box that describes the workbook. The Properties dialog box, which isn't shown here, also lets you collect and store information about the workbook. Excel users who create or share numerous workbooks may find it useful to explore this command and its dialog box on their own.

Exiting the Program

To exit Excel, you can click the Close button (the one with an X) in the upper right corner of the Excel program window. You can also choose the File menu's Exit command.

When you exit Excel, you are asked whether you want to save any workbooks with unsaved changes. If you indicate that you want to save your changes, Excel saves the workbooks.

Using Formulas and Functions

Excel's power stems from its ability to perform calculations on the values you've stored in a workbook—something you do with *formulas* and *functions*. This section describes how to construct formulas, use Excel's predefined formulas, called functions, and use range names in formulas. It also shows how to open saved workbooks.

Entering Formulas

Excel calculates formulas automatically. You enter them in a worksheet cell in the same way that you enter labels and values. In the cell, however, Excel displays not the formula, but its result. For example, if you enter a formula that says to add 4 and 2, Excel retains the formula and displays it in the formula bar when the cell is selected, but Excel displays the result, 6, in the worksheet itself.

Formula Fundamentals

Formulas must begin with the equal sign (=); that's how Excel distinguishes them from values and labels. You can construct formulas that subtract, multiply, divide, and exponentiate. The – symbol means subtraction, the * means multiplication, the / means division, and the ^ means exponential operation. Table 1-1 shows the different mathematical operators and the results they return.

FORMULA ENTERED	RESULT DISPLAYED IN CELL
=4+2	6
=4-2	2
=4*2	8
=4/2	2
=4^2	16

Table 1-1 A list of simple formulas illustrating the standard arithmetic operators.

Figure 1-8 shows a simple budgeting worksheet built from Figure 1-5. The formula used in cell C7 appears in the formula bar and the result is displayed in the worksheet.

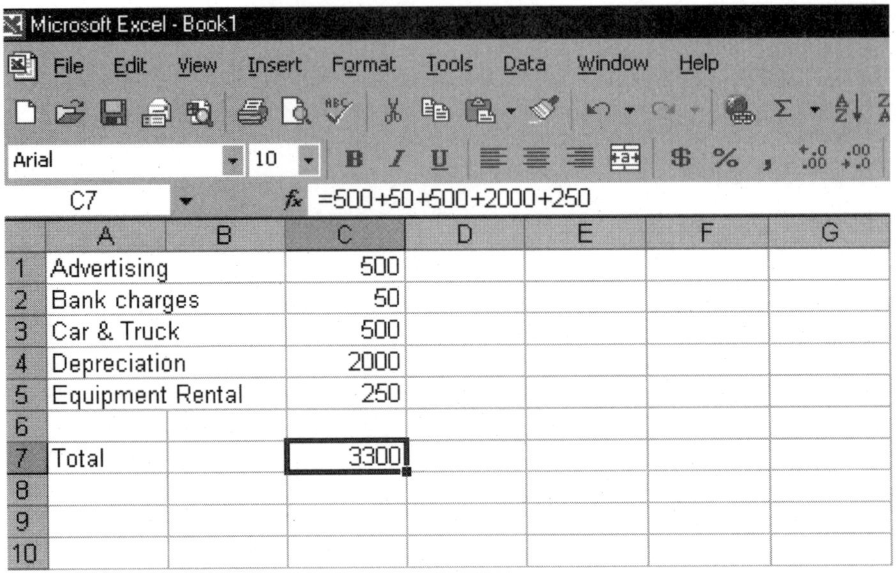

Figure 1-8 A budgeting worksheet with a formula entered and the result displayed.

To build more complicated formulas, you need to recognize the standard rules of operator precedence: Excel first performs exponential operations, then multiplication and division operations, and finally, addition and subtraction.

For example, in the equation =1+2*3^4, Excel first raises 3 to the fourth power to get 81. It then multiplies this value by 2 to get 162. Finally, it adds 1 to this value to get 163.

To override these rules, you must use parentheses. You can use multiple sets of parentheses in a formula as need be. Excel first performs the function in the innermost set of parentheses. Take the following formulas in Table 1-2 as an example:

FORMULA ENTERED	RESULT DISPLAYED IN CELL
=1+2*3^4	163
=(1+2)*3^4	243
=((1+2)*3)^4	6561

Table 1-2 A list of formulas that show how parentheses override operator procedure.

Using Cell References

In the budgeting worksheet, you could total the budgeted expenses by entering the formula =500+50+500+2000+250 in cell C7. There is, however, a practical problem with this approach: You would need to rewrite the formula each time any of the values changed. Because this approach is unwieldy, Excel also allows you to use cell references in formulas.

When a formula includes a cell reference, Excel uses the value that cell contains. For example, to add the budgeted amounts on your budgeting worksheet using a formula with cell references, follow these steps:

1. **Move the cell selector to C7.**

   You can do this by clicking cell C8. Or you can use the arrow keys.

2. **Type =C1+C2+C3+C4+C5.**

   If you make a mistake entering this formula, you can edit it in the same way that you edit any label or value.

3. **Press the Enter key, or click the Enter button.**

   Excel enters your formula in the cell, calculates the formula, and then displays the formula result.

To reference a cell on the same worksheet as the formula, you need to supply only the column-letter-and-row-number cell reference. To reference cell C1 on the same worksheet, for example, you enter C1.

You can also reference cells on other worksheets. To reference a cell on another worksheet in the same workbook, however, you need to precede the cell reference with the name of the worksheet and an exclamation point symbol. To reference cell C1 on the worksheet named Sheet2, for example, you enter Sheet2!C1.

You can reference cells in other workbooks, too. To do this most easily, open the other workbooks, begin building your formula as described earlier in this chapter, and then click the other workbook cell you want to reference at the point you want to include the reference. Excel then writes the full cell reference for you, which includes the workbook name. An external reference to cell C1 on the worksheet named Sheet2 in the workbook named Budget might be written as =[Budget.xls]Sheet2!$C$1.

Understanding Worksheet Recalculation

As you build and edit your worksheet, Excel automatically updates the formulas and recalculates their results. For example, in the budgeting worksheet, if you change the value in cell C1 from 500 to 600, Excel recalculates any formulas that use the value stored in cell C1. As a result, the formula in cell C7 returns the value 3400—an increase of one hundred.

In simple worksheets such as the one shown in Figure 1-9, recalculation takes place so quickly you won't even be aware it's occurring. In larger worksheets with hundreds or even thousands of formulas, however, recalculation is much slower. The mouse pointer changes to the hourglass symbol when Excel is busy recalculating.

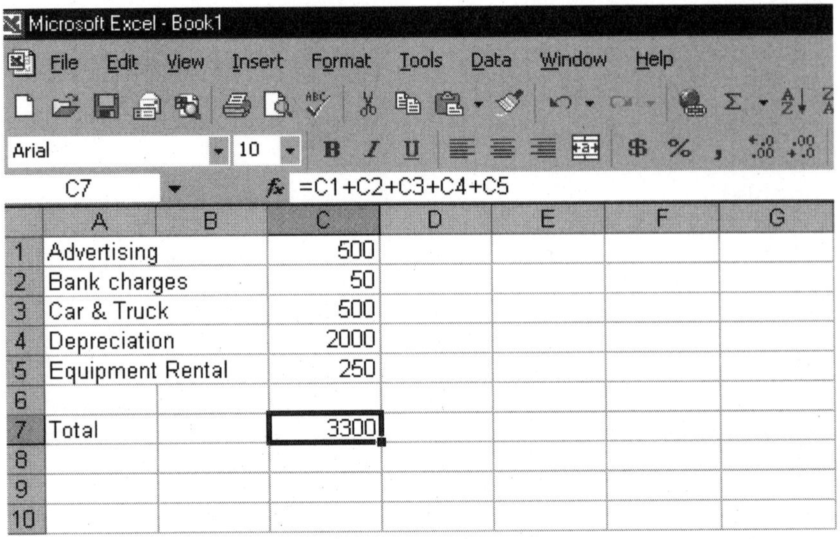

Figure 1-9 A worksheet with cell references used in a formula.

If you don't want Excel to automatically recalculate formulas as you're working, choose the Tools menu's Options command and click the Calculation tab. Then click the Manual option button under Calculation, and click OK. The word *Calculate* appears on the status bar when your worksheet needs to be recalculated. You can force recalculation by pressing the F9 key.

Formula Errors

It's possible to build an illogical or unsolvable formula. When you do, Excel displays an error message in the cell rather than calculating the result. The error message, which begins with the # symbol, describes the error. Suppose, for example, that you enter the formula =1/0 in a cell. Because division by zero is an undefined mathematical operation, Excel can't solve the formula. To alert you to this, Excel displays the error message #DIV/0!.

Another common error is a circular reference. This occurs when two or more formulas indirectly depend on one another to achieve a result. For example, if the formula in cell A1 is =A2 and the formula in cell A2 is =A1+A3+A4, A1 depends on A2 and A2 depends on A1. Excel displays a warning and the Circular Reference toolbar when you create a circular reference. Excel identifies circular references by displaying the word *Circular* on the status bar and showing the address of the cell whose formula completed the "circle." It also draws arrows between the cells causing the circle.

To fix a formula error, edit the erroneous formula using the same techniques as with label and value editing. Move the cell selector to the cell holding the formula, click the formula bar, and edit the formula. When the formula is correct, set it by moving the cell selector, pressing the Enter key, or clicking the Enter button.

NOTE *When a formula refers to a cell that contains an erroneous formula, both formulas return the error message. For example, if cell A1 attempts to divide by zero and cell A2 refers to cell A1, cell A2 returns the error message #DIV/0! as well.*

Using Functions

Excel provides several hundred pre-built formulas, called functions, that provide a shortcut to constructing complicated or lengthy formulas. In general, a function accepts input values, or arguments, then makes some calculation and returns a result.

Excel provides financial, statistical, mathematical, trigonometric, and even engineering functions. Each function has a name that describes its operation. The function that adds values is named SUM, for example, and the function that calculates an arithmetic mean, or average, is named AVERAGE.

Most functions require arguments, or input values, which you enclose in parentheses. The ROUND function, for example, rounds a specific value to a specified number of decimal places. To round the value 5.75 to the nearest tenth, you could use the function shown below:

```
=ROUND(5.75, 1)
```

Even if a function doesn't require arguments, you still need to include the parentheses. For example, the function PI returns the mathematical constant Pi. The function needs no arguments, but you still need to enter it as =PI().

Functions can use values, formulas, and even other functions as arguments. If entered in the budgeting worksheet shown in Figure 1-9, for example, each of the following functions returns the same result, 3300:

```
=SUM(C1:C5)

=SUM(C1,C2,C3,C4,C5)

=SUM(500,50,500,2000,250)

=SUM(SUM(C1),SUM(C2),SUM(C3),SUM(C4),SUM(C5))
```

NOTE *Because summing is such a common spreadsheet operation, Excel provides an AutoSum button on the toolbar; you can use it to enter an =SUM function in the active cell of a contiguous range of cells. If cell C6 in the worksheet shown in Figure 1-9 were empty, for example, and you selected the range C1:C6, you could click the AutoSum toolbar button to direct Excel to place the formula =SUM(C1:C5) in cell C6.*

TIP *To identify a toolbar button, point to the button. Excel displays the button name in a small box called a ToolTip. If you point to the button that shows the Greek sigma character, for example, Excel displays a ToolTip box identifying the button as the AutoSum button.*

To most easily insert complicated functions and reduce your chance of error, click the Insert Function button on the formula bar or choose the Insert menu's Function command. This displays the Insert Function dialog box shown in Figure 1-10. Search for a function or select a category using the upper box and select a specific function from the list in the lower box. Because some of the functions are a little difficult to recognize or distinguish by name, Excel describes what the selected function does at the bottom of the Insert Function dialog box. When you have found the function you want to use, click OK.

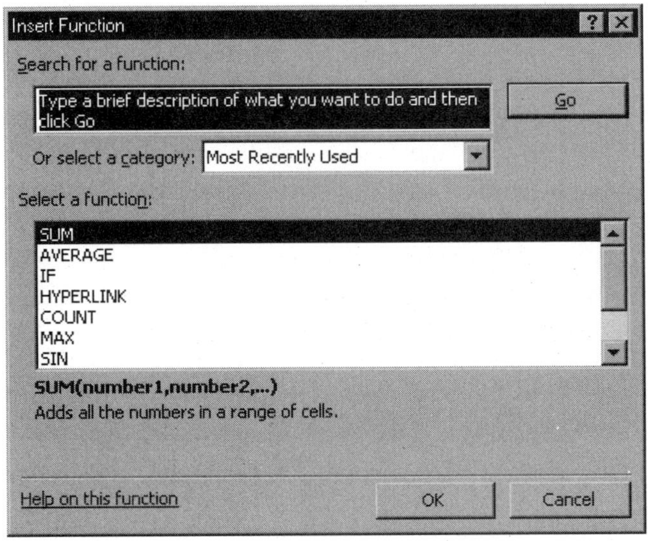

Figure 1-10 The Insert Function dialog box.

Excel displays the Function Arguments dialog box with text boxes you can use to identify or supply the arguments required for the function, as shown in Figure 1-11. If necessary, drag this dialog box to another portion of your screen to see the cells you want to include in the function. To enter cell data in an argument text box, click that box and then select the cell or range of cells in your worksheet that goes in the box. Excel highlights the cell or cells you selected with a flashing box. To enter cell data in another argument text box, click that box and select the cell or range in your worksheet that contains the data required for that box. Click OK when you're finished. Excel pastes the function in the cell.

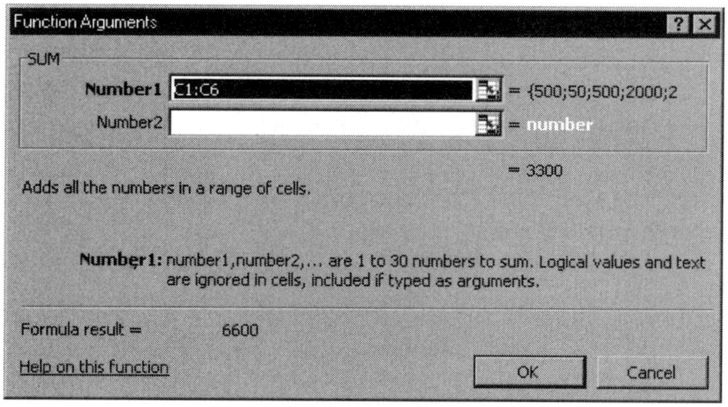

Figure 1-11 Selecting data required for a function.

NOTE *A range is simply any rectangular area of the worksheet, such as a two-cell by two-cell square, a five-cell by nine-cell rectangle, or even an entire worksheet. Excel uses opposite corner cell references and a colon to define ranges. For example, the range of cells from C1 and up to and including C5 is written as C1:C5. And the range of cells from C1 to D2 is written as C1:D2.*

Naming Cells and Ranges

In a small sample worksheet such as the one shown in Figure 1-9, it's not too difficult to remember that cell C1 contains the advertising expenses, C2 contains the bank charges, and so on. In the real world, however, Excel worksheets can be much more complex, and keeping track of what each cell represents becomes correspondingly more difficult. In this way, instead of referring to cell C1 in a formula, you could refer to Advertising if you first name the individual cell Advertising. For example, if you named cells C1, C2, C3, C4, and C5 Advertising, Bank, Car, Depreciation, and Equipment, respectively, the following two formulas would be identical:

```
=C1+C2+C3+C4+C5
```

```
=Advertising+Bank+Car+Depreciation+Equipment
```

To name a cell or range, follow these steps:

1. Select the cell or range of cells to be named.

You can select a cell by clicking it or by using the arrow keys to move the cell selector to the cell. You can select a range of cells by clicking on one corner of the range and then, while holding down the mouse button, dragging the mouse to the opposite corner of the range.

2. **Choose the Insert menu's Name command, and then choose Define.**

   Excel displays the Define Name dialog box shown in Figure 1-12.

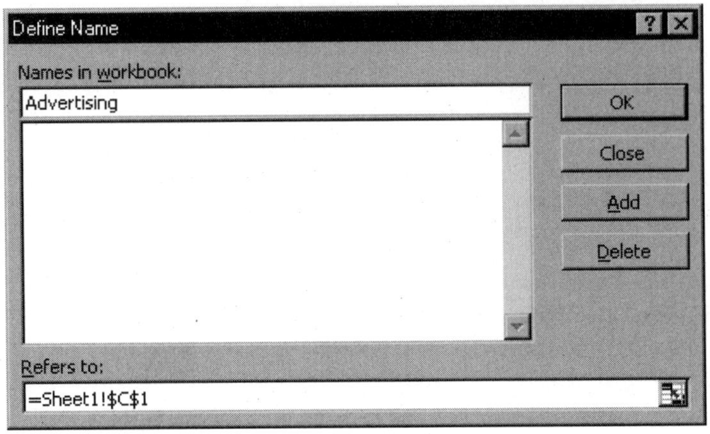

Figure 1-12 The Define Name dialog box.

3. **Enter a name in the Names In Workbook text box.**

   Range names must begin with a letter, not a number. They cannot include spaces, and they shouldn't look like cell references or function names.

4. **Click Add.**

   To create another name, click Add and then repeat steps 1 through 3. To finish creating names, click OK.

Range names are useful in formulas and functions, but that's not their only use. Once you name a range, you can use the name in place of the range definition whenever Excel asks you for a range. For example, if you use the Go To command, you could enter a name instead of a cell address.

Editing Workbook Data

Excel supplies many helpful commands that make creating and editing your workbooks easier and more efficient. If you anticipate spending any time at all working with Excel, it makes good sense for you to learn how these tools work and when they come in handy.

Erasing Cell Contents

You can erase the contents and formatting from a single cell or a range quickly and easily. To erase, follow these steps:

1. **Select the cell or range you want to clear.**

   You can select a cell by clicking it. You can select a range of cells by dragging the mouse from one corner of the range to the opposite corner of the range.

2. **Delete the cell contents.**

   Press the Delete key to erase all contents and formatting, or choose the Edit menu's Clear command to specify what you want to erase. Choose one of the three commands from the submenu, as shown in Table 1-3.

COMMAND	DESCRIPTION
All	Erases all contents and formatting
Formats	Erases formatting but leaves contents.
Contents	Erases the contents but leaves the formatting.
Comments	Erases any comments inserted using the Insert menu's Comment command.

Table 1-3 The Clear submenu's commands.

Undoing Mistakes

If you make a mistake while entering data or editing your worksheet, you can use the Undo toolbar button to reverse the effects of your last actions. You can also undo the Undo operation by clicking the Redo toolbar button. To reverse the effects of a series of most recent actions, click the arrow beside the Undo toolbar button and select multiple actions from the list. To redo a series of last actions, click the arrow beside the Redo toolbar button and select multiple actions from the list.

Copying, Cutting, and Pasting

You can copy or cut the contents of cells and ranges and then paste them into other locations. This means you don't have to repeatedly type a label, value, or formula. You can type the entry just once and then copy or move it.

TIP *With most programs, when you copy or cut something, the program places it on the Windows Clipboard. The only catch with the Windows Clipboard is that it can hold only one copied or cut piece of information at a time. So if you copy or cut another piece of information, the program replaces what the Clipboard previously stored. Office has a nifty feature called the Clipboard toolbar that allows you to store up to 12 pieces of copied or cut information at a time. To use the Clipboard toolbar, choose the View menu's Toolbars command and then choose Clipboard.*

Copying Labels and Values

Suppose, for example, that the numbers shown in column C of the budgeting worksheet represent the budgeted expenses for January and that the same figures are projected for February and March, as shown in Figure 1-13. Rather than reenter the same values, you could copy the values already stored in column C.

	A	B	C	D	E	F
1	Advertising		600			
2	Bank charges		50			
3	Car & Truck		500			
4	Depreciation		2000			
5	Equipment Rental		250			
6						
7	Total		3400			
8						
9						

Figure 1-13 The simple budgeting worksheet.

To copy the labels and values for such an operation, follow these steps:

1. **Select the cell or range to be copied.**

   In Figure 1-13, this would mean you select the range C1:C5. The easiest method for selecting a specific cell or range is by clicking or clicking and dragging the mouse.

2. **Click the Copy toolbar button, or choose the Edit menu's Copy command.**

   When you do this, Excel places a copy of the labels and values on the Clipboard.

3. **Select the destination cell or the cell in the upper left corner of the destination range.**

   If you want to duplicate the selected cells more than once, select the multiple destination ranges in their entirety. For the worksheet shown in Figure 1-13, for example, you would select the range D1:E5.

4. **Click the Paste toolbar button, or choose the Edit menu's Paste command.**

   When you do this, Excel copies the worksheet range from the Clipboard into the specified worksheet range.

NOTE *If you paste a copy of a single cell into a multiple-cell range, the contents of the cell are duplicated in each cell in the destination range.*

TIP *You can also copy a cell or range with the mouse. Just select the cell or range, hold down the Ctrl key, point to the black border around the cell or range so that the mouse pointer changes from a cross to an arrow, and then drag the cell or range to a new location.*

Copying Formulas

When you copy labels and values, Excel duplicates the contents of the copied cell or cells and pastes the data into the selected range. When you copy a formula, however, Excel adjusts any cell references used in the formula. This important difference can be illustrated by copying the formula in cell C7 of Figure 1-14, =C1+C2+C3+C4+C5, into cells D7 and E7. To do this, follow these steps:

1. **Select the cell or range with the formula(s) you want to copy.**

   In the example of the worksheet shown in Figure 1-14, you would select cell C7.

	A	B	C	D	E	F
1	Advertising		600	600	600	
2	Bank charges		50	50	50	
3	Car & Truck		500	500	500	
4	Depreciation		2000	2000	2000	
5	Equipment Rental		250	250	250	
6						
7	Total		3400			
8						
9						

Figure 1-14 A worksheet with two copies of C1:C5 pasted in D1:E5.

2. **Click the Copy toolbar button.**

   Excel moves a copy of the formula in cell C7 to the Clipboard.

3. **Select the destination range D7:E7.**

   In the example of the worksheet shown in Figure 1-14, you would select the range D7:E7.

4. **Click the Paste toolbar button.**

   Excel adjusts the formulas for the column in question and pastes the formula =D1+D2+D3+D4+D5 into cell D7 and the formula =E1+E2+E3+E4+E5 into cell E7. Figure 1-15 shows the worksheet after copying the formula.

	A	B	C	D	E	F
1	Advertising		600	600	600	
2	Bank charges		50	50	50	
3	Car & Truck		500	500	500	
4	Depreciation		2000	2000	2000	
5	Equipment Rental		250	250	250	
6						
7	Total		3400	3400	3400	
8						
9						

Figure 1-15 The budgeting worksheet after copying the formula in cell C7 into cells D7 and E7.

The formula changes that Excel makes aren't a mistake. Excel assumes—unless you tell it otherwise—that the cell references in your formulas are *relative.* When Excel copies and pastes a formula with relative cell references, it adjusts them.

To prevent Excel from automatically adjusting the relative references of copied formulas, you can make them *absolute.* Simply place a dollar sign ($) in front of the part or parts you don't want Excel to adjust. For example, to tell Excel not to adjust the formula at all, place a dollar sign in front of both the column letter and row number like this $A$1. To allow Excel to adjust row numbers but not column letters, put a dollar sign in front of the column letter but not the row number, like this: $A1. And to allow Excel to adjust column letters but not row numbers, put a dollar sign in front of the row number but not the column letter, like this: A$1.

Special Pasting Options

If you want to specify pasting options, instead of just clicking the Paste button after copying or cutting, choose the Edit menu's Paste Special command. Excel displays the Paste Special dialog box shown in Figure 1-16. To paste a row of cells as a column of cells or vice versa, select the Transpose check box. To paste only a portion of the copied or cut cells' contents, click a Paste option button other than All. For example, to paste only the comments in a cell, click the Comments option button under Paste. To add, subtract, multiply, or divide the values in the copied range with the values in the destination range, click the Add, Subtract, Multiply, or Divide option button under Operation. To tell Excel it shouldn't paste blank cells over values, select the Skip Blanks check box.

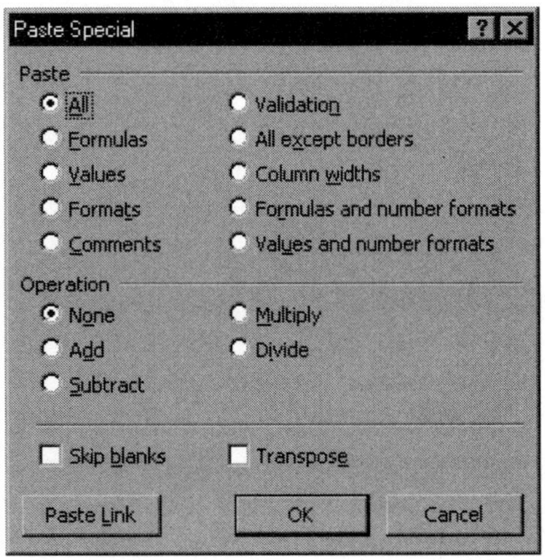

Figure 1-16 The Paste Special dialog box.

Moving Labels, Values, and Formulas

To move, rather than copy, a selected range, follow the same procedure, but click the Cut toolbar button or choose the Edit menu's Cut command instead of choosing the Copy command. Excel removes the selected contents from their original location and allows you to paste them in a new location.

NOTE *When you move a formula, Excel doesn't adjust the relative references used in the moved formula.*

You can also move a cell or range with the mouse by selecting the cell or range and pointing to the black border around the cell or range so that the mouse pointer changes from a cross to an arrow. Then drag the cell or range to a new location.

Filling Ranges

To continue a pattern you've begun, use the fill handle in the lower right corner of a cell or range. For example, if you begin the pattern 0, 5, 10 and want to continue it down a column, select the cells holding these values and click the little black square in the lower right corner of the range. The mouse pointer changes from a white outlined cross to a black cross. Now drag the mouse down the column as far as you want the pattern to go. This procedure also works for easily identifiable patterns of labels, such as months of the year and days of the week.

Inserting and Deleting Cells, Rows, Columns, and Worksheets

Excel lets you insert and delete cells, rows, columns, and worksheets in your workbook with speed and efficiency. You can easily delete what you no longer need or insert new items between existing entries when you need more space.

Using the Insert Command

To insert a row, click any cell in the row below where you want a row inserted. Then choose the Insert menu's Rows command.

To insert a column, click any cell in the column to the right of where you want a column inserted and choose the Insert menu's Columns command.

To insert a cell in a column or row, choose the Insert menu's Cells command. Excel displays the Insert dialog box shown in Figure 1-17. Click the Shift Cells Right button to insert a new cell in a row or click the Shift Cells Down button to insert a new cell in a column. After you've selected the appropriate option button, click OK.

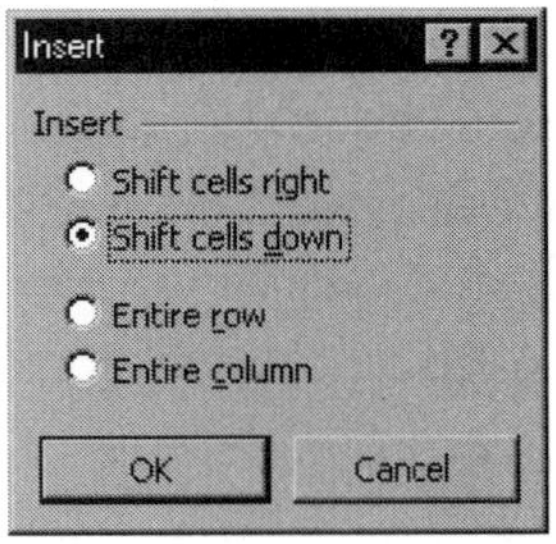

Figure 1-17 The Insert dialog box.

To insert a worksheet, display the worksheet in front of which you want to create a new worksheet and choose the Insert menu's Worksheet command.

Using the Delete Command

To delete a cell, range, row, or column, select the specific cell or range or any cell in the row or column you want to delete and choose the Edit menu's Delete command. Excel displays the Delete dialog box shown in Figure 1-18. Describe whether you want to shift the remaining cells up or to the left, or whether you want to delete the entire row or column, and click OK.

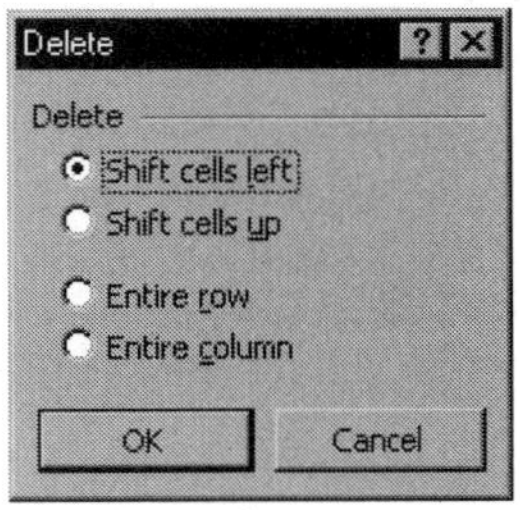

Figure 1-18 The Delete dialog box.

Excel attempts to adjust the cell references and range definitions used in formulas for row and column insertions and deletions. For example, if a formula uses values in column C and you delete column B so that column C becomes the new column B, Excel adjust the formulas to read column B. If you delete a cell referenced in a formula, however, Excel replaces the formula's reference with the error message #REF, indicating that the formula originally referenced a now-deleted cell.

Using Find and Replace

Excel provides two commands that you can use to search your workbook for specific entries. The Find command simply locates the contents you're looking for. The Replace command locates the contents and then gives you the option of replacing them with a new label, value, or formula.

Using the Find Command

To search your worksheet and locate specific entries, choose the Edit menu's Find command. Excel displays the Find And Replace dialog box with the Find tab displayed, as shown in Figure 1-19.

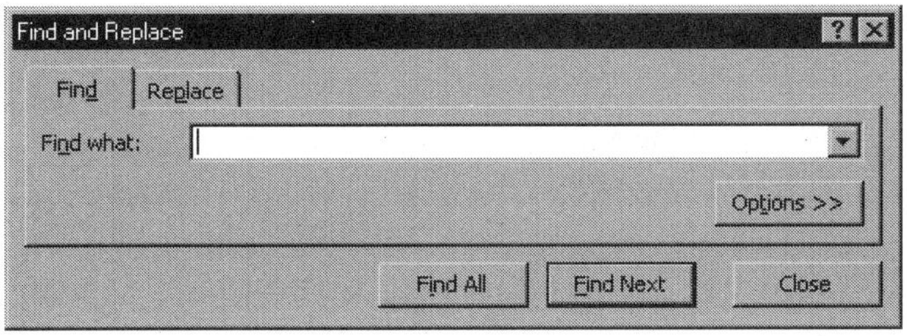

Figure 1-19 The Find And Replace dialog box.

Enter the label, value, or formula you want to find in the Find What text box, use the drop-down list boxes and check boxes to specify the parameters of your search, and then click Find Next to begin. If Excel finds an entry that matches your search parameters, it moves the cell selector to that cell. To resume searching, click Find Next again. Click Close when you're finished.

Using the Replace Command

When you choose the Edit menu's Replace command, Excel displays the Find And Replace dialog box with the Replace tab displayed, as shown in Figure 1-20.

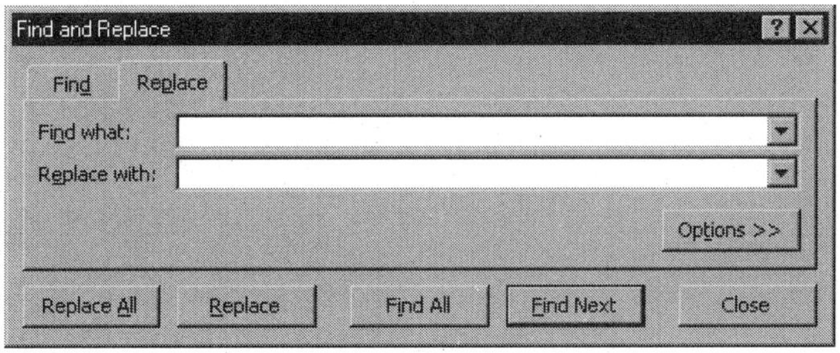

Figure 1-20 The Find And Replace dialog box.

Enter the item you want to find in the Find What text box and the label, value, or formula with which you want to replace it in the Replace With text box. Use the drop-down list box and check boxes to specify the parameters of your search.

Click Find Next and Replace to search for and replace entries one by one. Or click Replace All to have Excel automatically find and replace all occurrences of the entry without requesting verification from you. Click Close when you're finished.

TIP *With large or complex workbooks, you can streamline your find-and-replace efforts by first selecting the specific range you want to search. If you don't do this, Excel searches your entire workbook.*

Checking Your Spelling

Excel lets you check the spelling of a selected word, within a selected range or within an entire workbook. To check spelling, click the Spelling toolbar button. If Excel finds a word that's not in its dictionary, it displays the Spelling dialog box, as shown in Figure 1-21.

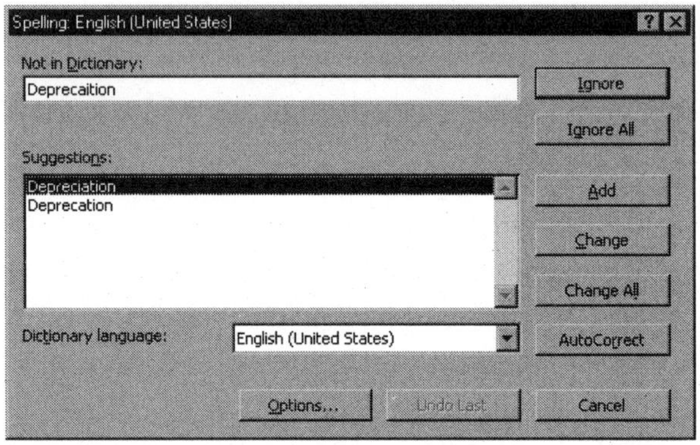

Figure 1-21 The Spelling dialog box.

If one of Excel's suggestions is correct, select it from the list box and click Change. If you want to change all occurrences of the misspelling to the suggestion you selected, click Change All. If you want to ignore the misspelling and continue, click Ignore. If you want to Ignore all occurrences of the spelling, click Ignore All. If you want Excel to recognize the word in future documents and spell checks, you can add it to the dictionary by clicking Add.

Formatting Workbooks

With proper formatting, your worksheets are easier to read and more visually attractive. Fortunately, Excel includes a rich set of easy-to-use tools for formatting your workbook data so it's more enjoyable and easier to read.

Using a Predesigned Format

Excel's AutoFormat feature performs many standard formatting tasks in a single operation: setting fonts, aligning labels, setting column width and row height, establishing numeric and date/time formats, and adding borders and rules.

To use AutoFormat, you first enter worksheet labels, values, and formulas, as shown in Figure 1-22.

	A	B	C	D	E
1		January	February	March	
2	Advertising	600	600	600	
3	Bank charges	50	50	50	
4	Car & Truck	500	500	500	
5	Depreciation	2000	2000	2000	
6	Equipment Rental	250	250	250	
7	Total	3400	3400	3400	
8					
9					
10					

Figure 1-22 The budgeting worksheet before an AutoFormat is applied.

To use the AutoFormat command, follow these steps:

1. Select the worksheet range you want to format.

In Figure 1-22, you would select the range A1:D7.

2. Choose the Format menu's AutoFormat command.

Excel displays the AutoFormat dialog box shown in Figure 1-23.

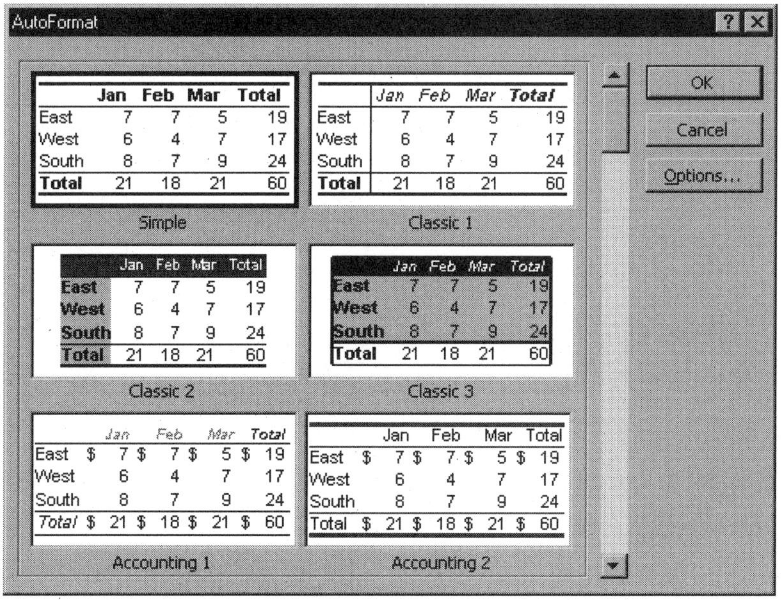

Figure 1-23 The AutoFormat dialog box.

3. **Select the AutoFormatting options you want to use.**

   Click the Options button if you want to specify which AutoFormatting options should be applied to your worksheet selection. When you do this, Excel adds Options check boxes to the AutoFormat dialog box. Select and clear these check boxes to selectively apply individual components of an AutoFormat.

4. **Select an AutoFormat by clicking it.**

   The AutoFormat pictures show roughly what the AutoFormat formatting looks like.

5. **Click OK to apply the format to the range you selected.**

   Figure 1-24 shows what the budgeting worksheet looks like after the AutoFormat selected in Figure 1-23 is applied.

	A	B	C	D	E
1		January	February	March	
2	**Advertising**	600	600	600	
3	**Bank charges**	50	50	50	
4	**Car & Truck**	500	500	500	
5	**Depreciation**	2000	2000	2000	
6	**Equipment Rental**	250	250	250	
7	**Total**	3400	3400	3400	
8					

Figure 1-24 A worksheet range with an AutoFormat applied.

TIP *If you like the AutoFormat feature and find yourself using it a lot, you can easily add the AutoFormat button to the toolbar. To do this, click the button with the arrows at the far right side of the toolbar. (This button is called More Buttons.) Click Add Or Remove Buttons from the box of buttons that pops up, and then select AutoFormat from the list of formatting buttons.*

Formatting Manually

As you create more complex and specialized worksheets, your formatting efforts require similar treatment. The following paragraphs briefly detail each of Excel's formatting features.

Aligning Labels and Values

Excel normally aligns numbers against the right edge of a cell and text against the left edge. You can override these default alignments by using the Left Align, Center, Right Align, and Merge And Center buttons on the toolbar.

The Left Align, Center, and Right Align toolbar buttons work as you might expect. For example, to left-align the contents of selected cells, click the Left Align button.

The Merge And Center toolbar button is a little more complex. It lets you center a label across a selection of cells. For example, you can enter a label in cell A1 of the budgeting worksheet, as shown in Figure 1-25, and then center it across the range A1:D1.

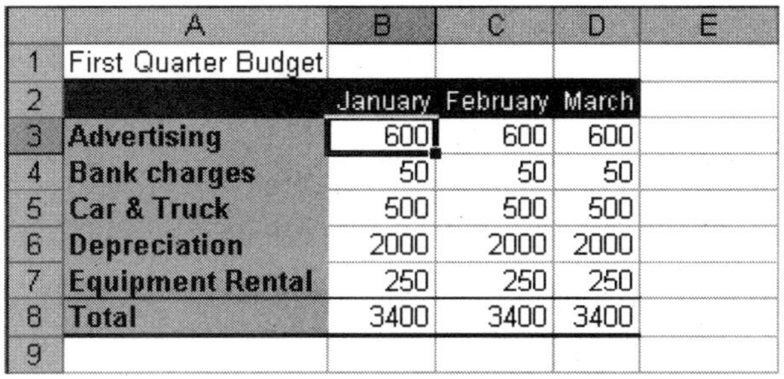

	A	B	C	D	E
1	First Quarter Budget				
2		January	February	March	
3	Advertising	600	600	600	
4	Bank charges	50	50	50	
5	Car & Truck	500	500	500	
6	Depreciation	2000	2000	2000	
7	Equipment Rental	250	250	250	
8	Total	3400	3400	3400	
9					

Figure 1-25 A label in cell A1.

To do so, first select the range and then click the Merge And Center toolbar button. Figure 1-26 shows the worksheet after making this alignment.

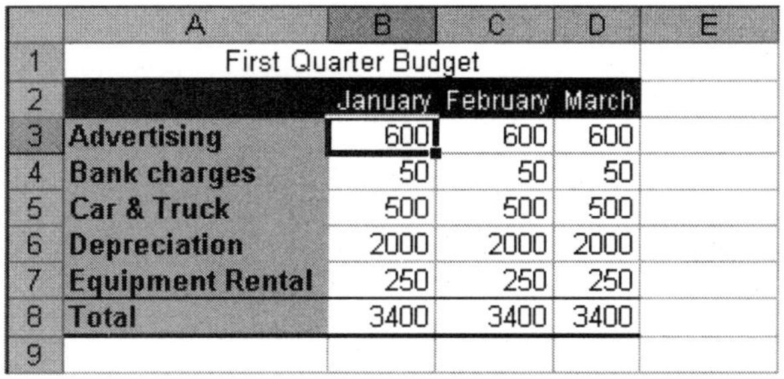

	A	B	C	D	E
1	First Quarter Budget				
2		January	February	March	
3	Advertising	600	600	600	
4	Bank charges	50	50	50	
5	Car & Truck	500	500	500	
6	Depreciation	2000	2000	2000	
7	Equipment Rental	250	250	250	
8	Total	3400	3400	3400	
9					

Figure 1-26 A label centered across the range A1:D1.

You can access a more sophisticated array of alignment features by selecting the cell or range you want to align, choosing the Format menu's Cells command, and clicking the Alignment tab, as shown in Figure 1-27. The Horizontal drop-down list box lets you align cell contents in the same ways as the Left Align, Center, Right Align, and Merge And Center tools do. The Vertical drop-down list box allows you to align cell contents at the top, center, or bottom of the cell. The Orientation box allows you to rotate the cell contents.

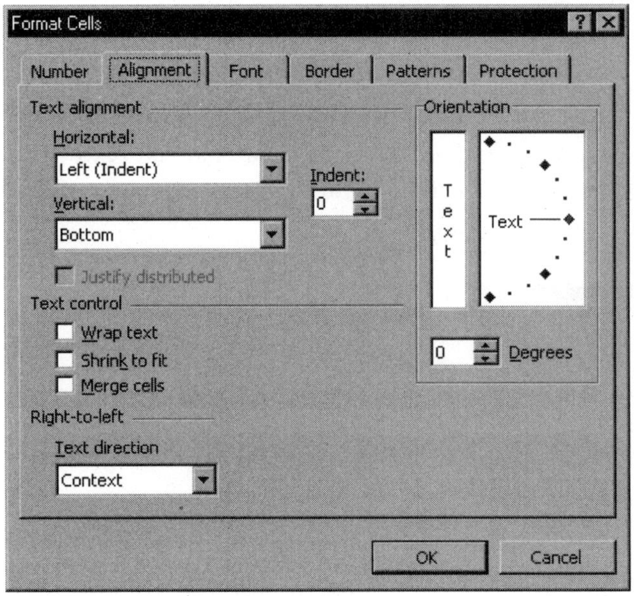

Figure 1-27 The Alignment tab of the Format Cells dialog box.

The Text Control boxes provide you with several more specialized alignment options. The Wrap Text check box allows you to wrap a long line of text into multiple lines in a single cell. The number of lines varies depending on the amount of text and the width of the cell. The Shrink To Fit check box allows you to decrease the size of the numbers or letters in a cell so that they fit in the current size constraints of the cell. The Merge Cells check box allows you to combine cells into larger, single cells.

Formatting Numbers

You can assign numeric formats such as dollar signs, percentage symbols, and commas. To quickly assign these specific common formats, select the cell or range you want to format and click the Currency Style, Percent Style, or Comma Style toolbar button. To assign other numeric formats, follow these steps:

1. **Choose the Format menu's Cells command, and click the Number tab.**

   Excel displays the Number tab of the Format Cells dialog box, as shown in Figure 1-28.

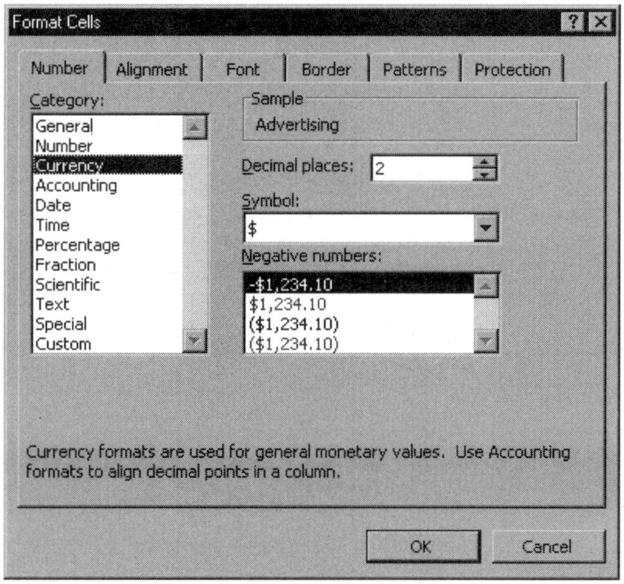

Figure 1-28 The Number tab of the Format Cells dialog box.

2. **Select a numeric formatting category from the list on the left.**

   In a budgeting worksheet, you would probably choose the Accounting category.

3. **Use the boxes and buttons for the category you chose to specify the exact formatting.**

   In a budgeting worksheet, for example, you might need to select a different currency symbol from the Symbol drop-down list box.

4. **Click OK.**

Changing Font and Font Size

Excel offers a wide variety of choices for changing a selected font's appearance, such as by adding boldfacing or underlining, for changing a font, and for specifying a different size.

To add effects such as boldfacing, italics, and underlining, you can use the Bold, Italic, and Underline font buttons on Excel's toolbar. To use any of these buttons, simply select the worksheet range you want to format and then click the button.

NOTE *If you're creating an Excel worksheet that you intend to publish on the World Wide Web, you probably don't want to use underlines in your formatting. Underlines are usually reserved for hyperlinks.*

To change the font of text, click the down arrow beside the Font toolbar button and select a font from the list. If you open the Font drop-down list box, Excel displays the font's name using the font itself, so you can preview what the font looks like, as shown in Figure 1-29. Fonts listed with a TT icon beside them are TrueType fonts. Fonts built into your printer have a printer icon next to them. If you use a TrueType font, the font you see on your screen will be the same one that the printer prints. If you use a scalable printer font and the printer you use doesn't support your selection, the printer uses the closest-matching font.

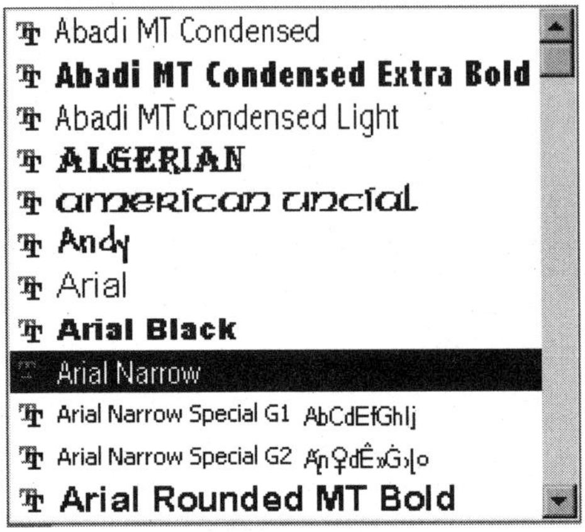

Figure 1-29 The Font drop-down list box.

To change the size of text, click the down arrow beside the Size toolbar button. Fonts are measured using points. One point is 1/72 of an inch. So a point size of 18 means that the font is ¼ inch tall. Excel's default point size is 10. You probably don't want to use fonts smaller than 10 points for legibility.

Adding Color to Cells and Text

Excel allows you to add color and shading to your data to help you organize, clarify, and emphasize the information on your worksheet—as well as to add interest.

To change the color of text, select the range you want to color, click the down arrow beside the Font Color toolbar button, and then select a color for the text.

To add a background color to a range of cells, select the range, click the down arrow beside the Fill Color toolbar button, and select a color for the cell background.

TIP *You can select a background pattern instead of, or in addition to, a background color. To do this, select the cell or range in which you want to have a background pattern, choose the Format menu's Cells command, and click the Patterns tab of the Format Cells dialog box. Select a pattern from the Pattern drop-down list box, and click OK.*

Creating Borders

To polish your worksheets and make them easy to read, you can add borders with the Borders toolbar button. To add a border to a cell or range, select the cell or range and click the down arrow beside the Borders toolbar button.

Excel displays the box shown in Figure 1-30, illustrating common border patterns and placements. To select a design for your cell or range, click it.

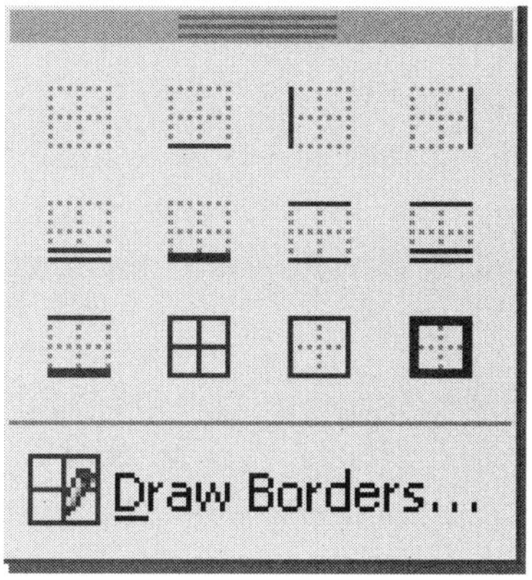

Figure 1-30 The border patterns and placements available from the Borders tool.

TIP *The border designs available from the Borders toolbar button are sufficient for most uses. If you can't find the pattern or placement you want, however, choose the Format menu's Cells command and click the Border tab. Then select a line style and place it where you want it in the range.*

Modifying Column and Row Size

As you reformat the labels and values in your worksheet, you may need to modify the standard column and row sizes to accommodate your formatting changes. To quickly increase the column width to accommodate all text in the column but include no extra white space, double-click the right border of that column heading. Normally, Excel automatically increases row height when you increase point size, but you can perform the same trick on rows by double-clicking the lower border of a row heading. This expands the row to the smallest height possible that still fits all entries within that row.

To specify exact column width, select any cell in that column, choose the Format menu's Column command, and then choose Width. Enter the width in characters in the Column Width text box, as shown in Figure 1-31, and click OK.

Figure 1-31 The Column Width text box.

To specify exact row height, select any cell in that row, choose the Format menu's Row command and then choose Height. Enter the height in points in the Row Height text box, and click OK.

To hide a row, select any cell in the row, choose the Format menu's Row command and then choose Hide. To redisplay a hidden row, select a range that includes cells in the rows above and below the hidden row. Then choose the Format menu's Row command, and choose Unhide.

To hide a column, select any cell in the column, choose the Format menu's Column command and then choose Hide. To redisplay a hidden column, select a range that includes cells in the columns to the left and right of the hidden column. Then choose the Format menu's Column command, and choose Unhide.

Using the Format Painter

Excel provides a feature that allows you to quickly copy the formatting from one cell to another while leaving the cell's contents intact. To copy cell formatting, select the cell with the formatting you want to copy. Next, click the Format Painter toolbar button, and then select the cell or range to which you want to apply the formatting.

Conditional Formatting

If you want to format only those cells that meet certain criteria, you can use Excel's Conditional Formatting feature. You might want to do this, for example, if you want to highlight cells in a budgeting worksheet that contain values larger than 200.

To apply conditional formatting, select the range of cells you want to include in the conditional formatting filters and then follow these steps:

1. **Choose the Format menu's Conditional Formatting command.**

   Excel displays the Conditional Formatting dialog box shown in Figure 1-32.

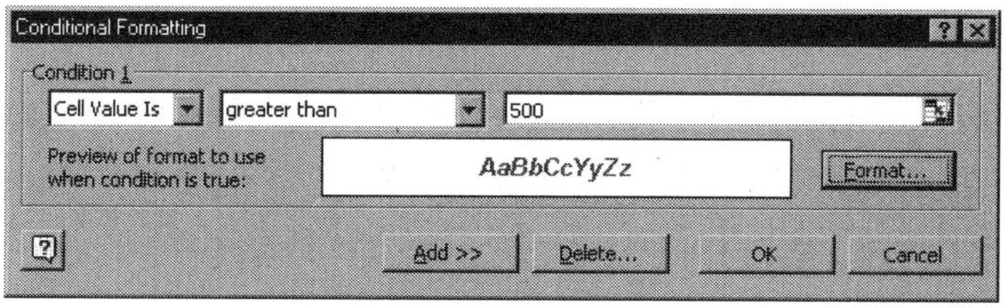

Figure 1-32 The Conditional Formatting dialog box.

2. **Enter the first criteria, using the drop-down list boxes and text boxes provided.**

   For example, if you want Excel to display values greater than $150,000 in red italic boldface, indicate that you want to conditionally format cells with values greater than 500, as shown in Figure 1-32.

3. **Click Format to describe how you want Excel to format the cells with contents that fit your criteria.**

   When you do this, Excel displays a variant of the Format Cells dialog box. Use it to specify the font, font size, font effects, and font color you want to use for cells that contain labels or values meeting your conditions. Click OK to close the Format Cells dialog box and return to the Conditional Formatting dialog box.

4. **Add the conditional formatting rule.**

   Click Add, and Excel adds the conditional formatting rule. If you want to specify multiple criteria, repeat steps 1 and 2 for the other criteria.

5. **Click OK.**

   Excel applies the conditional formatting, as shown in Figure 1-33. The budgeting worksheet displays values greater than 500 highlighted in red italic boldface.

	A	B	C	D	E
1	First Quarter Budget				
2		January	February	March	
3	**Advertising**	***600***	***600***	***600***	
4	**Bank charges**	50	50	50	
5	**Car & Truck**	500	500	500	
6	**Depreciation**	***2000***	***2000***	***2000***	
7	**Equipment Rental**	250	250	250	
8	**Total**	3400	3400	3400	
9					

Figure 1-33 Conditional formatting applied to values.

Printing Workbooks

Excel provides you with a wide variety of printing and presentation options, which is fortunate. As you move beyond the work of collecting and analyzing quantitative information, you'll usually want to share your information with others—typically by printing it.

TIP *If you want to print a worksheet immediately without specifying print settings (this technique tends to work fine for small, simple worksheets), just click the Print toolbar button.*

Setting Up Pages

The Page Setup dialog box, shown in Figure 1-34, gives you precise control over how your worksheet will print. Click the Setup button in the Print Preview window or choose the File menu's Page Setup command to display the dialog box.

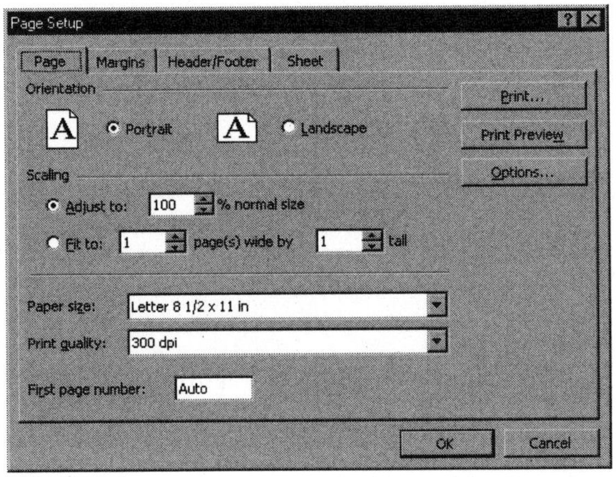

Figure 1-34 The Page Setup dialog box.

The Orientation option buttons allow you to select either the standard portrait or a horizontal landscape orientation for your printed worksheet pages. Use the Adjust To Scaling options to reduce or enlarge the worksheet proportionally, or use the Fit To Scaling options to fit the worksheet onto the number of pages you specify. Use the Paper Size drop-down list box to specify the size of paper you're using and the Print Quality drop-down list box to select the printer resolution. Higher print-quality settings, of course, look crisper and are more legible, but they take more time and toner to print. The maximum print quality setting you have available depends on your printer's capabilities.

Click the Margins tab, and use the Margins text boxes to enter the area in inches that you want to leave around the outside edges of the paper and between the spreadsheet and any header or footer. Use the Center check boxes to center your printed worksheet horizontally or vertically between the margins you specify.

Click the Header/Footer tab, and select a common header or footer from the Header And Footer drop-down list box. If you want to create your own header or footer, click Custom Header or Custom Footer and use the dialog box Excel displays to enter the header or footer text.

Click the Sheet tab, shown in Figure 1-35, to specify the print area, as well as any rows or columns you want to repeat on every page of a worksheet as titles. Select the Gridlines check box to print the gray worksheet gridlines that you see on-screen. Select the Black And White check box to print colors as black and white. Select the Draft Quality check box to print a fast, low-quality copy without most graphics. Select the Row And Column Headings check box to print the column letters and row numbers. Use the Comments drop-down list box to tell Excel if you want to print comments, and if so, where you want the text to appear on the printed page. Use the Page Order option buttons to specify the order in which multiple pages print.

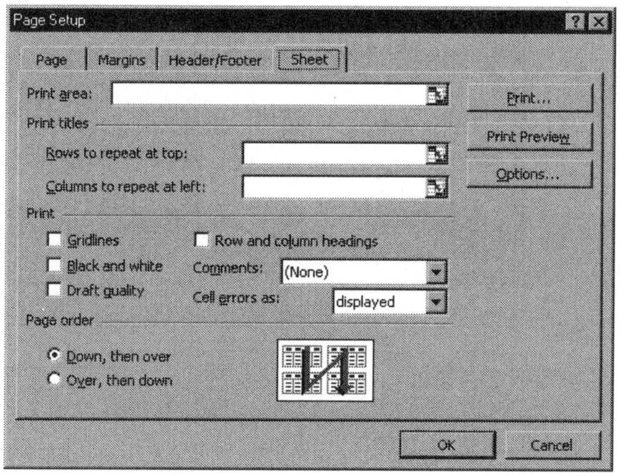

Figure 1-35 The Sheet tab of the Page Setup dialog box.

Previewing Before You Print

Previewing lets you see how a printed worksheet will look before you print it. When you preview a worksheet, for example, you can see how many pages it takes to print and whether or not all of the text fits as you think it does.

To preview a worksheet, click the Print Preview toolbar button or click Preview in the Print dialog box to display the Print Preview window, as shown in Figure 1-36.

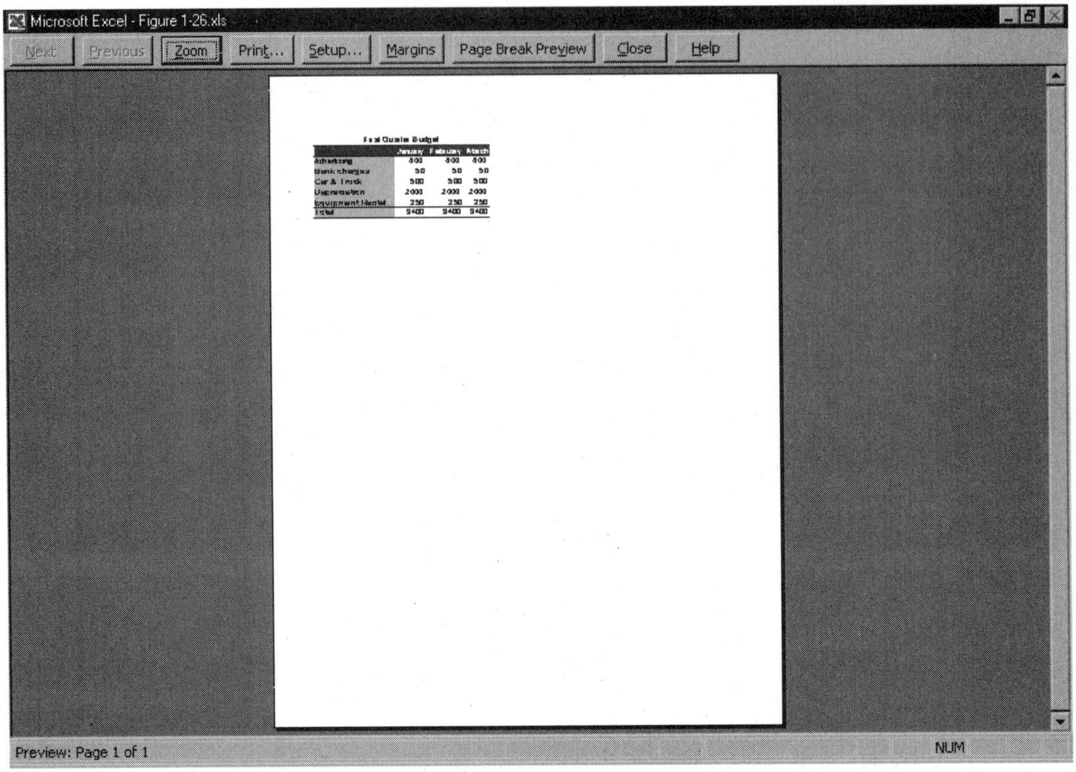

Figure 1-36 The Print Preview window.

The Next and Previous buttons allow you to page back and forth through a multipage worksheet. Click Zoom to zoom in on a page. Click Print to display the Print dialog box. Click Setup to display the Page Setup dialog box.

Click Margins to view the header, footer, and page margins. You can change these margins in the Print Preview window by dragging them. Click Page Break Preview to exit Print Preview and view the worksheet in Page Break Preview view. To change page breaks in Page Break Preview view, drag the breaks. To return to Normal view, choose the View menu's Normal command.

Click Close to go back to the regular application window. After you view a worksheet in Print Preview, Excel displays the page breaks in the worksheet as dotted lines.

Printing Workbook Pages

You have two options for printing worksheets: If you want to use Excel's default print settings, just click the Print toolbar button. If you want to specify print options, follow these steps:

1. **If you want to print only a specific area of a worksheet, select that area.**

   The easiest way to do this is by clicking and dragging the mouse.

2. **Choose the File menu's Print command.**

   Excel displays the Print dialog box, as shown in Figure 1-37.

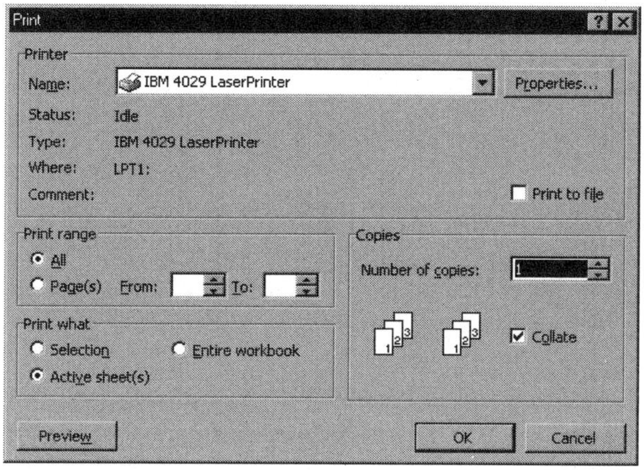

Figure 1-37 The Print dialog box.

3. **Specify which pages you want to print.**

   If a single worksheet is larger than one printed page, use the Print Range options to specify whether you want all pages or only some pages to print.

4. **Specify what portion of the workbook you want to print.**

   Use the Print What option buttons to tell Excel whether you want to print only the cells you selected, only the worksheet you currently have displayed, or all of the worksheets in the workbook.

5. **Specify how many copies Excel should print.**

   Use the Number Of Copies box to tell Excel how many copies you want to print. Select or clear the Collate check box to specify the order in which pages of multiple copies should print.

NOTE *The Print dialog box also lets you print to a file. When you print to a file, other people can print the file even if they don't have Excel. All they need to do is copy the file to their printer port.*

6. **Click OK.**

   Excel prints the workbook according to your specifications.

Skill 2

CHARTING

Featuring:

- Understanding Excel's Charting Terms
- Presenting Data with Charts
- Customizing Your Charts

Excel's Chart Wizard allows you to quickly and easily create professional, presentation-quality charts based on worksheet data. This chapter walks you through the steps you take to work with the Chart Wizard, paying particular attention to how you can use charts as powerful tools for better communicating complex information.

Understanding Excel's Charting Terms

In order to easily work with Excel's Chart Wizard, you'll want to learn both how Excel views to-be-plotted data and the terminology that Excel uses to refer to the parts of a chart.

How Excel Sees Chart Data

To easily use Excel for charting, you need to learn three key terms: *data points, data series,* and *data categories.*

The individual values you plot in a chart are called *data points.* Because a chart visually represents one or more numeric values, data points are always values. Note, however, that most formula results are also numeric, which means that you can also plot formulas. (Actually, in this case, you're really plotting the values that the formula calculates.)

The term *data series* refers to a collection of values that are all related—that are all part of the same set. That might sound complicated, but it's really not. If you want to chart monthly interest rates over the last 10 years, that collection of interest-rate percentages is a data series. If you want to plot advertising expenditures over the last 12 months, that collection of expense values is a data series.

Most charts you create will use more than one data series. For example, if you wanted to compare sales revenues of three competitors, each competitor's sales revenues would probably constitute its own data series. In the worksheet shown in Figure 2-1, you can see the annual sales revenues for three fictitious companies: Anderson Company, Baker Incorporated, and Carson Corporation. The data points that show Anderson's revenue represent a data series. The data points that show Baker's revenue represent another data. And the data points that represent Carson's revenue represent still a third and final data series.

	A	B	C	D	E	F	G
1		Year 1	Year 2	Year 3	Year 4	Year 5	
2	Anderson Company	1000000	1100000	1210000	1331000	1464100	
3	Baker Incorporated	3000000	2940000	2881200	2823576	2767104	
4	Carson Corporation	2000000	2050000	2100000	2150000	2200000	
5							

Figure 2-1 A simple worksheet with sales revenue data.

The term *data categories* refers to the secondary view, or perspective, on to-be-charted data. If you look at Figure 2-1 again, you can also see Year 1 data points, Year 2 data points, Year 3 data points, and so on. Each year's collection of data points represents a data category. The collection of Year 1 data points represents the Year 1 data category. Similarly, the Year 2 data points represent the Year 2 data category. The same thing is true of the Year 3, Year 4, and Year 5 data points.

People commonly get confused about the differences between data series and data categories (in part because Microsoft's product documentation typically hasn't done a very good job of defining and distinguishing these two terms). You can use the following tips to help distinguish between data series and data categories in your own charts:

- In general, if you look at a chart and ask, "What does this chart show," every concise answer identifies a data series. Figure 2-2 shows a simple line chart that plots the fictitious sales revenue from the worksheet shown in Figure 2-1. If someone asks you to describe what this chart shows, you'll probably say something like, "Well, it shows Anderson's revenue, Baker's revenue, and Carson's revenue." Which is not a coincidence; charts show data series. Anderson's revenue is a data series. And so is Baker's revenue, and so is Carson's revenue.

- Any chart that shows how some value changes over time is a time-series chart. In any time-series chart, the data categories will be some time interval, such as months or quarters or years. In Figure 2-2, for example, the chart plots sales revenue over a five-year period of time. Therefore, the chart is a time-series chart and uses time-interval data categories. In the case of Figure 2-2, the data categories are years.

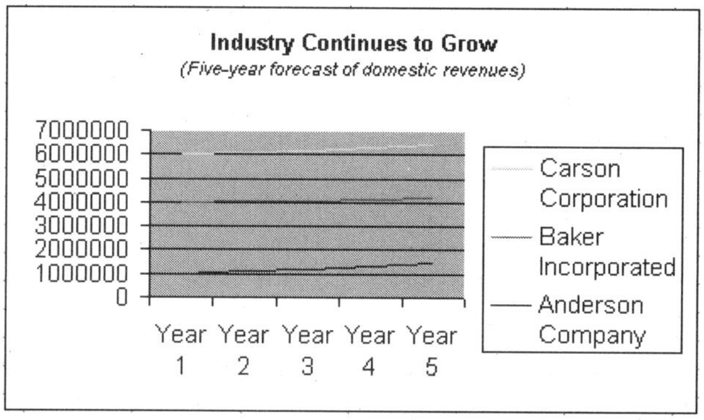

Figure 2-2 A line chart of the sales revenue data shown in Figure 2-1.

Now that you understand the three terms *data points, data series,* and *data categories,* you need to know just two final details about the to-be-charted Excel data. First, and as Figure 2-1 shows, you want not only to provide the actual data point values, but you also want to enter labels that name the data series and the data categories. In Figure 2-1, for example, you can see that cells A2, A3, and A4 hold labels that describe the names of the companies. In cells B1, C1, D1, E1, and F1, you see labels that identify the time intervals used as the data categories. Including data category and data series names in your worksheet is important. If you include this information in your worksheet, it's easily added later to your chart.

Second, note that Excel limits the number of data points and data series you can plot in a chart. A data series may hold no more than 4000 data points, for example. A chart may show no more than 255 data series. These constraints mean that you may sometimes need to arrange large data series or big sets of data series vertically by putting data series into worksheet columns rather than rows. Note that for smaller data series or small numbers of data series, a horizontal arrangement like that shown in Figure 2-1 works well.

Components of Excel Charts

Excel's Chart Wizard and documentation use several charting terms: *data markers, data-marker descriptions, legend, chart text, plot area,* and *chart area.* You'll find it useful to understand just what these words and phrases mean, so the bulleted list that follows provides definitions.

- *Data markers* are the graphical elements used to represent individual data point values in a chart. Figure 2-2, for example, uses symbols, or points, on a line to show data point values. Other types of charts in Excel use other data markers. A chart that uses columns or bars, for example, has column or bar data markers. A pie chart has pie-slice data markers, as shown in Figure 2-3, and so on.

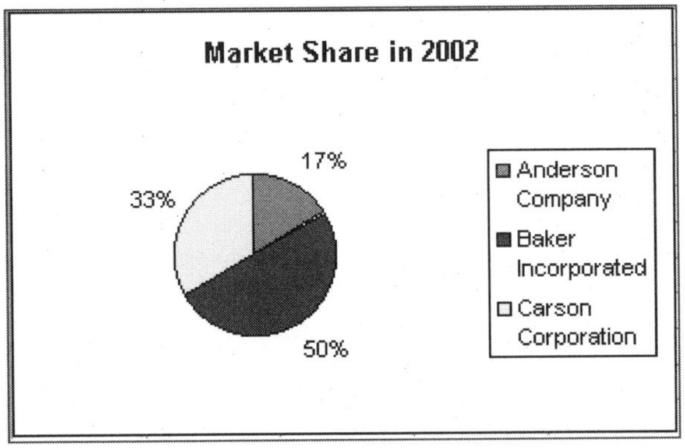

Figure 2-3 A simple pie chart.

- Excel typically describes and qualifies data markers using the *data-marker descriptions* such as axis scales and data labels. Different types of charts use different data-marker descriptions. Bar, column, and line charts use axis scales. (This is what Figure 2-2 shows, of course.) Pie and doughnut charts use data labels (see Figure 2-3).
- A *legend* names and identifies the data series you've plotted. In Figure 2-3, the legend names the data series and then shows which colors are used for which pie slices.
- *Chart text* describes a chart or some part of a chart. Figure 2-2, for example, shows a chart title (Industry Continues to Grow) and subtitle (Five-year forecast of domestic revenues).
- The *plot area* of a chart is the area that includes the data markers and data-marker descriptions. In Figure 2-2, the rectangle that shows the lines and scales represents the plot area. In the chart shown in Figure 2-3, the circle that shows the slices of pie and the data labels that identify the slices of pie comprise the plot area.
- The *chart area* includes plot area, any chart text, and a legend.

Presenting Data with Charts

Once you understand the terms that Excel uses to describe to-be-charted data and the parts of a chart, you can easily create charts. In essence, you need to simply select the worksheet data you want to chart, indicate where Excel should place the chart, and then tell the Chart Wizard to create the chart.

Using the Chart Wizard

To use the Chart Wizard, first enter your to-be-charted data in an Excel worksheet. As mentioned earlier, you want to include not only the data series data points but also the labels that identify the data series and the data categories. Figure 2-4 shows an example of how you might do this.

	A	B	C	D	E	F	G	H
1		January	February	March	April	May	June	
2	Revenues	1000000	750000	1200000	1300000	1100000	800000	
3	Expenses	550000	475000	610000	640000	580000	490000	
4								
5								

Figure 2-4 A simple worksheet with data you might plot in a chart.

Once you have the data in a worksheet, follow these steps to create a chart that visually depicts the data:

1. **Select the data you want to plot in the chart.**

   To select the data, select the worksheet range that includes the data series and any data series names and data categories names. In Figure 2-4, you would select the worksheet range A1:G3.

NOTE *If you arrange your data series in the way shown in Figure 2-4, Excel can usually correctly guess what the data series are, what labels show data series names, and what labels show the data categories' names.*

2. **Start the Chart Wizard.**

   You can do this by clicking the Chart Wizard button on the toolbar. Or you can choose the Insert menu's Chart command. Excel displays the first Chart Wizard dialog box, as shown in Figure 2-5.

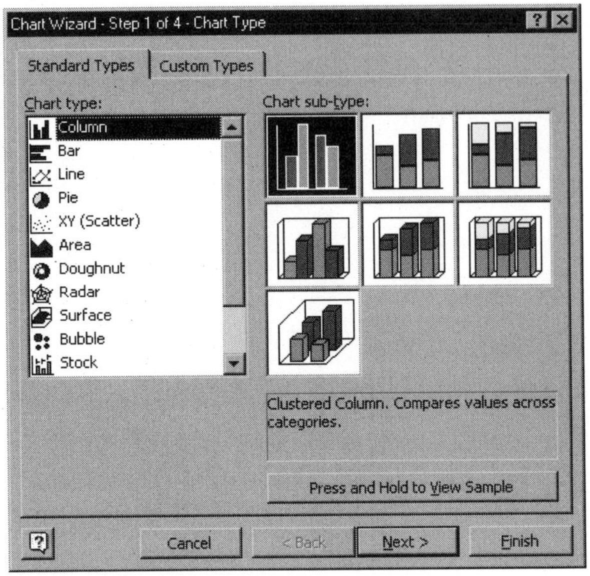

Figure 2-5 The first Chart Wizard dialog box.

3. Select the type of chart you want.

Select one of Excel's chart types from the Chart Type list box. Excel provides 14 different types of charts: Column, Bar, Line, Pie, XY (Scatter), Area, Doughnut, Radar, Surface, Bubble, Stock, Cylinder, Cone, and Pyramid.

TIP *The next section of this chapter, "Choosing the Right Chart Type," summarizes some of the rules of thumb that people often use to choose a particular chart type.*

4. Select the Chart sub-type.

After you select the Chart type, Excel displays the different versions available for the chart type as clickable buttons in the Chart Sub-type box. Excel displays a short description of the selected chart sub-type in the area below the Chart Sub-type box. To select a chart, click the button that looks like the chart you want. After making your selection, click Next.

NOTE *You can tell Excel to display a rough-draft version of the chart you're creating by clicking and holding the Press And Hold To View Sample button.*

5. **Verify that Excel has correctly interpreted the to-be-charted data.**

When Excel displays the second Chart Wizard dialog box, as shown in Figure 2-6, use it to verify that Excel is retrieving the correct data from the worksheet (this should be the case if you select the data correctly in step 1) and that it has correctly identified the data series. If Excel hasn't correctly interpreted the to-be-plotted data, click the worksheet button at the right end of the Data Range text box. When Excel minimizes the Chart Wizard dialog box, reselect the correct range. To restore the Chart Wizard dialog box, click the worksheet button a second time. If Excel has misinterpreted how you've organized your worksheet data—Excel assumes the chart has fewer data series than data categories—click the other Series In option button. Click Next when you're finished.

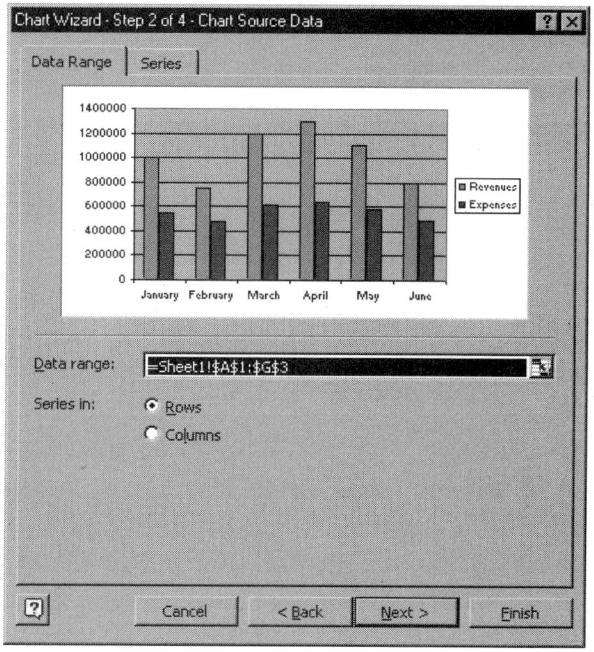

Figure 2-6 The second Chart Wizard dialog box.

NOTE *You can return to a previous Chart Wizard dialog box by clicking the Back button.*

6. **Add chart text as needed.**

When Excel displays the third Chart Wizard dialog box, as shown in Figure 2-7, you use its Titles tab to add a chart title and axis titles. To add such chart text, just click the appropriate text box and type the text you want. Click Next when you're finished.

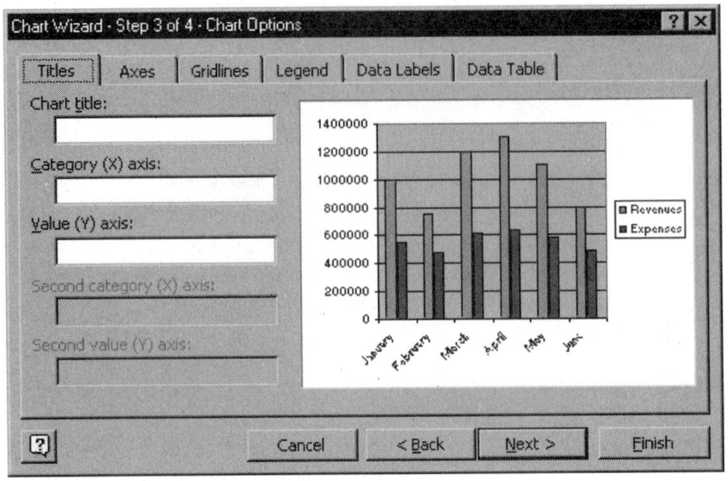

Figure 2-7 The third Chart Wizard dialog box.

NOTE *Excel updates the chart picture shown on the third Chart Wizard dialog box for any text you add.*

TIP *The other tabs of the third Chart Wizard dialog box provide options for changing and customizing the chart's appearance. The "Customizing Your Charts" section of this chapter describes how to use these tools to tailor Excel's charts to your requirements.*

7. Choose a location for the new chart.

Excel lets you place charts either as free-floating graphical objects in a worksheet or on their own individual chart sheets. You use the fourth Chart Wizard dialog box, as shown in Figure 2-8, to choose which location you want for your chart. To add a new sheet to the chart, click the As New Sheet option button and then enter a name for the new chart sheet. To add the chart as a free-floating object to an existing worksheet, click the As Object In option button and then select the worksheet from the As Object In drop-down list box. When you complete this step, you've finished creating the chart. Click Finish.

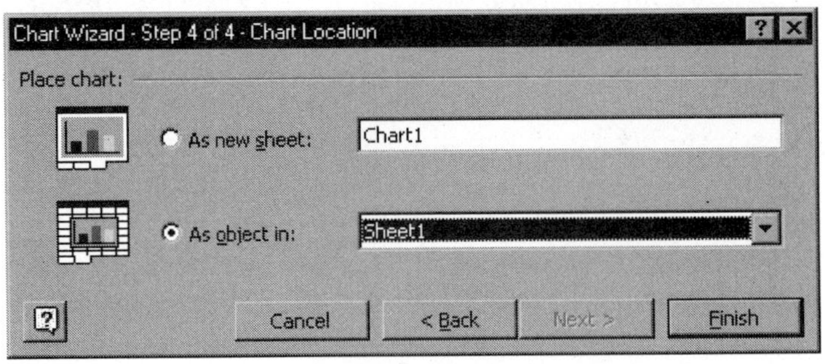

Figure 2-8 The fourth Chart Wizard dialog box.

Figure 2-9 shows how the worksheet data from Figure 2-4 looks in a column chart that resides on its own chart sheet. To view the chart, click its sheet tab. To print the chart in the selected sheet, simply click the Print toolbar button or choose the File menu's Print command.

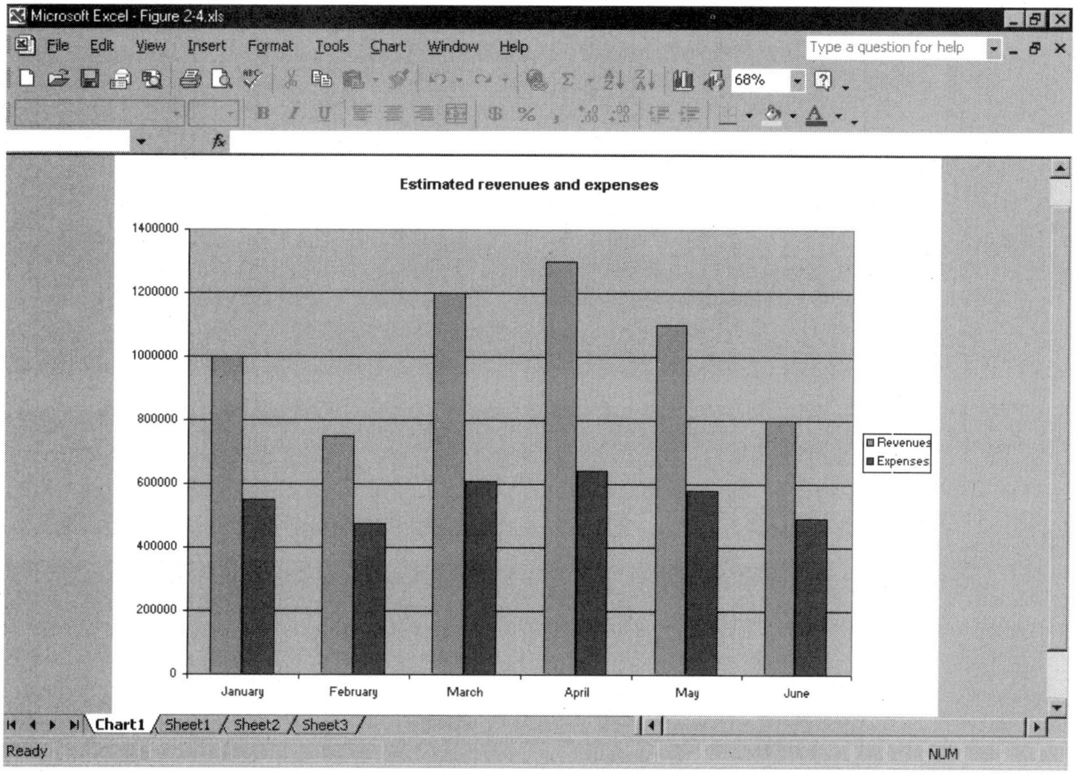

Figure 2-9 A column chart on a chart sheet.

Figure 2-10 shows the same worksheet data as that shown in Figure 2-9, except this time the worksheet data is depicted in an area chart that's free-floating as an object in a worksheet. You can resize any worksheet object, including a chart, by clicking the object and then dragging the square selection handles that appear on the sides and corners of the object.

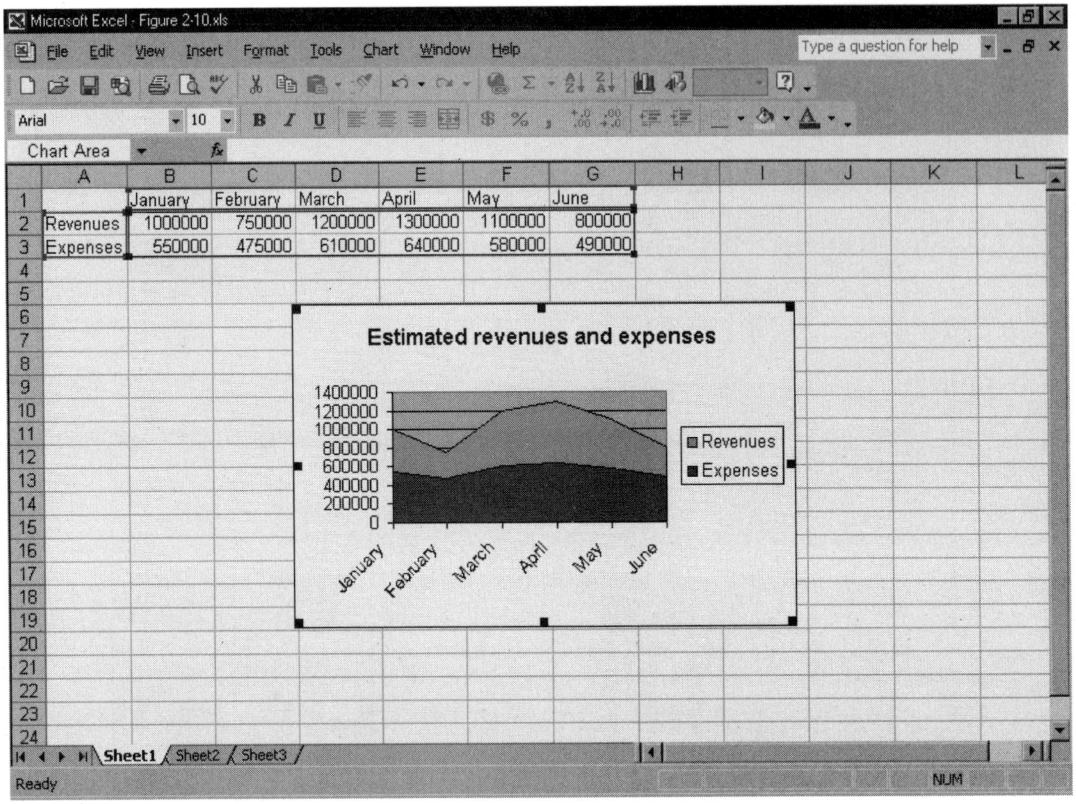

Figure 2-10 An area chart object in a worksheet.

To print a free-floating chart object, click it and then click the Print toolbar button or choose the File menu's Print command. You can also print the chart object by printing the worksheet over which it floats.

Choosing the Right Chart Type

Choosing the appropriate chart type is at least as much art as science. Nevertheless, it's still worthwhile to briefly discuss the three issues that you'll commonly want to consider as you choose a chart type: the basic data comparison that you want a chart to make, the principal message that you want a chart to communicate, and the relative strengths and weaknesses of the various chart types. All three factors greatly affect your choice of a chart type.

The Five Data Comparisons that Charts Make

Charts allow you to visually compare data in five ways, which means that your first step in determining the appropriate chart type is often simply to consider what data comparison you want to make. Suppose, for example, that you've collected detailed product sales revenue data for a golf equipment manufacturer. Using a chart, you might decide to look at this data in any of the ways summarized in Table 2-1.

COMPARISON	DESCRIPTION
Part-to-whole	Compares an individual data point value to the sum of a data series. Comparing sales of a particular golf club set to total sales, for example, is a part-to-whole comparison.
Whole-to-whole	Compares individual data point values to each other or data series to each other. Comparing sales of a starter men's golf club set to a starter women's golf club set, for example, is a whole-to-whole comparison.
Time-series	Compares data point values from different time periods to show how values change over time. Showing monthly sales over the last year, for example, is a time-series comparison.
Correlation	Compares different data series to explore correlation between the data series. Comparing industrywide sales to the average age of the population, for example, is a correlation comparison.
Geographic	Compares data values using a geographic map. Comparing sales by country, for example, is a geographic comparison.

Table 2-1 Summary of the five data comparisons made in charts.

Once you decide what data comparison you want to make, it's generally quite straightforward to identify the appropriate Excel chart types and sometimes even to identify appropriate chart sub-types.

- To make a part-to-whole comparison when working with just a single data series, you might choose a pie chart. (Pie charts plot only a single data series.) You might choose a doughnut chart or area chart if you're working with more than one data series.
- To make a whole-to-whole comparison, you might choose a chart that uses horizontal data markers, such as a bar chart or one of the cylinder, cone, or pyramid chart sub-types that uses a vertical data category axis and data markers. You might also choose a doughnut chart or radar chart.
- To make a time-series comparison, you would typically choose a chart that uses vertical data markers, such as a column chart, a line chart, or one of the cylinder, cone, or pyramid chart sub-types that uses a horizontal data category axis and data markers. You might also choose the stock chart if you're performing technical analysis of security prices. (Time-series charts typically use a horizontal data category axis because of the Western convention of using a horizontal axis to denote the passage of time.)
- To make a correlation comparison, you might choose the XY (scatter) chart if you're working with two data series or the bubble chart if you're working with three data series. You might also choose the surface chart if you want to explore trends in two dimensions.
- To make a geographic comparison, you would probably use the surface chart.

Importance of the Chart's Essential Message

A second important factor to consider is exactly what message you want to visually communicate with your chart. Typically, you can use the message as the chart title. But beyond this, you may want to experiment with different chart types and sub-types to see which best support your message.

NOTE *Of course, a chart can and should also be used to visually explore data. Oftentimes, information that's hidden in raw, tabular presentations of data suddenly becomes visible once you depict the data in a chart. This point is worth mentioning because when you are exploring data—something you might do by viewing data in different chart types—there probably shouldn't be any rules. Quite literally, thinking "outside the box" might often mean that you want to examine your data in unusual ways.*

Strengths and Weaknesses of Different Chart Types

A third factor you'll want to consider as you choose the best chart type is the relative strengths and weaknesses of each chart type. One could, of course, write an entire book on this subject. But you may find it useful to consider the strengths and weaknesses that people generally ascribe to the basic chart types as you choose a chart.

NOTE *In fact, someone has written a book—actually several books—about visually representing quantitative data. Edward Tufte has self-published several excellent books about the visual representation of data, including the bestseller* The Visual Display of Quantitative Information. *These books, available from online bookstores, will be of real interest and outstanding value to Excel users who frequently present data using charts. Note that one of Tufte's most elegantly argued points is that your charts shouldn't use more dimensions than your data—which essentially means that three-dimensional charts (with the exception of well-crafted surface charts) are usually just plain wrong.*

Area charts plot data point values using lines. Typically, they stack the lines so they show cumulative data point values and color the areas between the lines. Accordingly, area charts have two noteworthy strengths: They can show both the trend in the first data series and also the total of all the data series, and they can often create implicit total data series. Figure 2-11, for example, plots two data series: one for total expenses and one for profits. However, the total of these data series implicitly creates a third data series for total revenues.

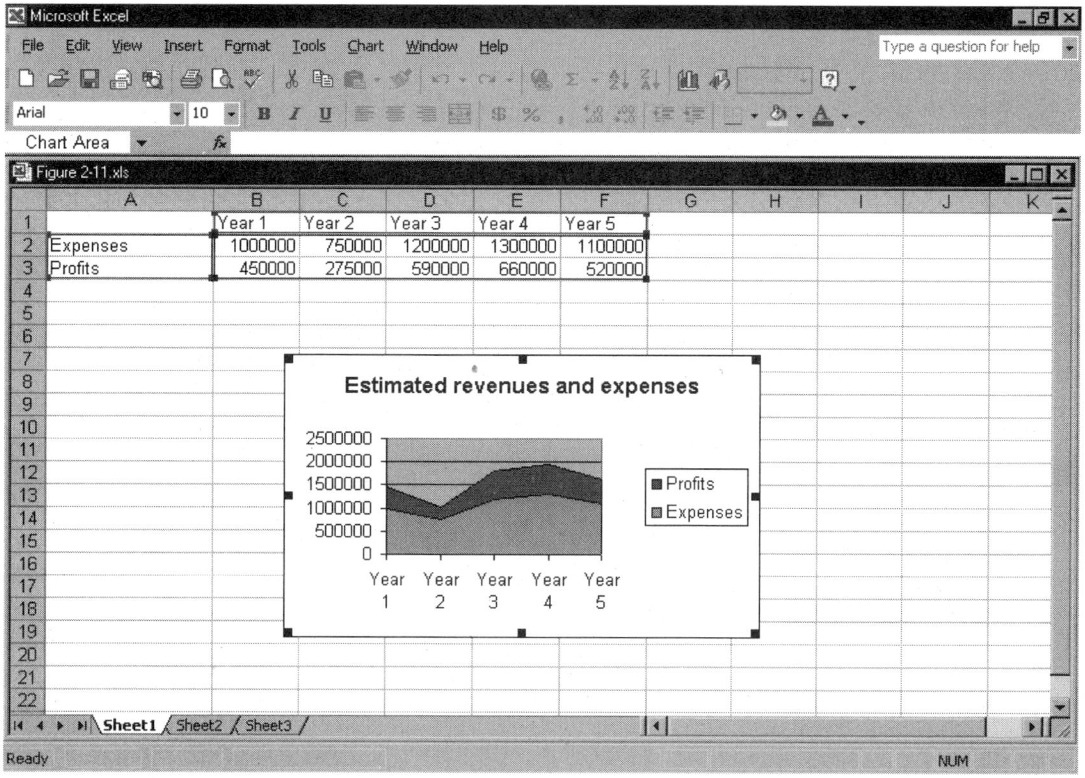

Figure 2-11 Area charts, which plot data series as stacked areas, also show the total data series.

NOTE *You have the option of not stacking the areas of an area chart, and sometimes you'll want to do this, too. In Figure 2-10, for example, an area chart plots revenues and expenses but doesn't stack the areas. Note that this arrangement also created an implied, third data series. In Figure 2-10, the visible portion of the revenue area shows profits.*

Area charts also suffer from several noteworthy weaknesses, however. They make it difficult to see the individual data point values (although this is a two-edged sword because the reduced emphasis on individual data point values also makes it possible to plot data series with large numbers of data point values). They make it next to impossible to compare data point values of the second and subsequent data series. (You can usually get a pretty good idea about the first data series data point values, though.)

NOTE *Area charts, as with any time-series graph, tend to suggest that time explains the apparent trends. This can be misleading, first, because there may not really be any trends and, second, because even if there are trends, the simple passage of time may likely not be the cause.*

Bar charts plot data point values in individual bars but arrange the bars so you calibrate them using a horizontal values axis. Accordingly, bar charts work really well when you want to compare data point values in a whole-item to whole-item data comparison and when the data categories are *not* time periods. Another feature of a bar chart is that the horizontal orientation of the chart makes it possible to comfortably use more lengthy data series names, as shown in Figure 2-12. Bar charts suffer from one weakness in particular: because they show each data point value with its own data marker, as you increase the number of data points you're plotting, the bars themselves become more narrow and less legible.

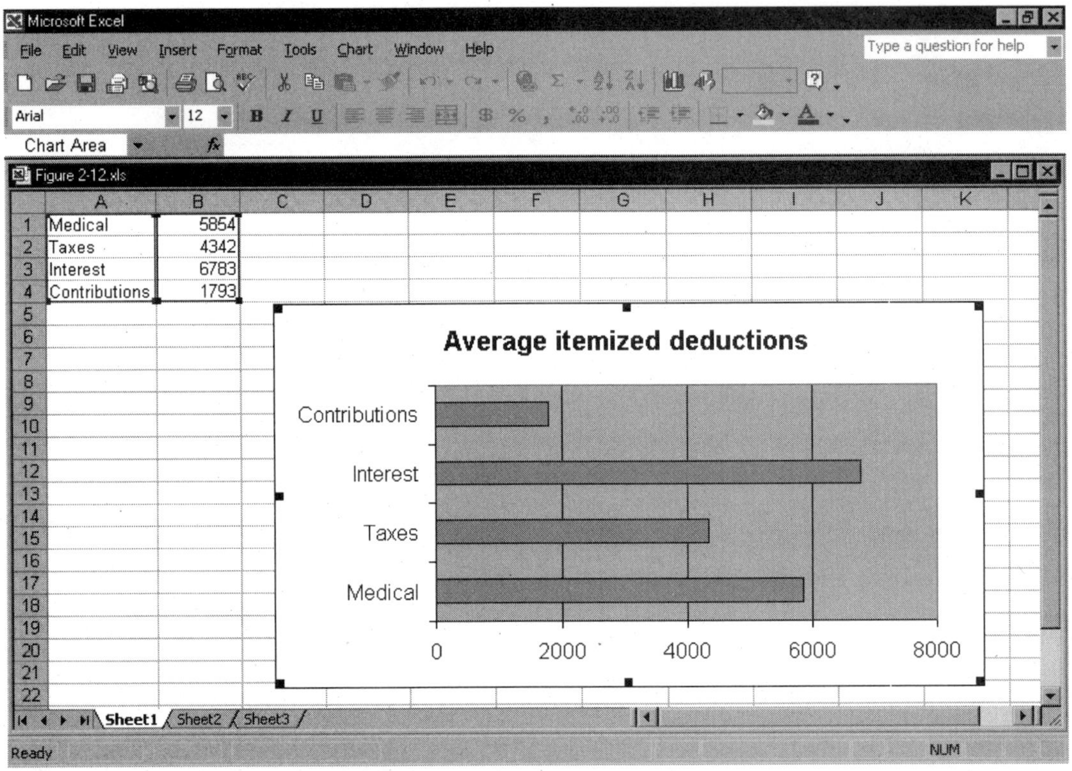

Figure 2-12 A simple bar chart that plots average tax deductions.

TIP *Cylinder, cone, and pyramid chart types possess the same general strengths and suffer from the same general weaknesses as do the bar and column charts. In addition, cylinder, cone, and pyramid chart types, because of their three-dimensionality, also suffer from an additional weakness. The added dimension, while admittedly interesting, often makes it more different to precisely compare data point values.*

Bubble charts let you visually explore the relationships between data series by treating the horizontal axis as a second values axis. To accomplish this, bubble charts plot pairs of data points. In Figure 2-13, for example, the chart shows income and contribution and suggests, perhaps surprisingly, that as people make more money, they only modestly increase their charitable giving. Bubble charts differ from XY charts, which also show this same information, in that Excel sizes the bubbles using the values of a third data point. While initially confusing, a bubble chart lets you explore the relationships between two data series. (The only other Excel chart type that lets you do this is the XY [scatter] chart.) If the bubble chart suffers from a weakness, it is that the chart may suggest correlations or relationships that don't exist.

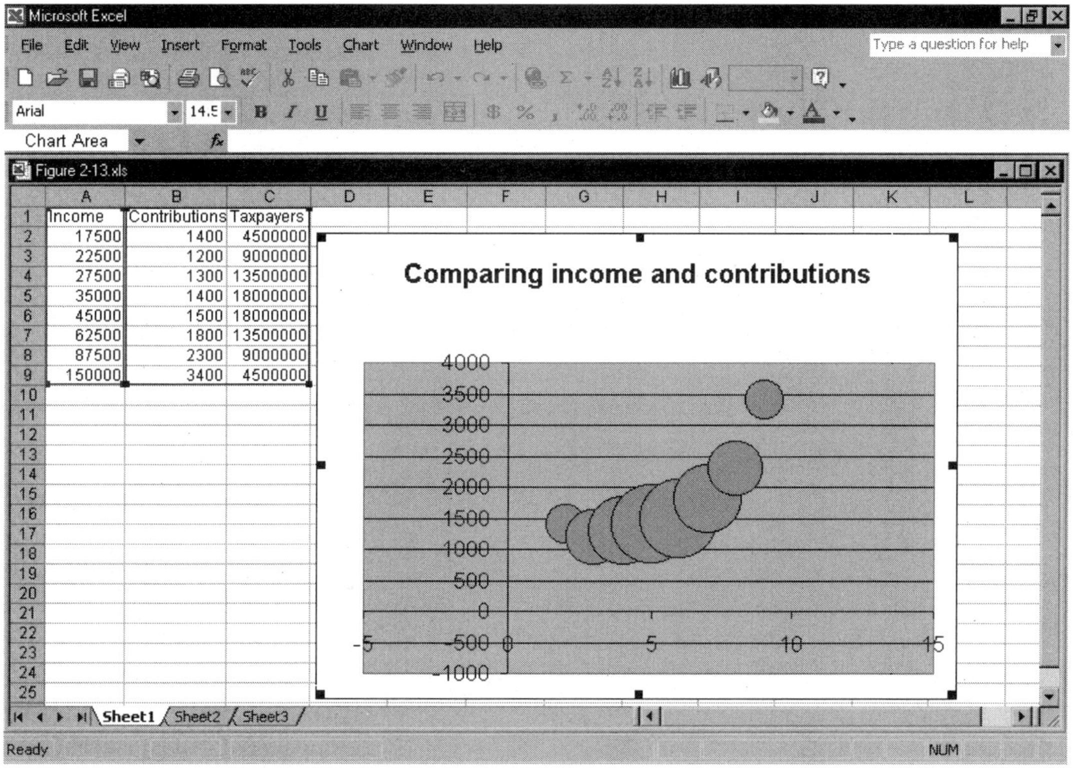

Figure 2-13 A simple bubble chart that shows U.S. Internal Revenue Service data on the relationship between income and charitable contributions.

NOTE *You can statistically examine correlations and relationships using Excel's regression analysis tools as discussed in Chapter 4.*

TIP *Compare the bubble chart shown in Figure 2-13 with the XY chart shown in Figure 2-21 on page 65 to see the other way you might choose to visually show a relationship between two data series.*

Column charts plot data point values in individual bars but arrange the bars so you calibrate them using a vertical values axis. Accordingly, column charts work really well when you want to view data point values in a whole-item to whole-item data comparison and when the data categories *are* time periods. Figure 2-14 shows a column chart that plots the future value of a retirement savings account based on $2,000-a-year contributions and a 9% annual return.

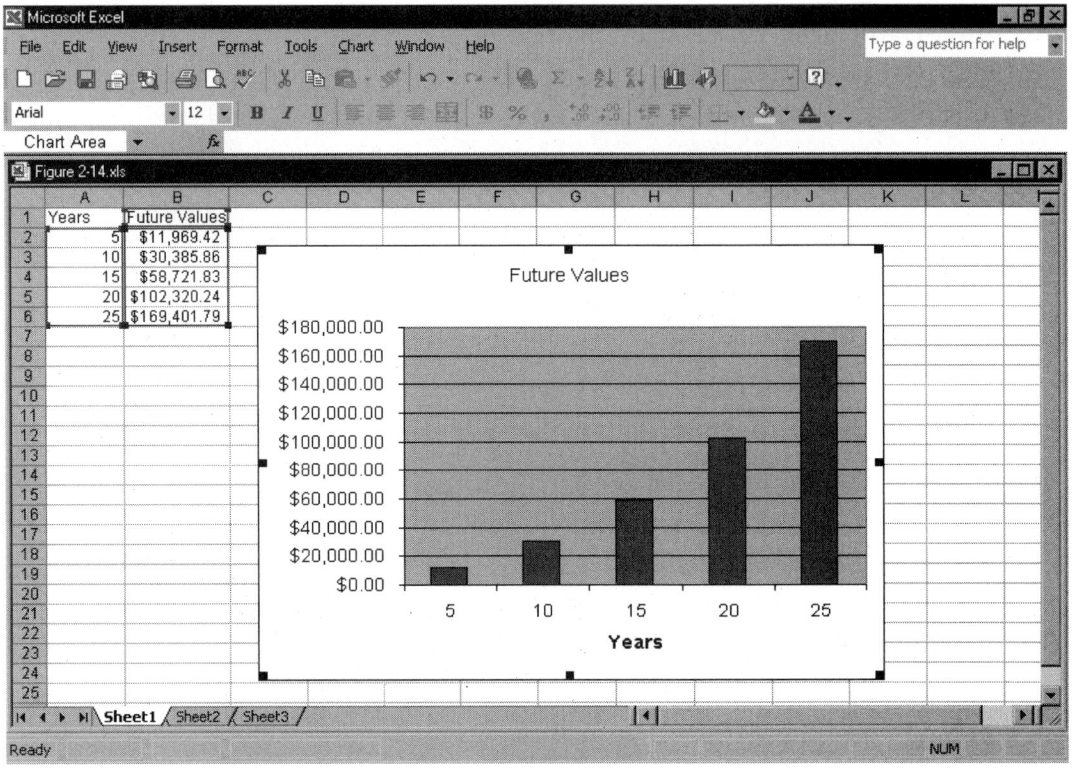

Figure 2-14 A simple column chart that plots future values of a retirement account at various points in the future.

Doughnut charts work similar to pie charts, plotting data series in concentric rings and showing each data point value as a segment, or bite, of the ring. Compared to pie charts, doughnut charts possess an advantage: they allow you to plot more than one data series. As a practical matter, they suffer from the same weaknesses as pie charts: they don't let you compare data point values between series (even though they paradoxically show multiple data series). They also limit you to small data sets. Almost always, something that appears in a doughnut chart should instead be shown with some other chart type. Figure 2-15, for example, compares the average deduction of taxpayers with $15,000 to $20,000 of adjusted gross income (shown with the inner doughnut) with those taxpayers with $100,000 to $200,000 of adjusted gross income (shown with the outer doughnut).

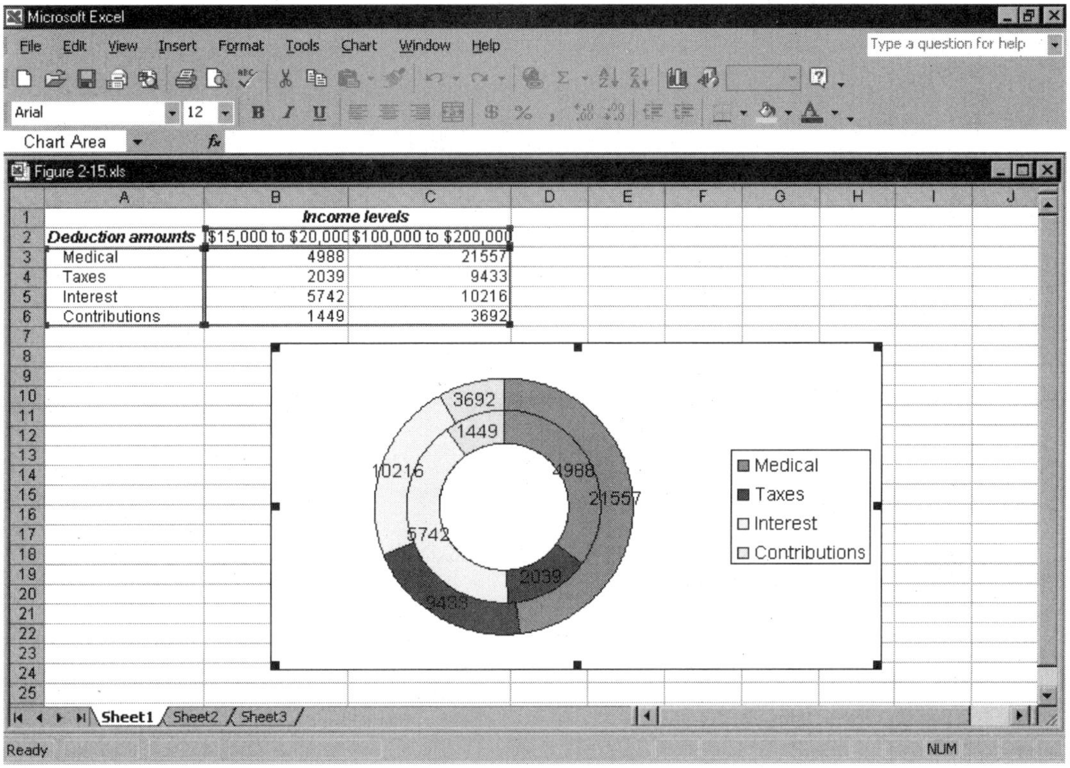

Figure 2-15 Doughnut charts let you plot data series in concentric rings.

Line charts generally plot individual data points in a line, using either different data marker symbols or different colored lines to distinguish the data series, and using a horizontal data category axis. Because line charts de-emphasize individual data point values, they work well for large data sets. With a line chart, you can literally plot thousands of data points. What's more, of all the Excel chart types, line charts tend to emphasize changes and trends in the data point values, which can be useful. Figure 2-16, for example, uses a logarithmic values axis, which means that it lets the viewer compare the rates of growth of a large company growing at 5% annually with a small company growing at 50% annually. Predictably, however, line charts suffer from some weaknesses: a de-emphasis of individual data point values which can camouflage inappropriately small data sets and make it impossible to compare individual data points, a tendency to show time-based trends that don't exist, and a tendency to show relationships between data series that don't exist.

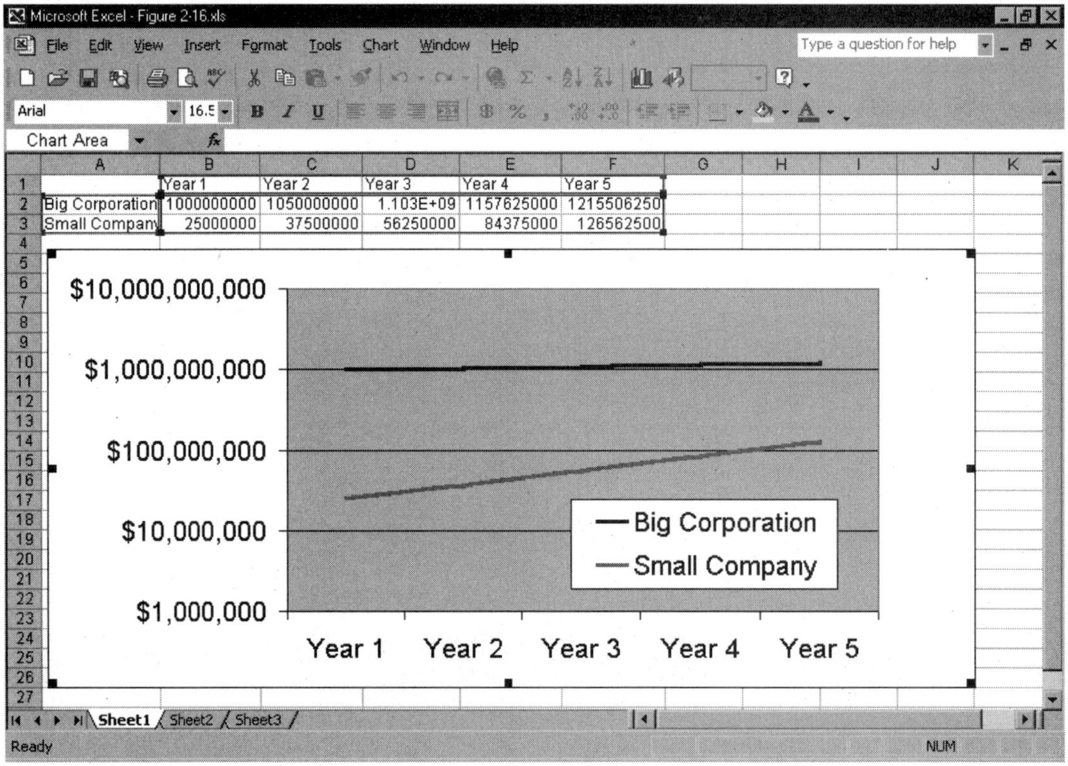

Figure 2-16 A line chart with a logarithmic values axis lets you visually compare a small company's 50% growth rate with a large company's 5% growth rate.

NOTE *In Figure 2-16, the small company's higher growth rate shows up in its sales line's greater slope. With regular arithmetic scaling, however, the difference in growth rates is hidden.*

Pie charts, as almost everybody knows, show a single data series and depict individual data points as segments of the circle, or slices of the pie. While this means that they allow people to compare individual data point values to the total of all the data point values—and one might argue this is a strength—in general, pie charts are without merit because they can show only a single small data series. Almost always, something that appears in a pie chart should instead be shown in a table. Figure 2-17, for example, uses both a table and a pie chart to show the same data set: populations of major English-speaking countries. You'll probably agree that the table shown in the worksheet range A1:B6 works much better as a communication tool than the pie chart.

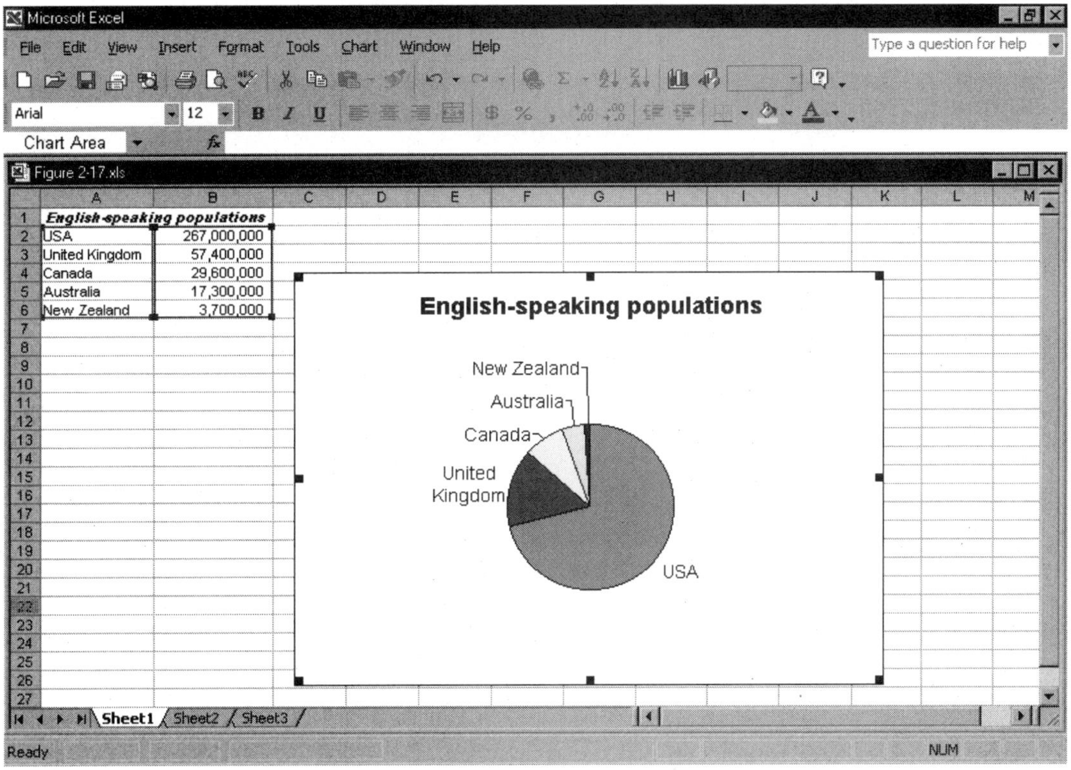

Figure 2-17 Although pie charts let you compare individual data point values to the total data point values in a data series, a table almost always presents the information more clearly.

Radar charts plot each data category's data point values on separate value axes and connect the data point values of each data series with a line, as shown in Figure 2-18. The strength of a radar chart is that it may make it possible to precisely compare individual data point values within a data category. The weakness of a radar chart is that it may make it difficult for you to compare data point values in different categories (although this isn't always a problem). You're also practically limited to a small set of data categories because the chart uses a separate value axis for each. (You obviously can't, for example, plot a set of data with two hundred categories.)

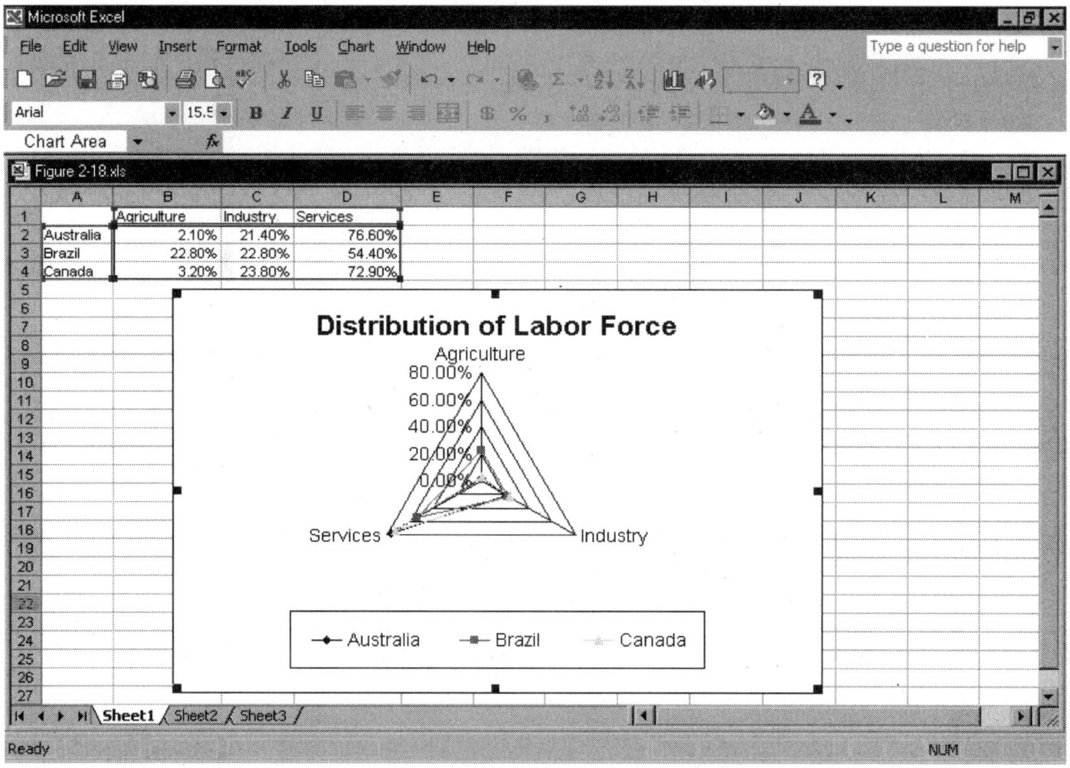

Figure 2-18 A radar chart that compares labor force distribution for Australia, Brazil, and Canada.

Stock charts plot security prices in a common open-high-low-close format, as shown in Figure 2-19. Note that if you do choose to create a stock chart, Excel expects you to organize your data series in this order: volume, opening price, high price, low price, and closing price, as shown in Figure 2-19.

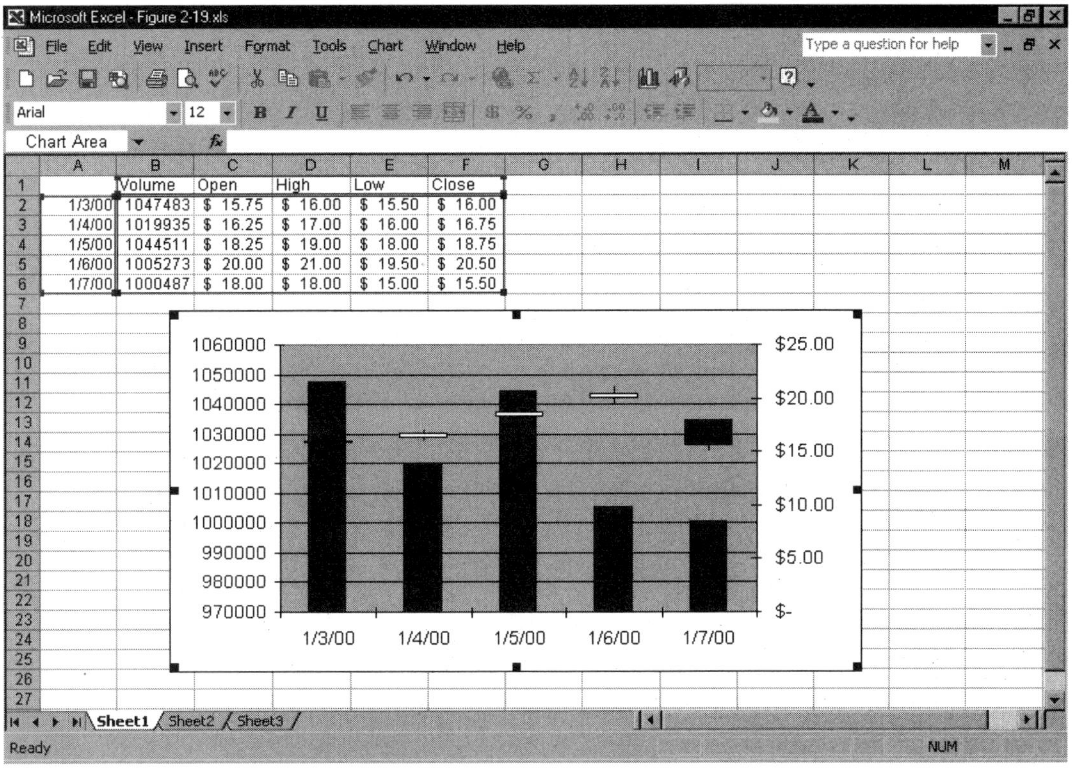

Figure 2-19 A stock chart lets you plot up to five data series in an open-high-low-close format.

NOTE *While this chart type comes from technical security analysis, the chart type can be useful even to people who don't chart security prices. One might use such a chart, for example, to plot daily temperatures.*

Surface charts plot data series in a three-dimensional grid, generally using color not to identify data series but rather to indicate value axis ranges. The principal strength of a surface chart is that it lets you show with equal emphasis both relationships within a data series and within a data category. A surface chart, however, also suffers from two weaknesses: One, because the chart does show a three-dimensional surface, it's easy for the topography of the plot area to hide data—for peaks to hide valleys. Two, although the surface uses color in its value calibrations, there isn't any agreed-upon order to colors. Is the color red "greater" than blue, for example? Is yellow "less than" green? Figure 2-20 shows a surface chart that plots labor force distribution data for Australia, Brazil, and Canada.

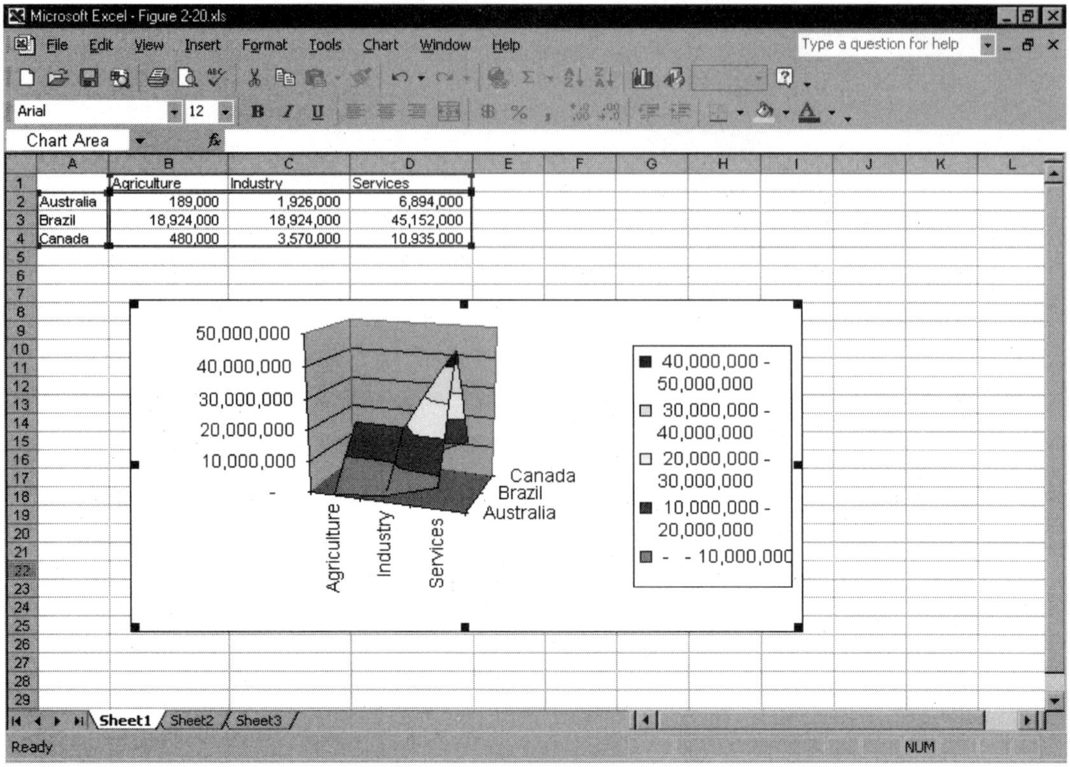

Figure 2-20 A surface chart that shows labor force distributions for Australia, Brazil, and Canada.

XY (Scatter) charts let you visually explore the relationships between data series by treating the horizontal axis as a second values axis. To accomplish this, XY charts actually plot pairs of data points. In Figure 2-21, for example, the chart shows years of education and monthly income and suggests, not surprisingly, that more educated people make more money. The huge strength of an XY chart is that it lets you explore the relationships—perhaps causation or simply correlation—between two data series. The XY chart is the only Excel chart type that lets you do this. If the XY chart suffers from a weakness, it is that the chart may suggest correlations or relationships that don't exist. (You can use Excel's regression analysis tools, discussed in Chapter 4, to examine whether two data series appear correlated.)

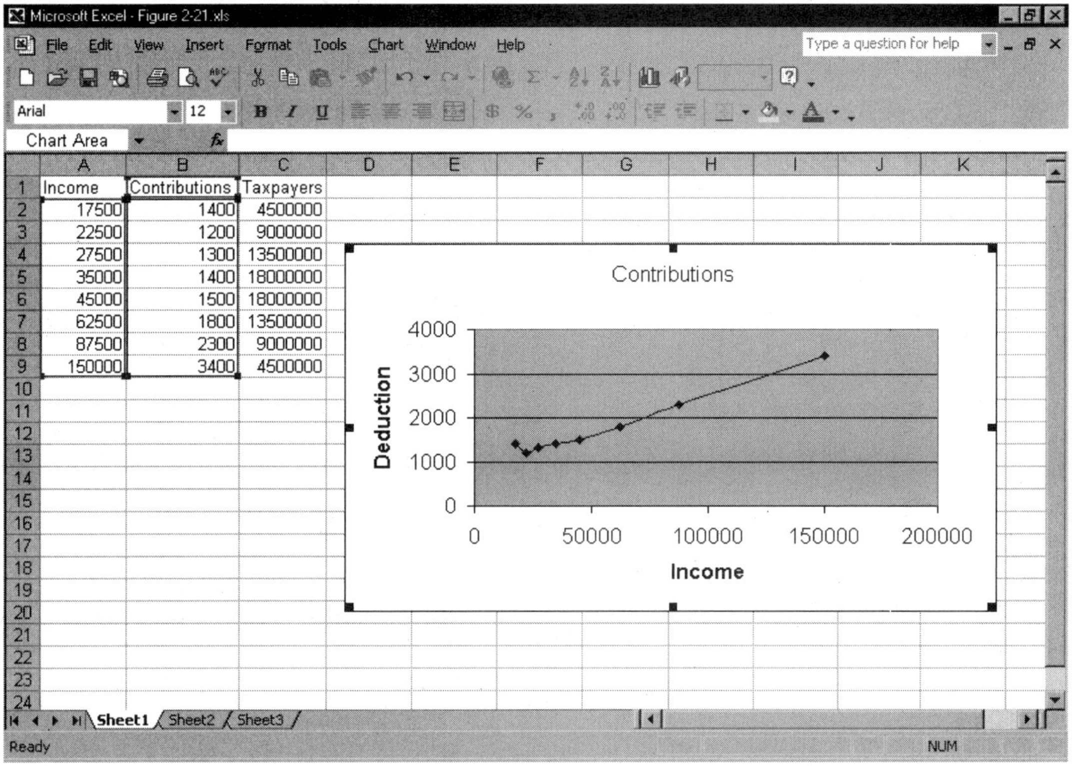

Figure 2-21 A simple XY chart that compares U.S. Internal Revenue Service data on the relationship between education and income.

NOTE *You aren't limited to showing a single data series in an XY chart. Each data series, however, must use the same pair of data point values.*

Customizing Your Charts

You can easily customize your charts so they better fit your needs. You can, for example, rerun the Chart Wizard. This approach is usually simplest. But you can also use Chart menu commands to change specific elements of a chart. The paragraphs that follow discuss each of the two approaches, because you'll find occasion to use both.

Using the Chart Wizard to Customize a Chart

To use the Chart Wizard to customize a chart, select the chart and then click the Chart Wizard toolbar button. Excel restarts the Chart Wizard, and you can step through the four dialog boxes (described earlier in this chapter) to make your changes.

Note that you can make changes not described in the earlier discussion of the Chart Wizard, too. Figure 2-22, for example, shows the Custom Types tab of the first Chart Wizard dialog box. The Custom Types tab displays a variety of hybrid charts in which different data series use different data markers and also charts that use unusual color schemes. To use one of these custom chart types, select it from the list.

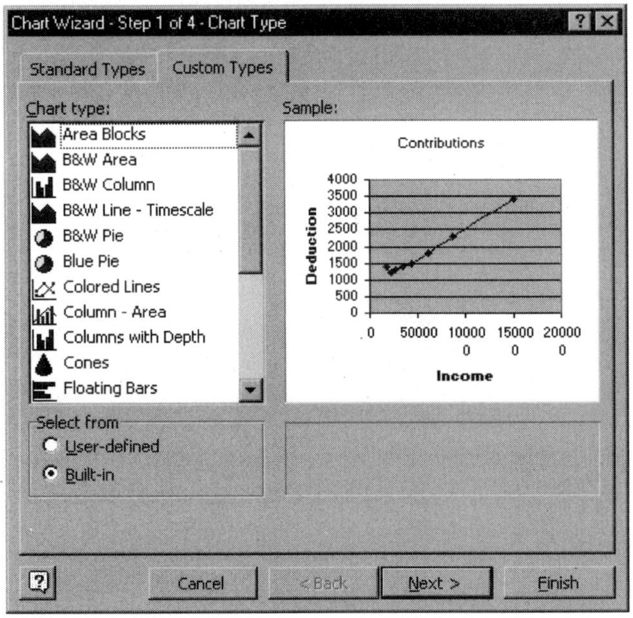

Figure 2-22 The Custom Types tab of the first Chart Wizard dialog box.

NOTE *You can also change the chart type by clicking a chart and then choosing the Chart menu's Chart Type command. When you do this, Excel displays a dialog box, which closely resembles the dialog box shown in Figure 2-22.*

You can add to or change the data series plotted in a chart using the Series tab of the second Chart Wizard dialog box, which is shown in Figure 2-23. To change a data series, click its name in the Series list box and then change the values in the Name and Values boxes. To add a data series to the chart, click Add, and then, after Excel adds the new series, use the Name and Values boxes to name the data series and identify the worksheet range holding the data series. To remove a data series, click the data series and then click Remove. Note, too, that the Series tab also provides a box you use to specify which worksheet range holds the data category names.

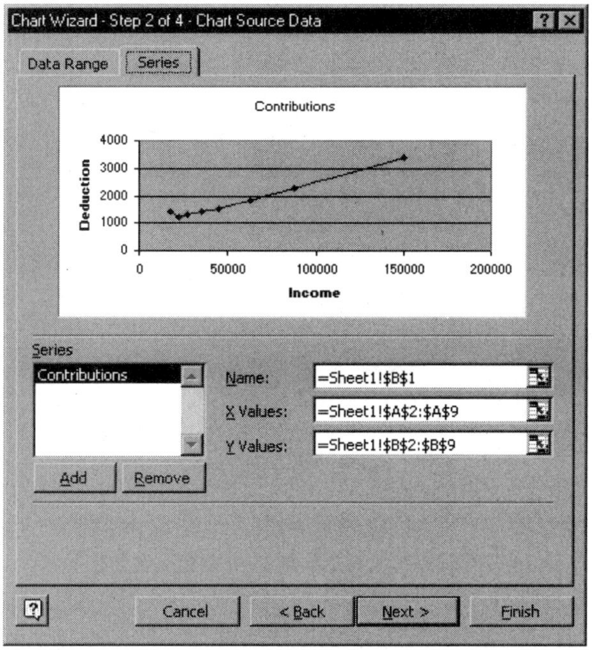

Figure 2-23 The Series tab of the second Chart Wizard dialog box.

TIP *If you click the worksheet button shown at the right end of the Name and Values boxes, Excel minimizes the dialog box. You can then select the cell or worksheet range holding the name, to-be-plotted data, or data category names.*

NOTE *You can also change the chart type by clicking a chart and then choosing the Chart menu's Source Data command. When you do this, Excel displays a dialog box, which closely resembles the dialog box shown in Figure 2-23.*

You can use the third Chart Wizard dialog box, shown in Figure 2-24, to change the text you've used to annotate the change, the appearance of the chart's axes, the gridlines used within the plot area, the location of a legend (and whether you even want one of these), whether data labels appear next to data markers, and whether a table of the plotted data also appears in the chart. Figure 2-24, for example, shows the Axes tab. You use its check boxes to indicate whether you want a Value (X) axis and a Value (Y) axis and, for the Value (X) axis, what formatting you want. Rather than reading about what each of these options does, experiment with them yourself. If your experimentation still leaves you with questions, click the Question button in the dialog box's upper right corner and then click the option you have a question about.

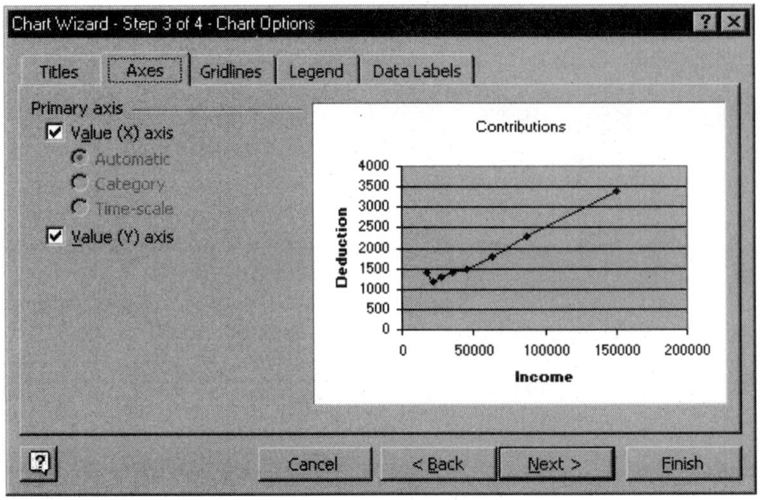

Figure 2-24 The Axes tab of the third Chart Wizard dialog box.

TIP *Typically you do want to apply common sense to your axes scaling, and especially the scaling of your Value (Y) axis. Using inappropriately small scaling factors, for example, can exaggerate differences in data point values and changes in values—as illustrated almost every night on the news report of the major stock market indexes. Similarly, using inappropriately large scaling factors can hide important differences in values and changes in values.*

NOTE *If you want to show the relative changes in values, you typically want to use logarithmic scaling of the values axis. To use the logarithmic scaling, right-click the axis you want to logarithmically scale, choose the shortcut menu's Format Axis command, click the Scale tab, and select the Logarithmic Scale check box.*

This book doesn't show pictures of the other tabs. You can easily see them yourself by clicking the appropriate tab. Note, however, what each of the other tabs allows you to do. The Gridlines tab displays check boxes you can select to add horizontal and vertical gridlines to plot the area of your chart. The Legend tab displays a Show Legend check box you can select to add a legend to the chart and then Placement option buttons—Bottom, Corner, Top, Right, or Left—which you can use to indicate where you want the legend placed. The Data Labels tab displays a set of option buttons you can use to indicate whether you want the actual data point values or equivalent percentages written next to their data markers.

Finally, the Data Table tab (if it appears) provides two check boxes you can select to add a table and, optionally, a legend of the data point values to the bottom of the chart area.

NOTE *You can also change the chart text, axes, gridlines, legend, data labels, or data table by clicking a chart and then choosing the Chart menu's Chart Options command. When you do this, Excel displays a dialog box, which closely resembles the dialog box shown in Figure 2-24.*

You can use the fourth Chart Wizard dialog box, shown in Figure 2-25, to relocate a chart. To do this, simply select the other option when you see this dialog box. For example, if the dialog box initially shows the As New Sheet option button selected, click the As Object In option button—or vice versa.

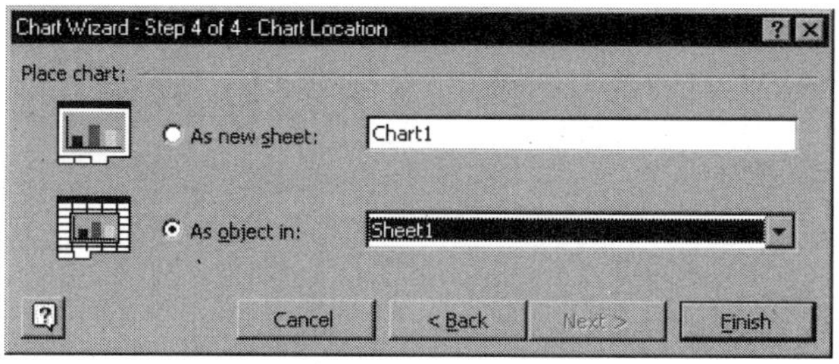

Figure 2-25 The fourth Chart Wizard dialog box.

NOTE *You can also change the chart location by clicking a chart and then choosing the Chart menu's Location command. When you do this, Excel displays a dialog box, which closely resembles the dialog box shown in Figure 2-25.*

Using the Shortcut Menu's Format Command

While you can use the Chart Wizard or some of the equivalent Chart menu commands to customize a chart, Excel doesn't allow you to make every change using just these methods. If you can't use the Chart Wizard or an equivalent command to change some element of a chart, you can right-click the part of the chart that you want to change and then choose the shortcut menu's Format command. For example, if you want to change the scaling of the values axis, you can right-click the values axis and then choose the Format Axis command. (Obviously, if you right-click other parts of a chart, Excel displays a different Format command which, in turn, displays a different dialog box.)

Some books on Excel spend pages describing the myriad changes you can make to each specific part of a chart. But you probably don't really need that level of instruction. In a nutshell, you make only a handful of changes to each part of a chart:

- *Patterns.* Many of the Format dialog boxes display a Patterns tab that you can use to select the colors and lines you want Excel to use to draw the chart object.
- *Fonts.* Any Format dialog box for an element that includes text provides a Font tab that you can use to choose font, font style, font point size, and special text effects.
- *Number.* Any Format dialog box for an element that includes numbers provides a Number tab that you can use to choose a numeric formatting style.
- *Alignment.* Any Format dialog box for an element that includes text provides an Alignment tab that you can use to align text.
- *Scale.* The Format dialog box for both the axes and the gridlines provides a Scale tab that you can use to specify how Excel should calibrate and draw the axis or grid.

TIP *Remember that if you have a question about how to work with some dialog box option, you can click the Question button and then click the option to get a brief but usually very helpful description. The Question button appears in the upper right corner of the dialog box and is marked with a question mark.*

Skill 3

DATABASES

Featuring:

- Understanding Databases
- Creating and Filling a Database
- Sorting and Filtering a Database
- Other Database Tools

Because Excel allows you to build tables quickly and easily, it is an excellent tool for creating and arranging flat databases, or basic lists of information. To create a more complex database with multiple tables linked together (called a *relational database*), you need a database management program such as Microsoft Access. Although relational databases require more time and effort to design and build, they reduce the amount of duplicate information you have to enter in the database as you work with it. For example, if you create a relational database for your customers, you can create a primary table for the customer list and related tables for customer orders. This way, when a customer places an order, you need only fill in the order information and not all of the information about the customer. However, when you use Excel's database capabilities, you are working in an environment in which you are familiar, and where you can take advantage of Excel's database tools and functions. In many cases, using Excel in this manner may be the only database you need.

Understanding Databases

A database is a table of information that you can search, sort, filter, and on which you can perform other operations. Each row of a database holds a record, and each column holds a field. For example, if you have a database of vendors, the various pieces of information about a single vendor make up a record; the rows store this information about the individual vendors. A piece of information, such as the payment term, is a field; the columns contain this same piece of information across all vendors.

Creating and Filling a Database

To work with a list of data in Excel, you first need to create the database so that Excel recognizes it as one. Then you can begin entering the data in the database. This section describes a couple of options Excel provides for doing so.

NOTE *If the data you want in your database already exists in electronic form, you can import it into Excel. See Skill 5 for more information on how to do so.*

Creating a Database

You create a database in Excel in much the same way you create any other spreadsheet. After you have created the database, you can rename, add, or delete worksheets in the workbook, and then save the workbook.

1. **Open a new blank workbook.**

   If you don't have Excel running, start the program to create a new workbook. If you have Excel running, click the New toolbar button to create a new workbook based on the Workbook template.

2. **Determine what each record should be. The information these records' hold becomes the records' fields.**

   For example, if you want to build a database of employees, each employee is a record, and the fields are probably first name, last name, Social Security number, address, birth date, hire date, and the like.

NOTE *Even if you don't have information for every field in a record, you can still include the field. For example, you can have a mobile phone-number field for a database of contacts even though only some contacts have mobile phone entries.*

3. **Enter the field labels in the first row of the worksheet.**

   Enter the field labels in the order in which you think you want them. You can easily change the order of the fields at a later time, if you find that you need to do so. Do not leave blank columns between fields. Figure 3-1 shows a worksheet with a list of field labels in row 1.

	A	B	C	D	E	F	G	H	I	J
1	ProductJD	Name	Size	Content	Color	Description	Cost	Vendor	Price	
2										

Figure 3-1 Creating a database.

TIP *For ease of use, use the shortest labels that clearly describe the contents of the field. It is not a good idea to use spaces in field labels, however, even though Excel allows it. It may cause problems if you ever need to export the database to another program.*

Filling a Database with Information

You can add information to the database the same way you add information to any other worksheet—by moving to the cell and typing the label, value, or formula. However, you can also use forms to enter the information record by record (i.e., row by row). To use forms for data entry, follow these steps:

1. **Choose the Data menu's Form command.**

   Excel displays the dialog box shown in Figure 3-2, named after the worksheet on which the form is based. The dialog box contains the form field labels you entered in the first row. If you've already entered some data in the database, Excel displays the first record you entered in the form field boxes. After you enter the first record, the upper right corner of the form tells you which record you're currently viewing and how many records you've entered (this number doesn't include the first row containing the field labels).

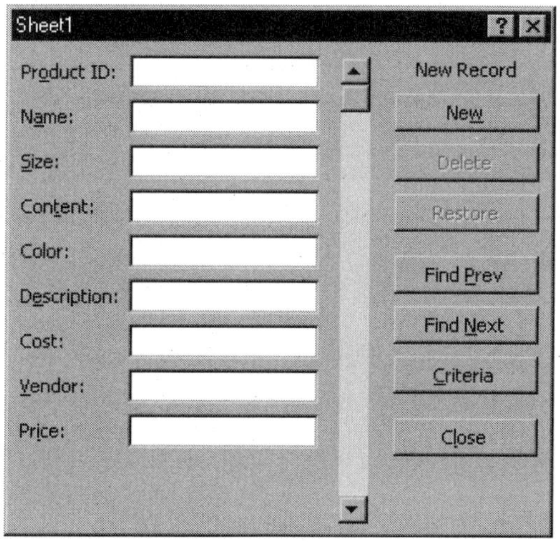

Figure 3-2 Using a form to enter data in a database.

NOTE *If you haven't yet entered any records, click OK in the warning message that Excel displays to use the first row as your field labels.*

2. **If the form field boxes are not blank, click New to create a New record.**

   Excel displays a blank form dialog box in which you can enter the new record's data.

3. **Fill in the information about the first record.**

   Enter the data in the appropriate boxes.

4. **Click New again to add the new record to the worksheet and display a new blank form.**

   When you add a new record to a database, Excel adds a new row to the worksheet.

5. **When you're finished using a form to enter records, click Close.**

   Excel closes the form and returns you to the worksheet containing the database.

TIP *To continue viewing field labels as you scroll down a database, you can use Excel's split feature. To create a horizontal pane, rest the mouse pointer over the narrow box at the top end of the vertical scroll bar so it becomes a double-sided arrow, and then drag to the line between the field label and the first record. Freeze this pane by choosing the Window menu's Freeze Panes command.*

Editing Database Records

After you've entered records, you can edit them by moving to the cell holding the information you want to change and entering new information. You can also redisplay the form and use it to edit records. To edit records using a form, follow these steps:

1. **Choose the Data menu's Form command to redisplay the form.**
2. **Move to the record you want to edit.**

   Click Find Prev to page backward through the records one by one, or click Find Next to page forward through the records one by one. You can also use the scroll bar to scroll through the database to the record you want to edit.
3. **Enter your changes in the form's fields.**

   If you make a mistake when editing a form, click Restore to undo all of your changes to the record.

NOTE *To delete a record, click Delete. Excel deletes this row from the worksheet.*

4. **Update the worksheet with your changes to the record.**

   Click Find Next or Find Prev to edit other records, click New to add a new record, or click Close to return to the worksheet.

Finding Records in a Database

To use a form to find records that match the criteria you specify, follow these steps:

1. **Choose the Data menu's Form command to display the form.**
2. **Click Criteria.**

   The upper right corner of the form now displays the word *Criteria,* as shown in Figure 3-3.

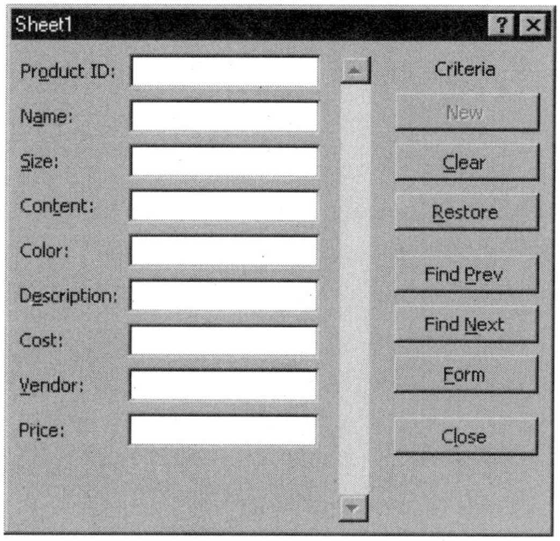

Figure 3-3 Finding a record in a database.

3. **Enter the search criteria in the form's fields.**
4. **Click Find Prev or Find Next.**

   Excel finds the previous or next record matching the criteria you specified.

NOTE *You can also use Excel's Find feature to find items in a database. Just choose the Edit menu's Find command. Chapter 1 describes finding and replacing information in Excel.*

Sorting and Filtering a Database

Once you have created a database, you can begin sorting and filtering so that you can access and analyze the information you need.

Sorting a Database

To sort a database, follow these steps:

1. **Click a cell in the database.**

   Doing so tells Excel that you want to sort all the fields in the database and keep the records intact.

WARNING *If you select a range that doesn't include all columns, Excel sorts the columns in your range but does not sort the other columns accordingly. This disassociates fields from the records to which they belong and attaches them to other records.*

TIP *To sort only a part of a database, select all rows for the records you want to sort.*

2. **Choose the Data menu's Sort command.**

   Excel displays the Sort dialog box shown in Figure 3-4.

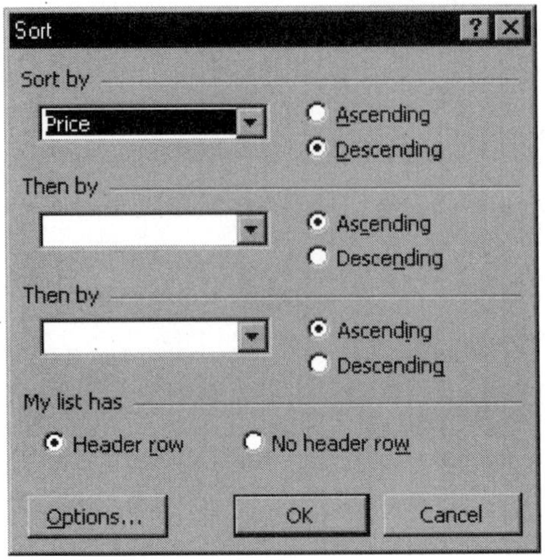

Figure 3-4 The Sort dialog box.

3. **Specify the first field by which you want to sort.**

   Use the Sort By drop-down list box to select the name of the field by which you want to sort the database.

TIP *To quickly sort a database by the entries in a single field, select a cell in the field's column and click the Sort Ascending or Sort Descending toolbar button.*

4. **Specify the order by which you want to sort the field.**

   Click the Ascending option button to sort with the lowest number, first letter of the alphabet, or earliest date at the top of the column. Click the Descending option button to sort in reverse numeric, alphabetic, or chronological order.

NOTE *Regardless of whether you click Ascending or Descending, blank fields appear at the bottom of the list.*

5. **Optionally, specify second- and third-level sorting.**

   If multiple entries in the field you're sorting by are the same, you can specify other fields by which you want to sort using the Then By drop-down list boxes and corresponding Ascending and Descending option buttons. For example, if you sort by the price field and have multiple items selling for the same price, you can sort within this group by name, by product identification number, or by cost.

6. **Make sure that the Header Row option is selected.**

   If you don't select the Header Row option, Excel sorts your field labels along with the data in the fields.

7. **Click OK.**

Creating Custom Sort Orders

To specify a nonnumeric, nonalphabetic, or nonchronological sort order, follow these steps:

1. **Choose the Tools menu's Options command, and click the Custom Lists tab.**

   Excel displays the Custom Lists tab of the Options dialog box, as shown in Figure 3-5.

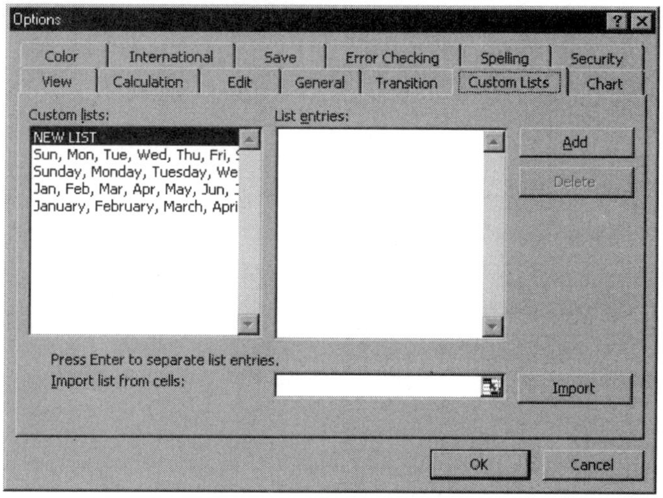

Figure 3-5 Creating a custom sort list.

2. **Select New List from the Custom Lists list.**

3. **Specify the items in the order you want to sort them.**

   To do this, enter the items in the List Entries box, pressing the Enter key after each item. Or, if you already have a range of cells in the worksheet that contains the items sorted in the order you want, click the Import List From Cells box, select the range, and click Import.

4. **Click Add.**

   Excel adds the list to the Custom Lists list.

5. **Click OK when you're finished.**

Filtering Databases

If your database contains large amounts of data, you may want Excel to display only the data you're interested in so you can focus on it better. To do this, you use Excel's Filter feature. When you filter a database, Excel doesn't delete the records that don't meet the criteria. It just hides them. To filter a database, follow these steps:

1. **Select a cell in the database.**
2. **Choose the Data menu's Filter command, and then choose AutoFilter.**

   Excel adds arrow buttons to the right side of your field labels in the first row, as shown in Figure 3-6.

	A	B	C	D	E	F	G	H	I	J
1	Product	Name	Si:	Content	Color	Descripti	Cost	Vendor	Price	
2	11236	Color Wheels	45	100 Cottor	Periwinkle	Swirl	3.23	Lucky	6.99	
3	11216	Color Wheels	45	100 Cottor	Periwinkle	Plain	2.89	Lucky	4.99	
4	21216	Color Wheels	60	100 Cottor	Periwinkle	Plain	2.92	Lucky	5.99	
5	11237	Color Wheels	45	100 Cottor	Forest	Swirl	3.23	Lucky	6.99	
6	11217	Color Wheels	45	100 Cottor	Forest	Plain	2.89	Lucky	4.99	
7	21217	Color Wheels	60	100 Cottor	Forest	Plain	2.92	Lucky	5.99	
8	11235	Color Wheels	45	100 Cottor	Sunflower	Swirl	3.23	Lucky	6.99	
9	11215	Color Wheels	45	100 Cottor	Sunflower	Plain	2.89	Lucky	4.99	
10	21215	Color Wheels	60	100 Cottor	Sunflower	Plain	2.92	Lucky	5.99	
11	11239	Color Wheels	45	100 Cottor	Chocolate	Swirl	3.23	Lucky	6.99	
12	11219	Color Wheels	45	100 Cottor	Chocolate	Plain	2.89	Lucky	4.99	
13	21219	Color Wheels	60	100 Cottor	Chocolate	Plain	2.92	Lucky	5.99	
14	48340	Collections	45	65/35	Purple	Stripes	3.43	JCC	7.29	
15	48344	Collections	45	65/35	Purple	Squares	3.43	JCC	7.29	
16	78340	Collections	45	65/35	Orange	Stripes	3.43	JCC	7.29	
17	78344	Collections	45	65/35	Orange	Squares	3.43	JCC	7.29	
18	28340	Collections	45	65/35	Navy	Stripes	3.43	JCC	7.29	
19	28344	Collections	45	65/35	Navy	Squares	3.43	JCC	7.29	
20	98340	Collections	45	65/35	Turquoise	Stripes	3.43	JCC	7.29	
21	98344	Collections	45	65/35	Turquoise	Squares	3.43	JCC	7.29	
22	22609	Fun spots	45	75/20/5	Pink	Stars	2.75	General Designers	5.49	

Sheet1 / Sheet2 / Sheet3

Ready NUM

Figure 3-6 Filtering field entries.

3. **Click the arrow for the field by which you want to filter records.**

   Excel displays a drop-down list of the entries in that field.

   - If you want to include only a single entry, select the entry from the list.
   - To display only a given top or bottom percent or number of entries, select Top 10 from the list. Excel displays the Top 10 AutoFilter dialog box. Use it to specify whether you want to view the top or bottom entries in the field and the number or percentage of entries you want to view. Click OK when you're finished.

- To customize the filter, choose Custom from the list. Excel displays the Custom AutoFilter dialog box shown in Figure 3-7. Use the first drop-down list box to select the operator. Use the second drop-down list box to enter the text or value on which you're basing the filter. Optionally, click the And or Or option button to specify another criteria and use the second row of drop-down list boxes to describe the second criteria. Click OK when you're finished.

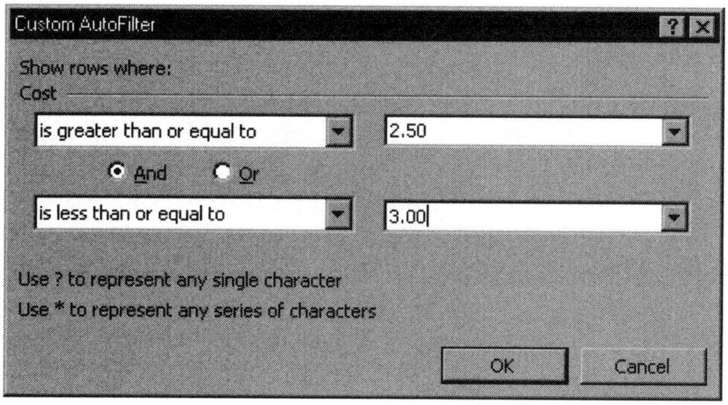

Figure 3-7 Displaying only records that show costs between $2.50 and $3.00.

4. If necessary, repeat the filtering procedure for another field.

For example, you could filter to display records that have cost entries fitting certain criteria and size entries fitting certain criteria.

5. Click OK.

If you want to save the filter criteria, save the database under a new name. To redisplay all records, choose the Data menu's Filter command and then choose Show All.

NOTE *You can tell that a database has been filtered because the row numbers appear in blue and skip values. The filtered field's arrow is also blue.*

Performing an Advanced Filter

For more advanced filtering options, you can use Excel's Advanced Filter feature. The Advanced Filter feature allows you to do the following:

- Filter criteria based on a computation. For example, you could display only those records with prices below the average price.
- Specify more than two criteria for a single column. For example, you may want to display all items that are from any one of three vendors.

- Specify criteria involving multiple columns and the conjunction OR. For example, you could filter to include items that either come from a particular vendor or are of a non-standard size.

To perform an advanced filter, follow these steps:

1. **Enter the filter criteria in a range of cells.**

   Place the criteria range either above or below the database so that it doesn't get hidden when you filter the database.

   Enter in a single row the criteria labels for the fields on which you want to base the filter. Make sure the criteria labels that you enter exactly match the field labels in the database. Then enter the criteria for each field in the rows below. Excel considers criteria on the same line to be joined by the conjunction AND and criteria on separate lines to be joined by OR. For numeric criteria, enter labels and operators such as <, <=, >, >=, and the value. For text criteria, enter a single letter to filter items that begin with that letter. Enter the operators < or > and a letter to filter items that come before or after that letter of the alphabet.

NOTE *Criteria based on formulas are a special case. When you use a formula to create a criterion, do not use a column label for a criteria label; either keep the criteria label blank or use a label that is not a column label in the list. For more information, choose the Help menu's Microsoft Excel Help command, click the Index tab, and select Advanced_Filter from the Keywords list.*

TIP *For filters based on computations, use absolute references to cells outside the database and relative references to cells within the database.*

Figure 3-8 shows how the criteria ranges would look for the three examples mentioned above.

M	N	O	P
Price			
=I2<AVERAGE(I2:I24)			
Vendor			
Lucky			
JCC			
General Designers			
Size	Size	Vendor	
<45	>60	Lucky	

Figure 3-8 Creating a criteria range.

2. **Select a cell in the database list, choose the Data menu's Filter command, and then choose Advanced Filter.**

   Excel selects the entire database and displays the Advanced Filter dialog box shown in Figure 3-9.

Figure 3-9 The Advanced Filter dialog box.

3. **Click an Action option button to specify where you want Excel to display the filtered database.**

   Click the first option button to display in the current database worksheet only those records that fit the filter criteria. Click the second option button to copy the records that fit the criteria to a different location.

4. **Verify that Excel selected the correct list in its entirety.**

   Make sure the List Range contains all the records and fields in the database and nothing but the database you want to filter.

5. **Enter the criteria range in the Criteria Range box.**

   You can either type the range in the box or click the box and then select the range in the worksheet.

WARNING *Make sure you don't select any blank rows in the range. When a cell in a criteria range is blank, Excel accepts any content for that field. So if a row is blank, Excel returns an unfiltered database.*

6. **If you chose to copy the filtered database to another location in step 3, specify the destination.**

   Enter the location in the Copy To box.

7. **Optionally, select the Unique Records Only check box to exclude duplicate records.**

8. **Click OK.**

   Excel filters the database according to your criteria and displays the filtered information in the location you specified.

To redisplay all records, choose the Data menu's Filter command and then choose Show All.

Other Database Tools

You can perform several other operations on databases in Excel. This section describes how you can create subtotals, validate database entries, and use functions specific to databases.

Subtotaling Databases

After you sort and filter your database as necessary, you can create subtotals to summarize details in your database. To subtotal information in a database, follow these steps:

1. **Select a cell in the database, and choose the Data menu's Subtotals command.**

   Excel displays the Subtotal dialog box shown in Figure 3-10.

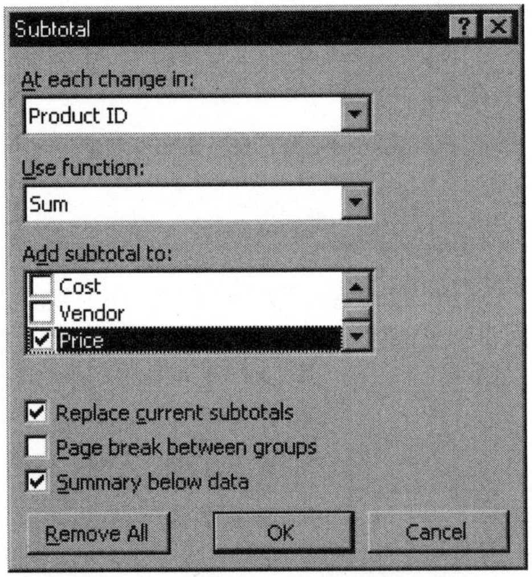

Figure 3-10 The Subtotal dialog box.

2. **Use the At Each Change In drop-down list box to specify the field by which you want the subtotals grouped.**
3. **Select a function from the Use Function drop-down list box.**

   Not only can the subtotal tool add groups of entries to create subtotals, but it can also perform other functions, such as calculating the average, counting the number of entries or blank items, or calculating the standard deviation or variation.

4. Select check boxes for the fields on which you want the subtotal operation performed.
5. Select the Replace Current Subtotals check box if you've created subtotals before.
6. Leave the Page Break Between Groups check box clear.
7. Select the Summary Below Data check box unless you want the subtotals to appear above rather than below the data they summarize.
8. Click OK.

   Excel adds subtotal and grand total rows to the database, as shown in Figure 3-11. To remove subtotals, choose the Data menu's Subtotals command and click Remove All in the Subtotal dialog box.

	A	B	C	D	E	F	G	H	I	J	K
1	ProductID	Name	Size	Content	Color	Description	Cost	Vendor	Price	Unit Sales	Revenue
2	11236	Color Wheels	45	100 Cotton	Periwinkle	Swirl	3.23	Lucky	6.99	35	244.65
3	11216	Color Wheels	45	100 Cotton	Periwinkle	Plain	2.89	Lucky	4.99	29	144.71
4	21216	Color Wheels	60	100 Cotton	Periwinkle	Plain	2.92	Lucky	5.99	35	209.65
5	11237	Color Wheels	45	100 Cotton	Forest	Swirl	3.23	Lucky	6.99	36	251.64
6	11217	Color Wheels	45	100 Cotton	Forest	Plain	2.89	Lucky	4.99	28	139.72
7	21217	Color Wheels	60	100 Cotton	Forest	Plain	2.92	Lucky	5.99	36	215.64
8	11235	Color Wheels	45	100 Cotton	Sunflower	Swirl	3.23	Lucky	6.99	20	139.80
9	11215	Color Wheels	45	100 Cotton	Sunflower	Plain	2.89	Lucky	4.99	15	74.85
10	21215	Color Wheels	60	100 Cotton	Sunflower	Plain	2.92	Lucky	5.99	15	89.85
11	11239	Color Wheels	45	100 Cotton	Chocolate	Swirl	3.23	Lucky	6.99	25	174.75
12	11219	Color Wheels	45	100 Cotton	Chocolate	Plain	2.89	Lucky	4.99	17	84.83
13	21219	Color Wheels	60	100 Cotton	Chocolate	Plain	2.92	Lucky	5.99	19	113.81
14								**Lucky Total**		310	1,883.90
15	48340	Collections	45	65/35	Purple	Stripes	3.43	JCC	7.29	41	298.89
16	48344	Collections	45	65/35	Purple	Squares	3.43	JCC	7.29	52	379.08
17	78340	Collections	45	65/35	Orange	Stripes	3.43	JCC	7.29	33	240.57
18	78344	Collections	45	65/35	Orange	Squares	3.43	JCC	7.29	37	269.73
19	28340	Collections	45	65/35	Navy	Stripes	3.43	JCC	7.29	43	313.47
20	28344	Collections	45	65/35	Navy	Squares	3.43	JCC	7.29	39	284.31
21	98340	Collections	45	65/35	Turquoise	Stripes	3.43	JCC	7.29	33	240.57
22	98344	Collections	45	65/35	Turquoise	Squares	3.43	JCC	7.29	33	240.57
23								**JCC Total**		311	2,267.19
24	22609	Fun spots	45	75/20/5	Pink	Stars	2.75	General Designers	5.49	70	384.30
25	23609	Fun spots	45	75/20/5	Pale Blue	Stars	2.75	General Designers	5.49	75	411.75
26	24609	Fun spots	45	75/20/5	Lime	Stars	2.75	General Designers	5.49	25	137.25
27								**General Designers Total**		170	933.30
28								**Grand Total**		791	5,084.39
29											

Figure 3-11 A database with subtotals.

TIP *You can hide and display groups by clicking the boxes with the plus and minus signs in the outline area on the left. You can also click the numbers at the top of the outline area to view specific levels of the outline.*

Validating Database Entries

Excel's Validation feature allows you to ensure that new records you add to a database fit certain criteria. This can help prevent someone from entering, for example, a product name in a numeric product ID field.

NOTE *The validation rules apply whether you enter data directly in the database worksheet or use a form.*

To set up validation criteria for your database, follow these steps:

1. **Select the range of cells to which you want the criteria to apply, and choose the Data menu's Validation command.**

   To set criteria for all entries in a field, select the entire field by clicking the column header. Excel displays the Data Validation dialog box, as shown in Figure 3-12.

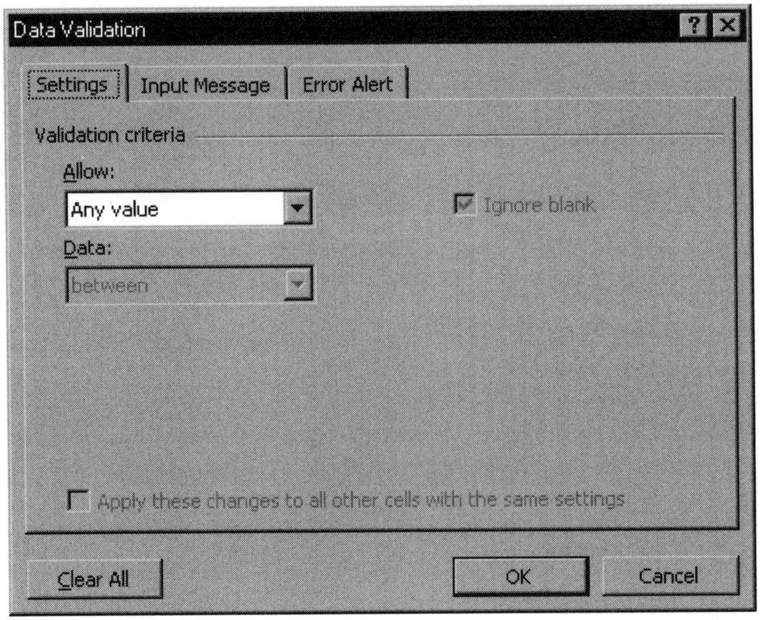

Figure 3-12 The Settings tab of the Data Validation dialog box.

2. **Click the Settings tab, and indicate which kind of data and which range of values is permissible.**

   Select a type of data from the Allow drop-down list box. After you select a data type, Excel displays other boxes, which allow you to constrain the type of data you selected. For example, if you selected Date, Excel prompts you to select the start- and end-date boundaries.

3. **Click the Input Message tab, and create a prompt to inform database users which input is allowable.**

   Optionally, enter a short title for the message in the Title box. Enter the message text in the Input Message box. If you enter records directly in the database and do not use a form, Excel displays the input message when you select a cell to which the validation criteria applies.

4. **Click the Error Alert tab to customize the pop-up error message that will appear if a person enters invalid data.**

   Select a symbol from the Style drop-down list box. Optionally, enter a title for the message in the Title box. Enter the message text in the Error Message box, as shown in Figure 3-13.

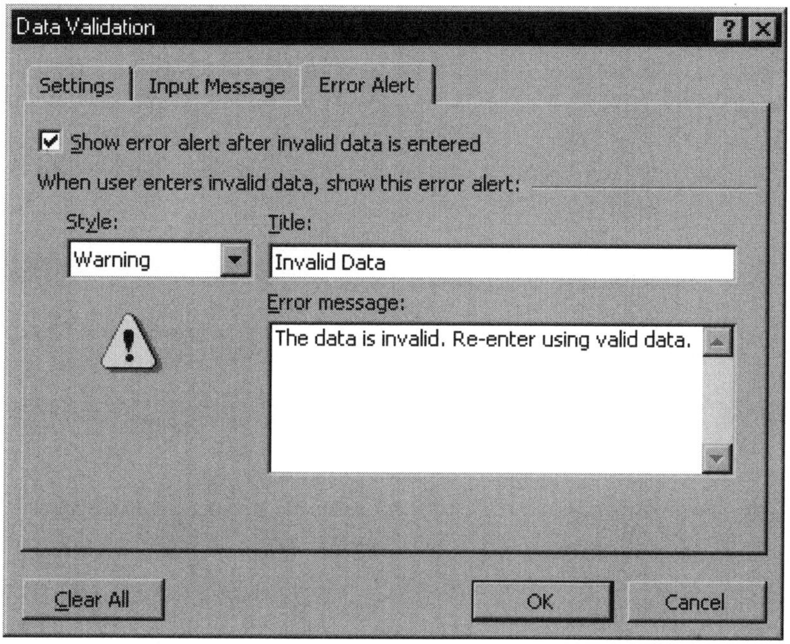

Figure 3-13 Creating an error message.

Excel's Database Functions

Excel comes with a collection of functions tailored especially for databases. To see these functions, display the Insert Function dialog box and select Database from the function category list. All of these functions begin with the letter D. The database functions work similarly to the standard worksheet functions except that they allow an extra parameter so you can specify the items to which a function applies. For example, the DSTDEV function works like the regular STDEV function to find standard deviation except that it uses the following syntax:

```
=DSTDEV(database,field,criteria)
```

where database is the range of cells that make up database, and field is the column on which you want the function performed. Enter the field parameter as text with the field label in quotation marks, such as "Product ID." Criteria is an optional range of cells containing criteria you specify.

TIP *When creating a criteria range, put it at the top or bottom of your database so that none of it is hidden if you filter the database. The "Performing an Advanced Filter" section earlier in the chapter contains more tips, information, and examples about creating criteria ranges.*

NOTE *The function DGET is unique to databases. It returns the value of any cell in a field that meets the criteria specified in the criteria range.*

Skill 4

BUSINESS MODELING

Featuring:

- What-If Analysis with Data Tables
- What-If Analysis with Scenario Manager
- Simple Modeling with Goal Seek
- Optimization Modeling with Solver

This chapter describes how Excel's standard business modeling tools work. Although you can do plenty of powerful analysis without ever touching these tools, you probably should explore them at least a little. They give you new, powerful, relatively easy-to-use ways to analyze issues, problems, and opportunities.

NOTE *Excel also provides another powerful tool for modeling and analyzing your data: the PivotTable tool. Chapter 8 describes the PivotTable tool, including its PivotChart component.*

What-If Analysis with Data Tables

Excel lets you easily create simple data tables that show how changing a formula input affects the formula result. You can, for example, build simple one-variable data tables that show how changing a single input value affects one or more formulas. And you can also create more complicated two-variable data tables that show how changing two input values affect a single formula.

Working with One-Variable Data Tables

One-variable data tables let you experiment with how changing a single input variable can affect a formula's result or even several formulas' results. For example, suppose that you wanted to see how a changing interest rate would affect the loan payment on a $100,000 mortgage. Or suppose that you wanted to see how a changing interest rate would affect the loan payments on a $100,000 mortgage with two different repayment terms: repayment over 15 years and repayment over 30 years. Within Excel, the easiest way to make these calculations would be with a one-variable data table. Both what-if analyses look at the effect of a single changing input value—the interest rate—on a formula or formulas.

Setting Up a One-Variable Data Table

To set up a one-variable data table, you arrange the input values along either the left or top edge of a worksheet range and the formula or formulas you want to calculate along the other edge (top or left). Figure 4-1 shows how this looks with the input values—8.00%, 9.00%, 10.00%, 11.00%, and 12.00%—stored along the left edge of the worksheet range in A2:A6. Along the other edge of the worksheet range—in Figure 4-1, this means B1:C1—enter the formulas you want to test using the input values. In Figure 4-1, you'll see two formulas for calculating a monthly mortgage payment.

B1 fx =PMT(A1/12,15*12,-100000)

	A	B	C	D	E
1		$555.56	$277.78		
2	8.00%				
3	9.00%				
4	10.00%				
5	11.00%				
6	12.00%				
7					

Figure 4-1 An Excel worksheet range set up for creating a one-variable data table.

NOTE *Excel provides financial functions for calculating common formulas, including the formula for a loan payment. The PMT function, which is used in the workbook shown in Figure 4-1, uses the following syntax: PMT(rate,term,loan) in which* rate *is the periodic interest rate,* term *is the number of payments, and* loan *is the loan amount. If you have questions about the PMT function or any other Excel financial function, refer to Chapter 5.*

Cell B1 holds the formula shown below to calculate the monthly payment on a 15-year, $100,000 mortgage:

```
=PMT(A1/12,15*12,-100000)
```

Cell C1 holds the formula shown below to calculate the monthly payment on a 30-year, $100,000 mortgage:

```
=PMT(A1/12,30*12,-100000)
```

The key point to note about both of these formulas—*this is the secret to using a one-variable data table*—is that they refer to the empty corner cell of the worksheet that holds the data table.

Once you've arranged the input values and the formulas as shown in Figure 4-1, finish the data table by following these steps:

1. **Select the worksheet range that includes the input values and the formulas.**

   In Figure 4-1, this means you select the worksheet range A1:C6.

2. **Choose the Data menu's Table command.**

   Excel displays the Table dialog box shown in Figure 4-2.

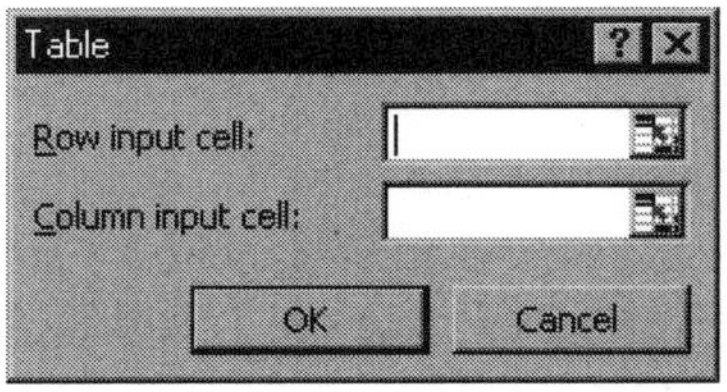

Figure 4-2 The Table dialog box.

3. **Provide the input cell location.**

   The input cell location tells Excel which cell address you've referenced in your what-if formulas. In the worksheet shown in Figure 4-1, the two what-if formulas use cell A1 as the changing, interest-rate input value. So this is the input cell. Because Figure 4-1 arranges the input values into a column, you enter this cell address in the Column Input Cell text box, as shown in Figure 4-2.

4. **Click OK.**

   Excel fills the data table with formula results for each input value, as shown in Figure 4-3. For example, Excel fills cell B2 by using the formula in cell B1 and the interest rate in cell A2 to calculate the monthly payment on a 15-year, $100,000 mortgage when the annual interest rate is 8.00%. Excel fills cell C3 by using the formula in cell C1 and the interest rate in cell A3 to calculate the monthly payment on a 30-year, $100,000 mortgage when the annual interest rate is 9.00%.

B1 =PMT(A1/12,15*12,-100000)

	A	B	C	D	E
1		$555.56	$277.78		
2	8.00%	$955.65	$733.76		
3	9.00%	$1,014.27	$804.62		
4	10.00%	$1,074.61	$877.57		
5	11.00%	$1,136.60	$952.32		
6	12.00%	$1,200.17	$1,028.61		
7					

Figure 4-3 The data table after calculating the what-if formula for each of the input values.

NOTE *Figure 4-1 and 4-3 show a one-variable data table that stores the input values along the left edge and the formulas along the top edge of the worksheet range. You can also store input values along the top edge and the formulas along the left edge. If you use this alternative organization, you enter the input cell address in the Table dialog box's Row Input Cell text box.*

Using the One-Variable Data Table

After you set up the one-variable data table, you can continue your what-if analysis without having to use the Data menu's Table command. Simply change the input values, and Excel updates the formula results for your changes. In the worksheet shown in Figure 4-3, for example, to see what loan payments would look like on a 15-year and 30-year, $100,000 mortgage at 6.5%, 7%, 7.5%, 8%, and 8.5%, enter these interest rate values in the worksheet range A2:A6.

While you might expect to have to reuse the Data menu's Table command to get Excel to recalculate the what-if formulas, you don't actually have to do this. When you initially choose the Data menu's Table command, Excel places the following formula in each of the cells inside the data table:

```
={TABLE(,A1)}
```

If you change an input value, Excel recalculates the TABLE function using the new input value.

Working with Two-Variable Data Tables

Two-variable data tables let you experiment with how changing two input variables can affect a single formula's result. For example, suppose that you wanted to see how a changing interest rate would affect the loan payment on 30-year mortgages of various sizes. For example, suppose that you wanted to calculate a loan payment using interest rates of 8%, 9%, 10%, 11%, and 12% and on mortgage amounts of $100,000, $200,000, and $300,000. Within Excel, the easiest way to make these calculations would be with a two-variable data table.

Setting Up a Two-Variable Data Table

To set up a two-variable data table, you arrange the two sets of input values along the left and top edge of a worksheet range. You then place the what-if formula in the top-left corner cell of the worksheet range. Figure 4-4 shows how this looks with the interest rate input values—8%, 9%, 10%, 11%, and 12%—stored along the left edge of the worksheet range in A2:A6 and the mortgage balance input values stored along the top edge of the worksheet range in B1:D1.

A1 =PMT(A8/12,30*12,A9)

	A	B	C	D
1	$0.00	$100,000.00	$200,000.00	$300,000.00
2	8.00%			
3	9.00%			
4	10.00%			
5	11.00%			
6	12.00%			
7				

Figure 4-4 An Excel worksheet range set up for creating a two-variable data table.

Cell A1 holds the formula shown below to calculate the monthly payment on a 30-year mortgage:

```
=PMT(A8/12,30*12,A9)
```

NOTE *The PMT function uses the syntax PMT(rate,term,loan) in which* rate *is the periodic interest rate,* term *is the number of payments, and* loan *is the loan amount. If you have questions about the PMT function or any other Excel financial function, refer to Chapter 5.*

The key point to note about this formula—*and this is the secret to using a two-variable data table*—is that the formula refers to two empty cells below the worksheet range, A8 and A9, that will be used to store temporarily the what-if data as Excel makes its calculation.

Once you've arranged the input values and the formula as shown in Figure 4-4, finish the data table by following these steps:

1. **Select the worksheet range that includes the input values.**

   In Figure 4-4, this means you select the worksheet range A1:D6.

2. **Choose the Data menu's Table command.**

   Excel displays the Table dialog box shown in Figure 4-5.

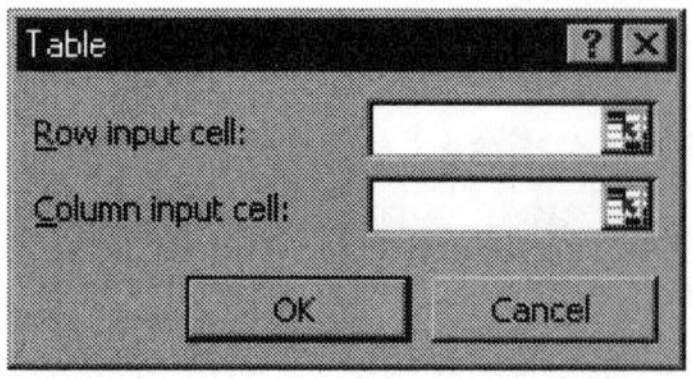

Figure 4-5 The Table dialog box.

3. **Provide the input cell location for the input values you've stored in a row.**

   You provide the input cell location for the input values you've stored in a row by clicking the Row Input Cell text box (to select the text box) and then clicking the empty cell you've used to refer to the variable that should be stored in this cell. Figure 4-4 stores mortgage amounts in a row, so you click the cell that the what-if formula uses to refer to the mortgage balance, which is cell A9.

4. **Provide the input cell location for the input values you've stored in a column.**

   You provide the input cell location for the input values you've stored in a column by clicking the Column Input Cell text box (to select the text box) and then clicking the empty cell you've used to refer to the variable that should be stored in this cell. Figure 4-4 stores interest rates in a row, so you click the cell that the what-if formula uses to refer to the interest rates, which is cell A8.

5. **Click OK.**

   Excel fills the data table with formula results for each input value, as shown in Figure 4-6. For example, Excel fills cell B2 by using the mortgage amount in cell B1 and the interest rate in cell A2 to calculate the monthly payment on a $100,000 mortgage when the annual interest rate is 8.00%. Excel fills cell C3 by using the mortgage amount in cell C1 and the interest rate in cell A3 to calculate the monthly payment on a $200,000 mortgage when the annual interest rate is 9.00%. Excel fills cell D4 by using the mortgage amount in cell D1 and the interest rate in cell A4 to calculate the monthly payment on a $300,000 mortgage when the annual interest rate is 10.00%.

A1 =PMT(A8/12,30*12,A9)

	A	B	C	D	E
1	$0.00	$100,000.00	$200,000.00	$300,000.00	
2	8.00%	($733.76)	($1,467.53)	($2,201.29)	
3	9.00%	($804.62)	($1,609.25)	($2,413.87)	
4	10.00%	($877.57)	($1,755.14)	($2,632.71)	
5	11.00%	($952.32)	($1,904.65)	($2,856.97)	
6	12.00%	($1,028.61)	($2,057.23)	($3,085.84)	
7					

Figure 4-6 The data table after you calculate the what-if formula for each of the input values.

Using the Two-Variable Data Table

As with a one-variable data table, you can continue your what-if analysis even after you've set up the two-variable data table—but without having to use the Data menu's Table command. Simply change the input values, and Excel updates the formula results for your changes. In the worksheet shown in Figure 4-6, for example, to see what loan payments would be using the same interest rates but with mortgage balances equal to $125,000, $150,000, and $175,000, simply enter these values in the worksheet range B1:D1.

What-If Analysis with Scenario Manager

Data tables, as discussed in the earlier sections of this chapter, let you perform what-if analysis when you change one variable and explore the effect on a small handful of formulas or when you change two variables and explore the effect on a single formula. But this approach doesn't work except in the simplest of situations. In most complex situations, you'll want to change several variables at a time and explore the effect on large numbers of formulas.

Suppose, for example, that you're using a workbook like the one shown in Figure 4-7 to perform break-even analysis. Each of the values in the worksheet range B4:B24 is an input to the formulas that show in the break-even analysis schedule contained in D2:G18. If you want to test several sets of input values, use Scenario Manager.

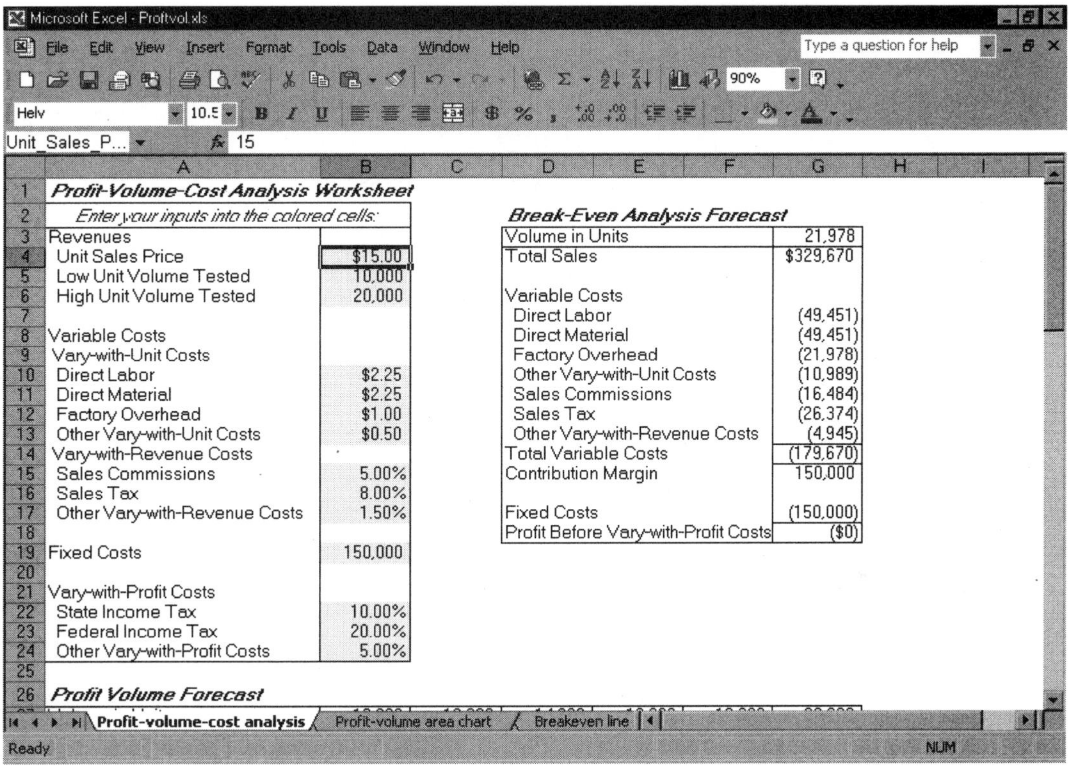

Figure 4-7 A simple profit-volume-cost analysis workbook.

Creating a Scenario

To use Scenario Manager, you create sets of inputs called *scenarios*. To create a scenario, follow these steps:

1. **Choose the Tools menu's Scenarios command.**

   Excel displays the Scenario Manager dialog box.

2. **Click the Add button.**

   Excel displays the Add Scenario dialog box shown in Figure 4-8.

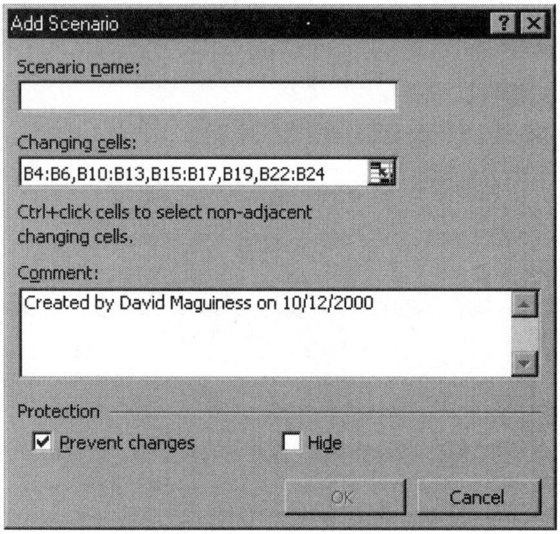

Figure 4-8 The Add Scenario dialog box.

3. **Name the scenario.**

   Give the scenario a name by typing a description in the Scenario Name text box.

4. **Identify the scenario inputs.**

   Enter the worksheet range that holds the cells you want to change in the Changing Cells text box of the Add Scenario dialog box (see Figure 4-8) by using the mouse to select the worksheet range. If you want to enter several worksheet ranges, as would be required for the worksheet shown in Figure 4-7, hold down the Ctrl key as you select ranges. When you finish, click OK. Excel displays the Scenario Values dialog box shown in Figure 4-9.

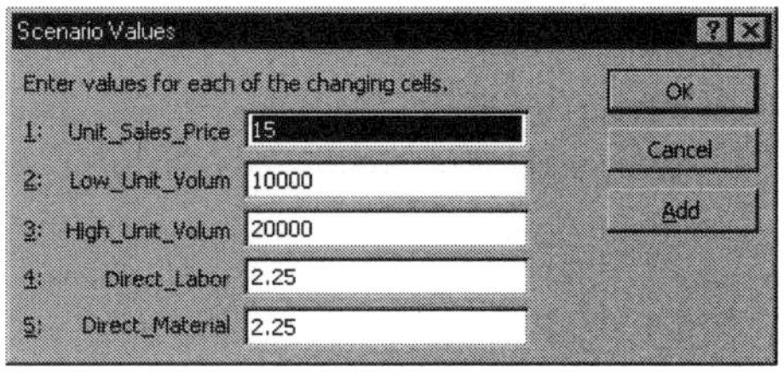

Figure 4-9 The Scenario Values dialog box.

5. Provide the input values.

Enter the input value you want to use for each scenario value. If you've selected more input cells than will fit within the Scenario Values dialog box, you'll need to scroll through the list. Click OK when you finish. Excel redisplays the Add Scenario dialog box.

Repeat steps 2 through 5 to create additional scenarios. After you complete step 5 for the last time, click Close.

Using a Scenario

Once you've created a scenario—again, this is just a set of input values—you can tell Excel to use the input values. To use a scenario, follow these steps:

1. Choose the Tools menu's Scenarios command.

Excel displays the Scenario Manager dialog box, which now displays the newly created scenario, as shown in Figure 4-10.

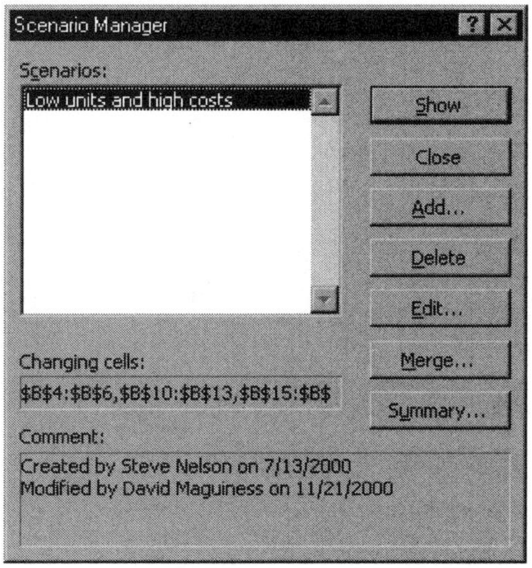

Figure 4-10 The Scenario Manager dialog box.

2. Select a scenario.

Select the scenario you want to explore by clicking its name in the Scenarios list box.

3. **Click the Show button.**

   Excel inputs the scenario values in your workbook and recalculates its formulas. You can repeat this step to experiment with or explore other scenarios. When you finish, click Close.

Editing a Scenario

As you would suspect, you can easily edit the scenarios you've created. You can also easily remove scenarios you no longer want to work with.

To remove an existing scenario, choose the Tools menu's Scenarios command so that Excel displays the Scenario Manager dialog box. Then select the scenario you want to delete, and click Delete.

To edit an existing scenario, follow these steps:

1. **Choose the Tools menu's Scenarios command.**

   Excel displays the Scenario Manager dialog box.

2. **Select a scenario.**

   Select the scenario you want to edit. You can do this most easily by clicking.

3. **Click the Edit button.**

   Excel displays the Edit Scenario dialog box, which closely resembles the Add Scenario dialog box shown in Figure 4-8.

4. **Optionally, edit the scenario name.**

   You can do this by editing the contents of the Scenario Name text box.

5. **Optionally, change the scenario inputs.**

   You can do this by editing or replacing the worksheet range or worksheet ranges shown in the Changing Cells text box of the Edit Scenario dialog box. When you finish, click OK. Excel displays the Scenario Values dialog box (see Figure 4-9).

6. **Provide the input values.**

   Edit or replace the input values you want to use for each scenario value. Click OK when you finish, and Excel redisplays the Add Scenario dialog box.

   Repeat steps 2 through 6 to edit additional scenarios. After you complete step 6 for the last time, click Close.

Summarizing Scenarios

Excel's Scenario Manager includes a Summary feature, which you can use to create either a separate worksheet or a PivotTable that lists selected input values and formula results. To create such a summary, follow these steps:

1. **Choose the Tools menu's Scenarios command.**

   Excel displays the Scenario Manager dialog box.

2. **Click the Summary button.**

   Excel displays the Scenario Summary dialog box, which asks whether you want to display a scenario summary or a PivotTable. Select the button that corresponds to the type of scenario summary you want. Then click OK.

3. **Click the Summary button.**

   Excel displays the Scenario Summary dialog box, shown in Figure 4-11, which asks whether you want to display a scenario summary or a PivotTable. Click the option button that corresponds to the type of scenario summary you want. Do not click OK until after step 4.

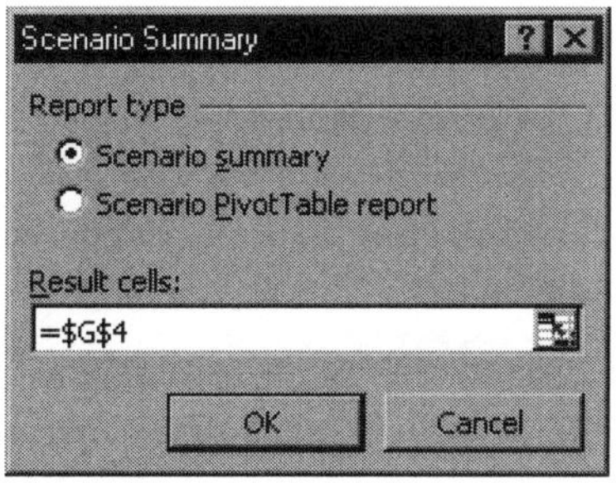

Figure 4-11 The Scenario Summary dialog box.

4. **Select the Result cells.**

   Specify which Result cells you want to see in the summary—these are the cells with the formulas that change as you explore different scenarios—by selecting them with the mouse. You can select nonadjacent cells by holding down the Ctrl key as you click. Click OK when you finish. Excel adds a scenario summary to your workbook that shows the scenario values and the selected Result cells, as shown in Figure 4-12.

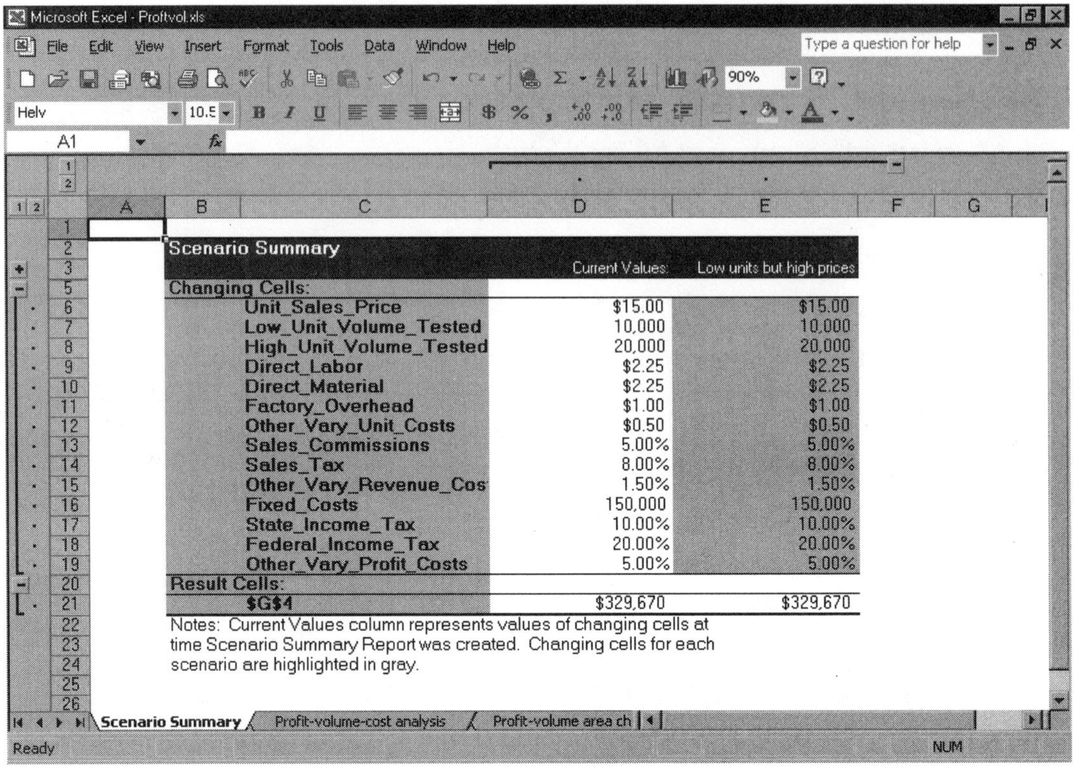

Figure 4-12 A Scenario Summary worksheet.

Merging Scenarios from Other Workbooks

If two workbooks use the same set of input cells, you can copy, or merge, a scenario from one open workbook to another open workbook. To merge scenarios, follow these steps:

1. **Activate the workbook to which you'll add a scenario.**

   When you merge scenarios, both workbooks need to be open, and you work from the workbook to which you'll add the scenarios.

2. **Choose the Tools menu's Scenarios command.**

   Excel displays the Scenario Manager dialog box.

3. **Click the Merge button.**

   Excel displays the Merge Scenarios dialog box shown in Figure 4-13.

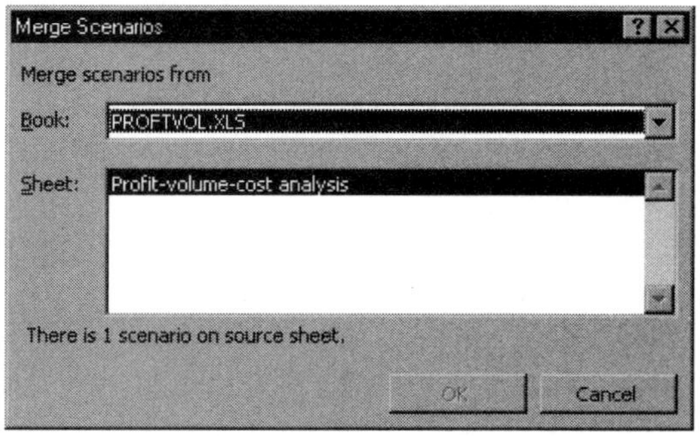

Figure 4-13 The Merge Scenarios dialog box.

4. **Identify which workbook holds the scenarios you want.**

   Use the Book drop-down list box to select the workbook from which you want to retrieve a scenario.

5. **Identify which scenario you want.**

   Use the Sheet list box to select the scenario you want to retrieve.

6. **Click OK.**

   Excel merges the scenarios from the source workbook into the active workbook. You can now use these scenarios in the same way as those you create from scratch.

Simple Modeling with Goal Seek

You can use the Goal Seek command to determine which input value for a formula produces a specified formula result. Goal Seek, then, lets you quantify what needs to happen in order to achieve some specified result. Rather than supplying a set of formula inputs and letting Excel calculate the result, you supply a formula result, all of the input values except one, and then let Excel iteratively determine what the missing input value needs.

For example, suppose you want to determine the interest rate that would result in a $1,400-a-month payment on a $100,000 loan with a 10-year repayment term using the workbook shown in Figure 4-14. Cells B1, B2, and B3 hold values. Cell B5 holds the formula shown below to calculate the monthly interest payment:

```
=PMT(B1/12,B2,-B3)
```

B5 | =PMT(B1/12,B2,-B3)

	A	B	C	D
1	Annual interest rate	8%		
2	Term in months	120		
3	Loan balance	100000		
4				
5	Payment	$1,213.28		
6				
7				

Figure 4-14 A simple loan payment workbook.

NOTE *If you have questions about the PMT function or any other Excel financial function, refer to Excel's online help.*

To determine the rate input value required for your specified formula result, follow these steps:

1. **Choose the Tools menu's Goal Seek command.**

   Excel displays the Goal Seek dialog box shown in Figure 4-15.

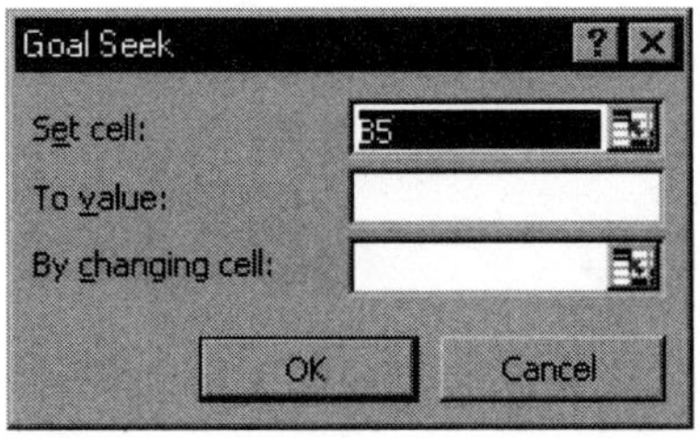

Figure 4-15 The Goal Seek dialog box.

2. **Specify which cell's formula you want to return a specified result.**

   Use the Set Cell text box to specify the cell that holds the formula Excel will attempt to set to the specified value. For the example workbook shown in Figure 4-14, you would specify the Set cell as B5.

3. **Specify this result.**

   Use the To Value text box to specify the formula result you want. For the example workbook shown in Figure 4-14, you would specify the To Value as 1400.

4. **Indicate which input cell should be adjusted.**

   Use the By Changing Cell text box to specify the input cell that Excel should adjust in an attempt to calculate the formula result you want. For the example workbook shown in Figure 4-14, you would specify the By Changing cell to B1. Then click OK. Excel adjusts the input cell to a value that produces the desired formula result and displays the results in the Goal Seek Status dialog box, as shown in Figure 4-16.

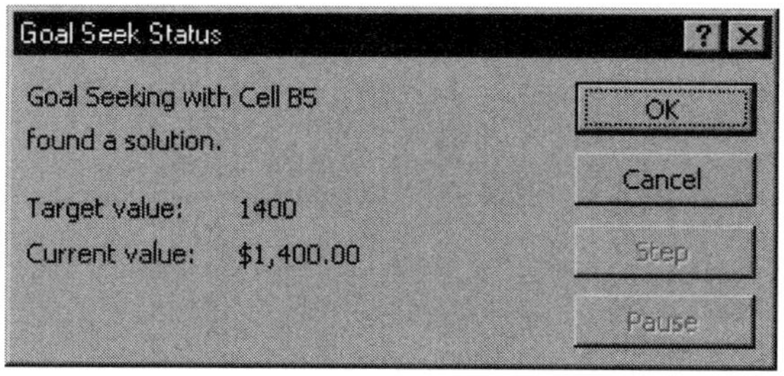

Figure 4-16 The Goal Seek Status dialog box.

Goal Seek typically finds the correct input cell value in a fraction of a second. If your calculations are very cumbersome, however, Goal Seek may take longer. When this happens, you can click the Goal Seek Status dialog box's Stop button to terminate the search. Or you can click the Pause button to temporarily suspend the search.

NOTE *Commonly, Goal Seek's calculations become more complicated or cumbersome when you have it calculate a string of formulas. For example, this might happen when you ask Goal Seek to calculate the input cell value to a first formula, which supplies a result to the second formula, which supplies a result to a third formula, which is the formula you want to produce a specified result.*

Optimization Modeling with Solver

Excel's Solver tool lets you solve optimization-modeling problems, also commonly known as linear programming problems. With an optimization-modeling problem, you want to optimize an objective function but at the same time recognize that there are constraints, or limits. While this abstract definition sounds complicated, at least at the conceptual level, optimization modeling makes common sense once you provide a concrete example.

EasyRefresher™: How Optimization Modeling Works

Suppose, for example, that you're a residential real-estate developer and contractor. You create and sell two products: building lots and houses. Suppose that you make $20,000 on each home you build and $15,000 on each building lot you develop and then sell. Your principal financial objective is to maximize your profits, and this objective can be expressed as an objective function, or equation, that you want to maximize:

```
$15,000*Lots+$20,000*Houses=Profits
```

Of course, any objective function is limited by certain constraints. To continue with the fictional case of residential development, suppose that you have two principal limiting factors: working capital and bulldozer capacity. Your working capital of $1,200,000 limits the number of lots and houses you can annually sell because every lot requires a $50,000 cash investment and every house requires a $25,000 cash investment. The fact that you have a single bulldozer available for only 3,000 hours each year also limits the number of lots and houses you can annually sell because every lot requires 80 hours of bulldozing and every house requires 200 hours of bulldozing. These two constraints can also be expressed as equations. For example, the working capital constraint can be expressed as follows:

```
$50,000*Lots+$25,000*Houses<=$1,200,000
```

This formula says the result of the formula $50,000 times the number of lots plus $25,000 times the number of houses must be less than or equal to the working capital limit of $1,200,000. The less than or equal to symbol is represented by the <= operator.

The bulldozer capacity constraint can be expressed as follows:

```
80*Lots+200*Houses<=3000
```

This formula says the result of the formula 80 times the number of lots plus 200 times the number of houses must be less than or equal to the bulldozer-hours limit of 3,000. Again, the less than or equal to symbol is represented by the <= operator.

Typically, you also have policy constraints when you work with an optimization-modeling problem. Suppose that as a matter of policy you want to maintain a certain level of activity both in developing lots and building houses. You might say, for example, that because you must maintain your team's expertise in both raw land development and residential contracting that you want to develop at least 10 lots every year and build at least 5 houses. These two constraints also need to be expressed as equations. The minimum-number-of-lots policy constraint can be expressed as follows:

```
Lots>=10
```

This formula says that you want to develop at least 10 building lots. Or, restated, this formula says that the *lots* variable must be greater than or equal to 10. The greater than or equal to symbol is represented by the >= operator.

The minimum-number-of-houses policy constraint can be expressed as follows:

```
Houses>=5
```

This formula says that you want to build at least 5 houses. Or, restated, this formula says that the *houses* variable must be greater than or equal to 10. Again, the greater than or equal to symbol is represented by the >= operator.

With the information provided in the preceding paragraphs of this EasyRefresher, we've described your fictional optimization-modeling problem. You want to maximize your profits, which can be described using the following objective function:

```
$15,000*Lots+$20,000*Houses=Profits
```

but you can't develop unlimited numbers of building lots or build unlimited numbers of houses. You are subject to the following constraints:

```
$50,000*Lots+$25,000*Houses<=$1,200,000

80*Lots+200*Houses<=3000

Lots>=10

Houses>=5
```

You can solve this equation in a variety of ways, including graphically, iteratively, or using a technique like simplex algebra. Or, you can provide the objective function and the constraint equations to Excel and have it solve the problem, which is the solution technique described in the paragraphs that follow.

Solving an Optimization Problem

To use Excel's Solver, you first build a workbook that describes your optimization-modeling problem, including its objective function and any constraints, and then you tell Solver to look for an optimal solution. As long as you understand the concepts of optimization modeling, as described in the preceding EasyRefresher, this process is simple.

Setting Up Your Workbook for Solver

You take three steps to set up a workbook for Solver: provide guesses of the variables that optimize your objective function, supply the objective function, and then supply the constraint functions. Figure 4-17 shows a workbook set up to solve the example problem discussed in the EasyRefresher.

B5 =15000*Lots+20000*Houses

	A	B	C
1	***Solver variables***		
2	Lots	15	
3	Houses	10	
4			
5	***Objective function***	=15000*Lots+20000*Houses	
6			
7	***Constraints***	*Formula*	*Constant*
8	Cash required limit	=Lots*50000+Houses*25000	1200000
9	Bulldozer hours limit	=Lots*80+Houses*200	3000
10	Minimum number of lots policy	=Lots	10
11	Minimum number of houses policy	=Houses	5
12			

Figure 4-17 A workbook set up for optimization modeling.

To build this or any optimization model workbook, follow these steps:

1. **Optionally, tell Excel to display the actual formulas rather than results.**

   You don't have to take this step, but because with optimization modeling you're really more interested in what the formulas look like as opposed to the results they produce, you probably want to tell Excel to display formulas rather than formula results. To do this, choose the Tools menu's Options command, click the View tab, and select the Formulas check box.

NOTE *Figure 4-17 displays formulas instead of formula results.*

2. **Provide starting guesses for the variables.**

   You need to provide starting guesses for the variables you're trying to optimize. You can do this simply by entering values in cells, but we recommend you create a small schedule of variable names and variable guesses, as shown in Figure 4-17 in the worksheet range A1:B3.

   If you set up a worksheet range like that shown in Figure 4-17—and you really should—you'll also want to name the cells that hold your guesses. In this case, you can do this by selecting the worksheet range that holds the variable names (Lots, Houses) and guesses—A2:B3 in Figure 4-17—and then by choosing the Insert menu's Name command and then choosing Create. When Excel displays the Create Names dialog box, select the Left Column check box and click OK.

3. **Describe the objective function.**

   In Figure 4-17, the worksheet describes the equation with the following formula located in cell B5:

   ```
   =15000*Lots+20000*Houses
   ```

   Because the cells holding the variable guesses have been named Lots and Houses, the objective function uses these names in place of cell references. Note that the label in cell A5 identifies the equation, but you need to enter only the actual equation shown in cell B5.

4. **Describe each constraint.**

   In Figure 4-17, the constraints are described in the worksheet range B8:C11.

   To describe a single constraint, you enter the constraint equation in one cell and the limiting constant value in another cell. For example, the working capital constraint mentioned in the earlier EasyRefresher says the formula $50,000 times the number of lots plus $25,000 times the number of houses must be less than or equal to $1,200,000 (the limiting constant).

To describe this first constraint, you enter the following formula in cell B8:

```
=Lots*50000+Houses*25000
```

and you enter the constant value which limits this formula in cell C8:

```
1200000
```

To describe the second constraint—the one that quantifies the limit on bulldozer capacity—you enter the following formula in cell B9:

```
=Lots*80+Houses*200
```

and you enter the constant value which limits this formula in cell C9:

```
3000
```

To describe the third constraint—which comes from your minimum-number-of-lots policy constraint—you enter the following formula in cell B10:

```
=Lots
```

and you enter the constant value which limits this formula in cell C10:

```
10
```

Finally, to describe the fourth constraint—which comes from your minimum-number-of-houses policy constraint—you enter the following formula in cell B11:

```
=Houses
```

and you enter the constant value which limits this formula in cell C11:

```
5
```

Once you've completed the preceding steps, you're ready to use Solver to look for an optimal solution to your objective function.

Using Solver

If you set up your workbooks similar to the one shown in Figure 4-17, you will find Solver easy to use. You simply follow these steps:

1. Choose the Tools menu's Solver command.

Excel displays the Solver Parameters dialog box shown in Figure 4-18.

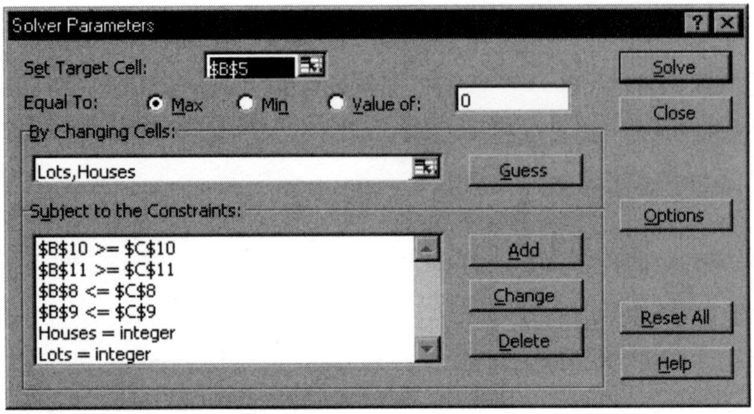

Figure 4-18 The Solver Parameters dialog box.

NOTE *If you don't see the Solver command on your Tools menu, it means the Solver add-in isn't yet installed. To install Solver, choose the Tools menu's Add-Ins command. When Excel displays the Add-Ins dialog box, scroll down the Add-Ins Available list box until you see the Solver Add-in entry. Select the Solver Add-in check box, click OK, and then if Excel requests it, provide the Excel or Office installation CD.*

2. **Identify the objective function.**

   Enter the address of the cell that holds your objective in the Set Target Cell box. For example, in Figure 4-17, cell B5 holds the objective function, so you would enter *B5* in the Set Target Cell box.

3. **Describe how Solver should optimize the objective function.**

   Use the Equal To option buttons to specify how Solver optimizes the objective function. In the case of a profit function, for example, you want to maximize the function, so you click the Max button. This is the case for the workbook shown in Figure 4-17. If your objective function described costs, you would instead want to minimize the function and so would click the Min button. You may also have situations in which you want to have the objective function return a specific value, and so you would click the Value Of button and then provide the specified value.

4. **Tell Solver which cells hold your variable guesses.**

   Use the By Changing Cells box to tell Excel where you've stored the variables used in the objective function and constraint equations. In Figure 4-17, for example, the workbook stores these variables in cells B2 and B3, so you could enter these two cell addresses in the By Changing Cells box. If you've named the variable cells, you can also type the cell names, as shown in Figure 4-18. Cell B2 is named Lots, and cell B3 is named Houses.

5. **Tell Solver you want to begin describing constraints.**

   Click the Add button. Excel displays the Add Constraint dialog box shown in Figure 4-19.

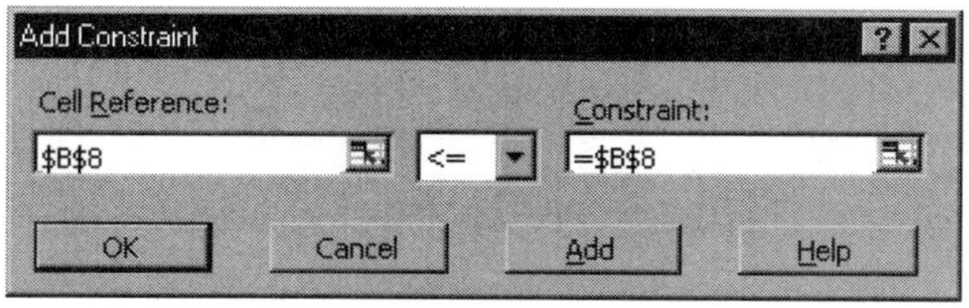

Figure 4-19 The Add Constraint dialog box.

6. **Describe the first constraint.**

   To add a constraint, use the Cell Reference box to identify the cell holding the first constraint's equation, use the unnamed operator box to select an appropriate constraint operator, and then use the Constraint box to identify the cell holding the first constraint's constant value. In the case of the workbook shown in Figure 4-17, for example, you might do this by clicking the Cell Reference box and then clicking cell B8, by selecting the <= operator, and then by clicking the Constraint box and then clicking cell C8. Figure 4-19 shows how the Add Constraint dialog box should look to specify this constraint. Click Add to add the constraint. Then repeat this task to add more constraints.

NOTE *The unnamed drop-down list box provides five constraint operators: <= for indicating less than or equal to, = for indicating equal to, >= for indicating greater than or equal to,* int *for indicating that a variable must be an integer, and* bin *for indicating that a variable must be binary (equal either to 1 or 0).*

7. **Add any implicit integer constraints.**

   In many optimization-modeling problems, you'll also have implicit integer constraints. What this means, for example, is that you can't use decimal values as part of the optimal solution. For example, you might say that you must develop an integer number of building lots or build an integer number of houses. Or restated slightly, you might say that you can't get to the end of the year and have one of your building lots only half-done or one of your houses only partially complete. To specify an integer constraint, use the Cell Reference box to identify the variable cell that must be an integer and then select the *int* operator from the unnamed drop-down list box. Figure 4-20 shows how the Add Constraint dialog box looks when you specify an integer constraint. Note that you don't enter the word *integer* in the Constraint box. Excel does that.

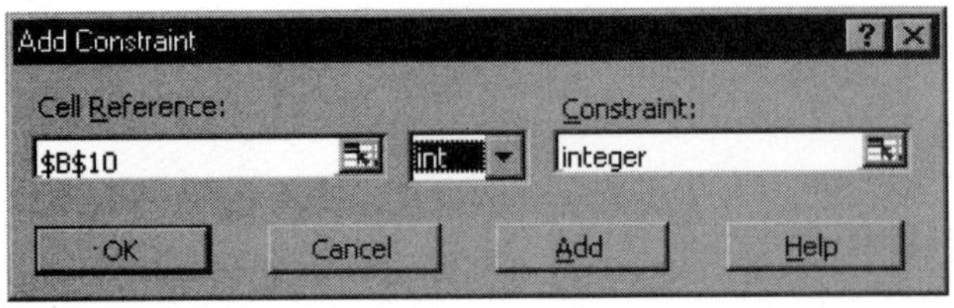

Figure 4-20 The Add Constraint dialog box, this time showing how an integer constraint looks.

8. **Add any binary constraints.**

   In a handful of optimization modeling problems, you may also have binary constraints. A binary constraint is one in which the variable must equal either 0 or 1. To specify a binary constraint, use the Cell Reference box to identify the variable cell that must be binary and then select the *bin* operator from the unnamed drop-down list box.

9. **Tell Excel you're done adding constraints.**

   To leave the Add Constraint dialog box after you finish describing your last constraint, click OK. Excel closes the Add Constraint dialog box and returns you to the Solver Parameters dialog box. Any constraints you've added show in the Subject To Constraints list box.

NOTE *If you add a constraint and later want to delete it, display the Solver Parameters dialog box, select the constraint, and then click the Delete button. If you add a constraint and later want to edit it, display the Solver Parameters dialog box, select the constraint, and then click the Change button. When Excel displays the Edit Constraint dialog box, use it to make your changes. The Edit Constraint dialog box works like the Add Constraint dialog box.*

10. **Tell Excel to look for a solution.**

    Click the Solve button to direct Excel to look for a solution to your optimization-modeling problem. Excel looks for a solution and then displays the Solver Results dialog box shown in Figure 4-21.

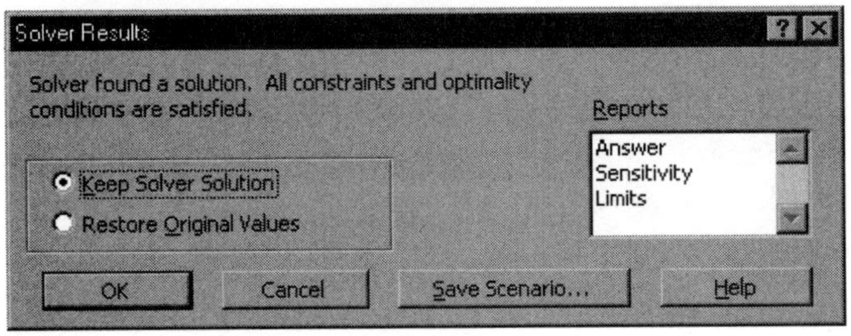

Figure 4-21 The Solver Results dialog box.

This dialog box identifies the variable values that optimize your objective function and asks what you want to do with these values.

- To save the solution, click the Keep Solver Solution option button and click OK.
- To discard the solution, click the Restore Original Values option button and click OK.
- To save the solution as a scenario, click the Save Scenario button and then provide a scenario name when prompted.

NOTE *The earlier section, "What-If Analysis with Scenario Manager," discusses how scenarios work.*

Reviewing Solver Reports

The Solver Results dialog box gives you the option of generating several reports on the optimization modeling that Solver performs. To generate these reports, select the report or reports you want from the list in the Solver Results dialog box, as shown in Figure 4-21.

NOTE *Excel does not allow integer constraints in Sensitivity and Limits Reports. You will need to return to the Solver Parameters dialog box (see Figure 4-18) and delete the integer parameters for Houses and Lots to get these reports. These reports involve graphing several parameters in several equations. When you graph a complex equation, not all of the results will have integer values.*

Understanding the Answer Report

The Answer Report, which Excel places on a separate worksheet, provides information about how close the optimal solution is to your original guesses and about which constraints bind, or limit, optimization. Figure 4-22 shows an example Answer Report. At the top of the report, Excel compares the original objection function formula result with the objection function result provided by original variable values. In Figure 4-22, for example, Excel shows the original objective function value as 425000 and the final objective function value as 440000. Solver, in this case, improves the objective function by 15000.

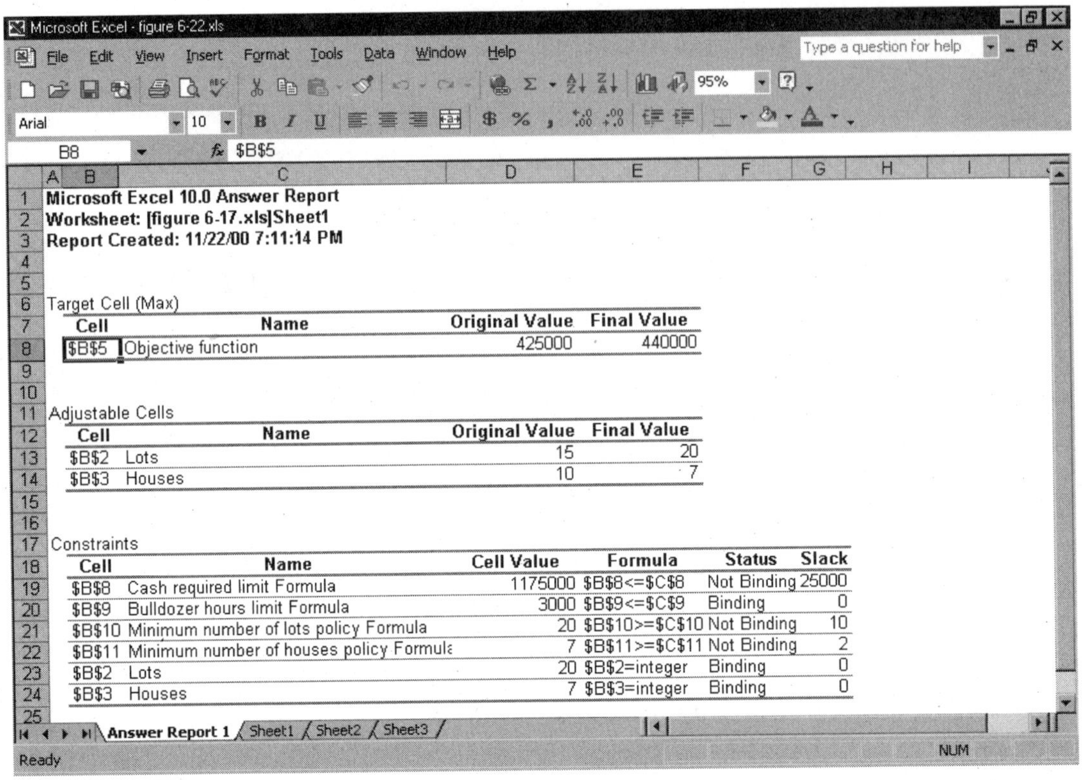

Microsoft Excel 10.0 Answer Report
Worksheet: [figure 6-17.xls]Sheet1
Report Created: 11/22/00 7:11:14 PM

Target Cell (Max)

Cell	Name	Original Value	Final Value
$B$5	Objective function	425000	440000

Adjustable Cells

Cell	Name	Original Value	Final Value
$B$2	Lots	15	20
$B$3	Houses	10	7

Constraints

Cell	Name	Cell Value	Formula	Status	Slack
$B$8	Cash required limit Formula	1175000	$B$8<=$C$8	Not Binding	25000
$B$9	Bulldozer hours limit Formula	3000	$B$9<=$C$9	Binding	0
$B$10	Minimum number of lots policy Formula	20	$B$10>=$C$10	Not Binding	10
$B$11	Minimum number of houses policy Formul:	7	$B$11>=$C$11	Not Binding	2
$B$2	Lots	20	$B$2=integer	Binding	0
$B$3	Houses	7	$B$3=integer	Binding	0

Figure 4-22 The Answer Report.

Beneath the comparison of the original and final values of the objective function's formula results, Excel compares the original values and final values of the variables (see Figure 4-22). This information lets you see exactly by how much Excel adjusts the variables in order to optimize your objective function.

At the bottom of the Answer Report, Excel analyzes the constraints by calculating the formula results for the constraints and then comparing these formula results to the constraint constants. This sounds like busywork at first blush, but this information is often very useful in two important ways: First, you can use the status information to see which constraints are binding, or limiting. In Figure 4-22, the binding constraint is the bulldozer hours. Second, you can use the slack information to see how close a given constraint comes to becoming binding. In Figure 4-22, the working capital constraint shows only 25000 for slack; in other words, you have only a 2% margin of error with your working capital ($25,000 / $1,200,000).

Understanding the Sensitivity Report

The Sensitivity Report, which Excel also places on a separate worksheet, shows reduced gradients for the variables and the Lagrange multipliers for the constraints, as shown in Figure 4-23. A reduced gradient value shows how the objective function would change if the variable value increased by 1. The Lagrange multiplier shows how the objective function would change if the constraint constant increased by 1.

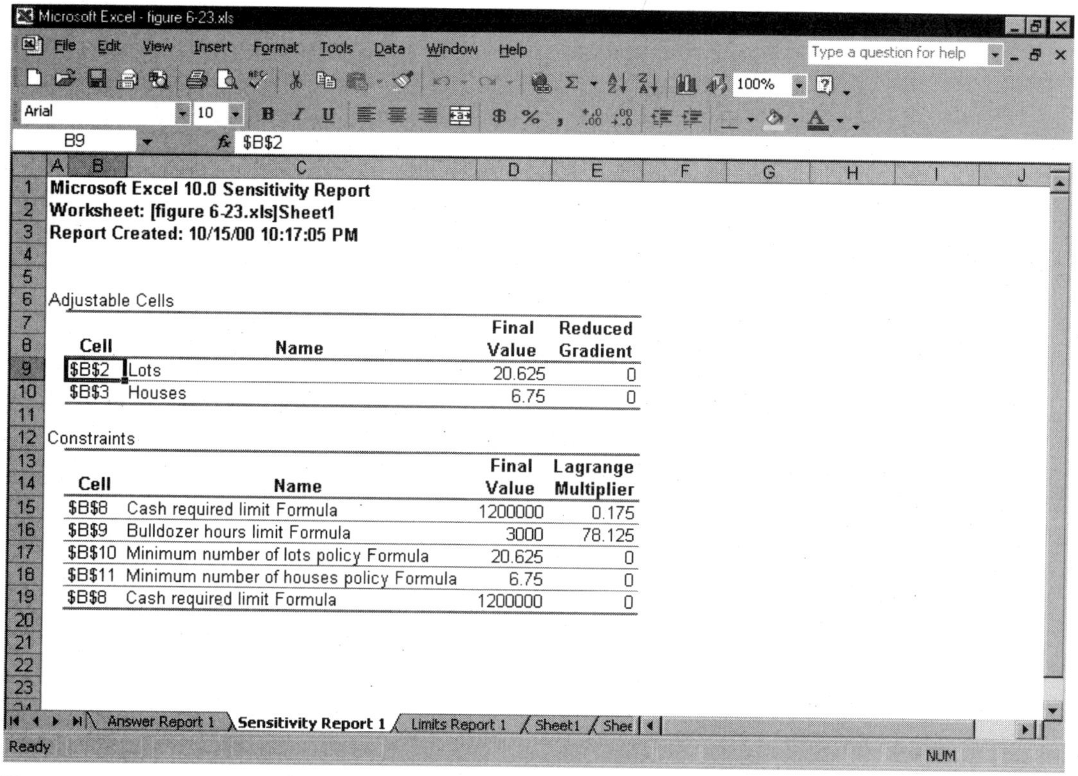

Cell	Name	Final Value	Reduced Gradient
$B$2	Lots	20.625	0
$B$3	Houses	6.75	0

Cell	Name	Final Value	Lagrange Multiplier
$B$8	Cash required limit Formula	1200000	0.175
$B$9	Bulldozer hours limit Formula	3000	78.125
$B$10	Minimum number of lots policy Formula	20.625	0
$B$11	Minimum number of houses policy Formula	6.75	0
$B$8	Cash required limit Formula	1200000	0

Figure 4-23 The Sensitivity Report.

NOTE *Some reduced gradient values and some Lagrange multipliers will always show as 0. The reduced gradient equals 0 if the variable value can't be increased, and the Lagrange multiplier shows as 0 if a constraint constant isn't binding.*

A closer inspection of the Sensitivity Report shown in Figure 4-23, for example, shows that the reduced gradient values for both the Lots and Houses variables equal 0. This indicates that neither value can be increased. The Sensitivity Report does show Lagrange multipliers for the working capital constraint and for the bulldozer-hours constraint. The Lagrange multiplier for the bulldozer-hours limit, 78.125, indicates that a 1 hour increase in the number of bulldozing hours available increases the objective function (your profits) by 78.125.

If you've created a linear optimization model—and we'll discuss linear models briefly in the next section, "Customizing Solver's Operation"—your Sensitivity Reports include several additional pieces of information, including reduced costs, shadow prices, objective coefficients, and constraint right-hand side ranges.

Understanding the Limits Report

The Limits Report, which Excel places on still another worksheet, shows you how much your variable values can change but still stay within your constraints, as shown in Figure 4-24. For each variable, the Limits Report shows the calculated optimal value, the lowest possible value that is allowable, and the highest possible value that is allowable. In Figure 4-24—and this would often be the case—the lower limit and upper limit values equal the optimal values. This shows that these variable values can be changed without affecting the optimal solution or violating constraints. Note, however, that some optimization problems do allow you to change variable values while continuing to optimize the function and continuing to stay within the stated constraints. This happens when there are multiple sets of variable values that optimize the equation.

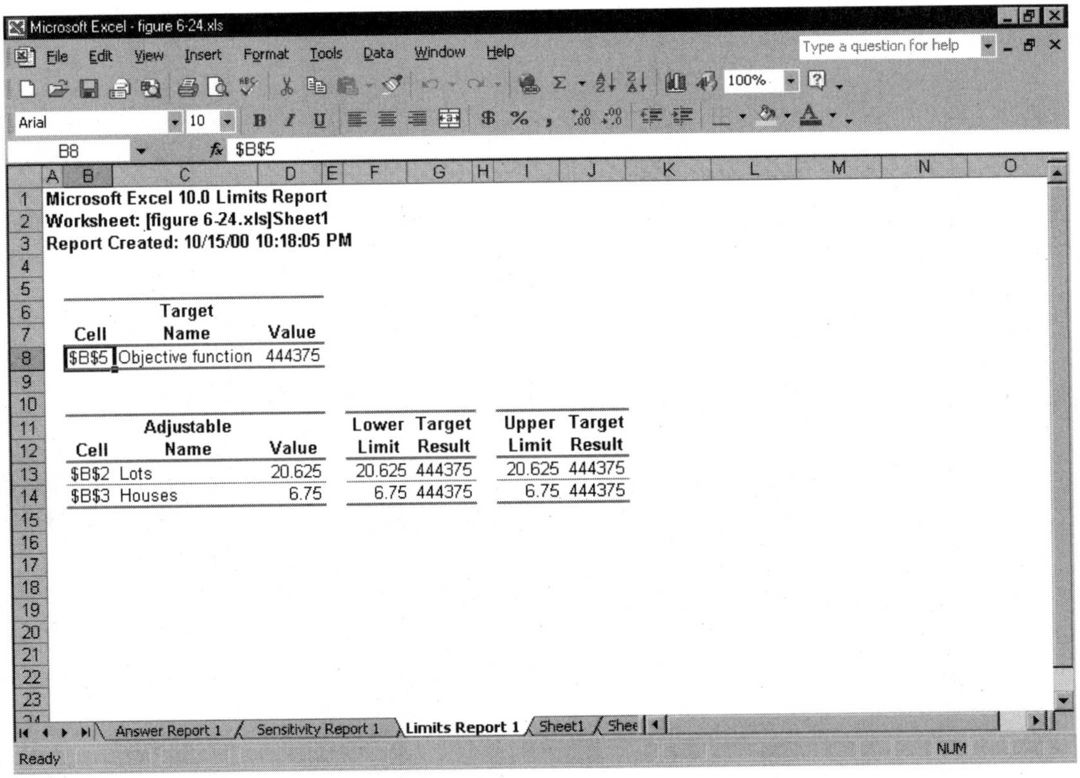

Figure 4-24 The Limits Report.

Customizing Solver's Operation

The Solver Parameters dialog box provides an Options button that you can click to display the Solver Options dialog box shown in Figure 4-25. The Solver Options dialog box lets you customize the way in which Solver works out your problem. The paragraphs that follow briefly describe each of the Solver options along with how and why you might change their settings.

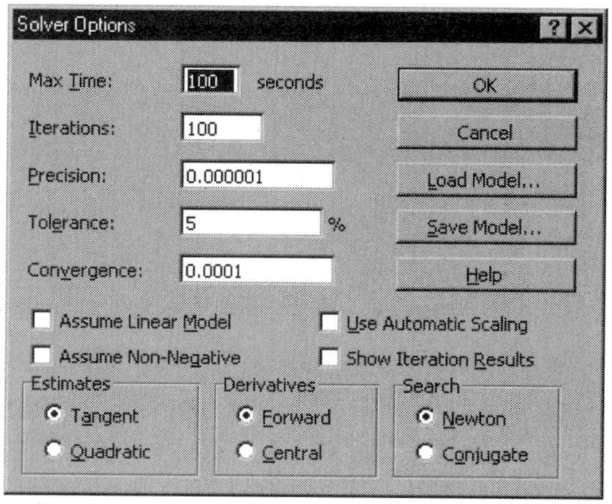

Figure 4-25 The Solver Options dialog box.

Max Time and Iterations

A handful of these options are essentially self-descriptive. The Max Time box, for example, lets you specify how long Solver should work on a problem, and it can be set as high as 32,767 seconds (which is over nine hours). The Iterations box lets you specify how many iterations Solver should work on a problem, and it can be set as high as 32,767.

Precision

The Precision box lets you specify how precise Solver should be in checking a possible optimal solution against your constraints. A precision setting of 0.000001, the default setting, tells Excel that if a constraint formula value is within 0.000001 of the constraint constant, it meets the constraint. You can set the Precision box to any value from 0 to 1. To loosen your precision, use a larger Precision value. To tighten your precision, use a smaller Precision value. As you boost your precision, predictably, Excel takes longer to reach a solution.

Tolerance

The Tolerance box lets you specify how precise Solver should be in making sure that any integer constraints are met. The default Tolerance setting of 5, or 5%, means that if an objective function variable is within 5% of an integer value—from 95% to 105%, in other words—Excel can consider it to be an integer. The Tolerance setting, by the way, applies only to optimization problems that use integer constraints. As you increase your precision, predictably, Excel takes longer to reach a solution.

Convergence

The Convergence box lets you indicate when Excel should stop looking for a better solution. You can set the Convergence value to any fractional value between 0 and 1. When the change in the objective function is less than the value shown in the Convergence box, Excel stops looking for a better solution. The Convergence setting, by the way, applies only to nonlinear optimization-modeling problems. As you reduce the convergence setting (i.e., increase the precision), predictably, Excel takes longer to reach a solution.

Assume Linear Model

If the relationships in your optimization are linear, you can select the Assume Linear Model check box. By doing this, you simplify the calculations that Excel has to make and, thereby, speed things up.

Assume Non-Negative

If you want to tell Excel that your variables must be equal to or greater than zero when you haven't set a lower limit constraint, you can select the Assume Non-Negative check box. In effect, when you check this box, you tell Excel to create another, implicit, set of constraints.

Use Automatic Scaling

You should select the Automatic Scaling check box when you're working with variables and formula results that differ in magnitude. An example of this situation is when you're solving for a rate of return (a percentage) using a set of large dollar variables.

Show Iteration Results

You can select the Show Iteration Results check box to direct Excel to pause after each calculation iteration. After each calculation iteration, Excel displays a Show Trial Solution dialog box. You can save the trial solution by clicking the Save Scenario button. Or you can continue to work toward the solution by clicking the Continue button. To terminate the iterations, click the Stop button.

Estimates

You use the Estimates option buttons—Tangent and Quadratic—to choose the approach that you want Excel to use to come up with the first trial solution. Select Tangent if you want Excel to extrapolate linearly from a tangent vector. Select Quadratic if you want Excel to extrapolate quadraticly—a technique which may yield better results for nonlinear optimization-modeling problems.

Derivatives

You use the Derivatives option buttons—Forward and Central—to specify the differencing used to estimate partial derivatives of the objective function and constraint function formulas. Typically, you can click the Forward button. However, if an optimization problem can't be solved with Forward derivatives, you can click the Central button. Using differentials near the center of a target often takes more calculations to solve, but can be better with highly constrained problems, such as airline ticket prices.

Search

The Search option buttons—Newton and Conjugate—let you choose the algorithm Excel uses to find an optimal solution. If your personal computer has lots of free memory, click the Newton button to reduce the number of calculation iterations (albeit at the expense of using more memory). If your personal computer doesn't have extra memory, click the Conjugate button to allow more time so that your computer doesn't use as much memory.

NOTE *Changing your Search setting to Conjugate should be necessary only on large, complicated optimization problems.*

Save Model and Load Model

The Save Model and Load Model buttons let you save an optimization model description. To save a model—such as the equations that you set up for the scenario with houses, lots, working capital, and bulldozers—click the Save Model button and then specify the empty worksheet range that Excel should use to save the model. To load a model, click the Load Model button and then specify the worksheet range holding the model.

Understanding Solver Error Messages

For most simple optimization problems, Excel rather quickly finds a solution to your problem and displays the Solver Results dialog box. In more complicated problems—unfortunately, those you're likely to encounter in real life—Excel may encounter difficulties. In these cases, it may display one of the error messages described in the following paragraphs.

Solver has converged to the current solution

This message means that while Excel has found what it appears to be a solution, there may be a better solution. To direct Excel to look for a better solution, reduce the Convergence setting using the Solver Options dialog box, as described in the preceding section, "Customizing Solver's Operations."

Solver cannot improve the current solution

This message indicates that Excel has calculated a rough, appropriate solution, but there may be a better solution. To direct Excel to look for a better solution, adjust the Precision setting to a larger value using the Solver Options dialog box. Again, the preceding section explains how to do this.

Stop chosen when the maximum time limit was reached

This message indicates that Excel ran out of time. You can attempt to retry solving the solution using a larger MaxTime setting. To specify a larger MaxTime value, use the Solver Options dialog box.

NOTE *To save the work that Excel has already performed when you encounter either this message or the next one, click the Keep Solver Results button.*

Stop chosen when the maximum iteration limit was reached

This message indicates that Excel ran out of iterations. You can attempt to retry solving the solution using a larger Iterations setting. To specify a larger Iterations value, use the Solver Options dialog box.

The Set Target Cell values do not converge

This message indicates that the objective function continues to increase or decrease even though all the constraints are already satisfied. In other words, with each iteration, Excel gets a better objective function value, but doesn't appear any closer to a final objective function value. If you encounter this error, review your objective function and constraints to make sure that you've correctly described the optimization-modeling problem.

Solver could not find a feasible solution

This message probably indicates that your optimization-modeling problem has no answer. Alternatively, this error message may suggest that you've incorrectly described the objective function or, perhaps more likely, one or more of the constraints. In the previous model, if your working capital was limited to $600,000, you would not have enough cash to work the minimum required number of lots and houses. There would be no feasible solution.

Conditions for Assume Linear Model are not satisfied

This message indicates you selected the Assume Linear Model check box, which appears on the Solver Options dialog box, but Excel, after reviewing the calculation results, concludes your model isn't linear. If you see this message, first display the Solver Options dialog box and select the Use Automatic Scaling check box. Then attempt to solve your optimization model again. If you get the message error a second time, display the Solver Options box again, but this time clear the Assume Linear Model check box. Then attempt to solve your problem again.

Solver encountered an error value in a target or constraint cell

This message indicates that one of your formulas results in an error value or that you've incorrectly specified an integer or binary constraint. To address this Solver problem, you need to fix the incorrect formula.

NOTE *The earlier section, "Using Solver," describes one way to correctly set up integer and binary constraints.*

There is not enough memory available to solve the problem

This message, as you would suspect, indicates that Excel doesn't have enough memory to successfully run Solver. To free up memory, try closing open documents and any other open programs. You may also want to add memory to your personal computer.

Skill 5

SHARING WORKBOOKS

Featuring:

- Using OLE with Excel
- Sharing Workbook Files
- Sharing Excel Data over the Web
- Retrieving External Data with Excel

One of Excel distinguishing new features relates to sharing information—both between programs and within a workgroup. Excel now fully recognizes that many users—you may be one—use several programs in their work and use Excel in a workgroup environment. This chapter describes the tools and features that Excel provides for sharing data among users and between programs.

Using OLE with Excel

Microsoft Windows itself provides a powerful and easy-to-use tool for sharing data known as OLE, or Object Linking and Embedding. With OLE, you can transfer data between Excel and other Windows programs, as described in the paragraphs that follow.

How OLE Works

In order to make sense of OLE, it's helpful both to understand the basic operation of the Windows Clipboard and the terminology of OLE. The following paragraphs provide this background information.

The Clipboard is simply a temporary storage area in memory that's provided by Windows. Anytime you use the Copy or Cut command, Windows stores your copy of the copied or cut selection using the Clipboard. When you later choose the Paste command, the Windows program—this might be Excel, for example—retrieves whatever it stored on the Clipboard and pastes it into the worksheet at the location of the cell marker or insertion bar.

While you most often use the Clipboard to move and copy data within a program like Excel, you can also use the Clipboard to move and copy data between programs. In fact, the Clipboard is often the quickest and most convenient way to transfer data between programs.

NOTE *Microsoft Office programs store multiple selections on the Clipboard. When you choose the Paste command and the Clipboard holds multiple copied or cut selections, you can choose which selection gets pasted.*

Because the contents of the Clipboard are stored until you exit Windows, you can copy Excel data or formulas, leave Excel, start another program, and in that program choose the Edit menu's Paste command to paste the contents of the Clipboard into that program's document.

NOTE *Rather than exiting the Windows program before starting another one, you can run several applications at the same time.*

Once you understand the basic mechanics of the Clipboard, the terminology of OLE is easy to grasp. OLE is simply the name that Microsoft has given to this Clipboard-based method of sharing document data.

OLE works in roughly this way: The *source* (the document that contains the data you want to transfer elsewhere) in the *server application* (program used to create server document) provides data (such as a paragraph of text, a spreadsheet, or a chart) to the *container* (where you want to data to go) in the *client application* (the application used to create the container document).

For example, with OLE you can use a chart from an Excel workbook in a Microsoft Word document. In this case, Excel is the server application, the Excel workbook is the source, Word is the client application, and the Word document is the container.

OLE objects can be either static, or embedded, which means that what gets stored in the container document is simply a copy. And OLE objects can also be dynamic, or linked, which means that the client application actually retrieves a picture of the actual data from the server application. With a linked object, this "picture" changes as the data changes.

NOTE *You choose between embedded objects and linked objects on the basis of whether you want the object to change. If you don't want the object to change—perhaps because the container document shouldn't be revised—you embed. If you want the object to change—because you automate updating of the container document—you link.*

Although OLE provides you with powerful opportunities to share data between programs, you'll find it easy to use. You create an OLE connection by copying and pasting the data you want to share. Windows hides the complexity from you and takes care of the actual work of data sharing.

Creating an Embedded OLE Object

As an example of how to create an embedded OLE object, suppose that you do want to use an Excel chart in a Word document. To easily create such an embedded OLE object, follow these steps:

1. Open both the source and destination documents.

To most easily create embedded OLE objects, start both the server application and the client application. You should also open both the source document and the container document. If you're working with brand-new, as-yet unsaved documents, first save them.

NOTE *To easily create OLE connections, you need to run more than one program at the same time, which is called* multitasking. *The Windows Taskbar lets you easily run multiple programs at once. To start a second program, for example, use the Start button to start the program in the usual way. To switch between running programs, use the task buttons on the Taskbar.*

2. Select the chart object.

To select an object, simply click it. For example, to select the chart object shown in Figure 5-1, just click the chart.

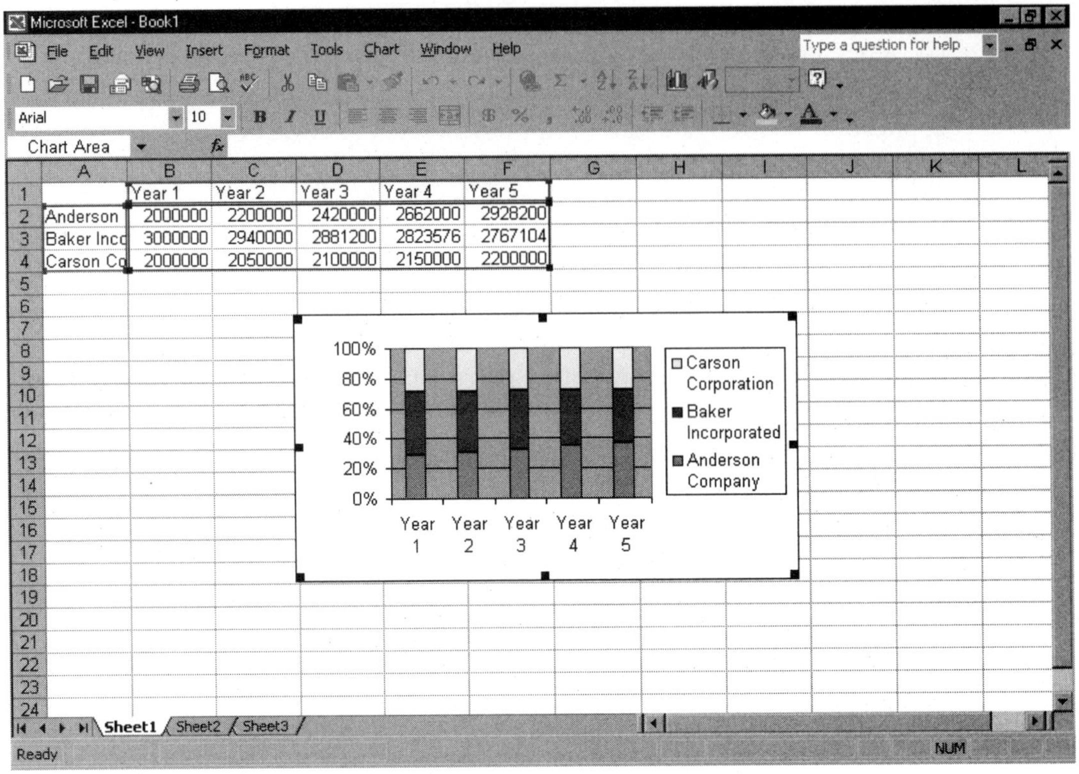

Figure 5-1 An Excel chart such as you might use for an OLE source document.

3. **Copy the object to the Clipboard.**

   You can copy an object to the Clipboard by clicking the Copy toolbar button. Or you can choose the Edit menu's Copy command.

4. **Display the source document.**

   You could do this by clicking the document's button on the Taskbar. If you wanted to copy the object to a Word document named Report, you would click the Report taskbar button.

5. **Position the insertion point at the location where you want to paste the object.**

   You can typically position the insertion point by clicking the point in the document where you want to place the object. For example, if you wanted to paste a chart object after the first paragraph, as shown in Figure 5-2, you would click on the line following the first paragraph.

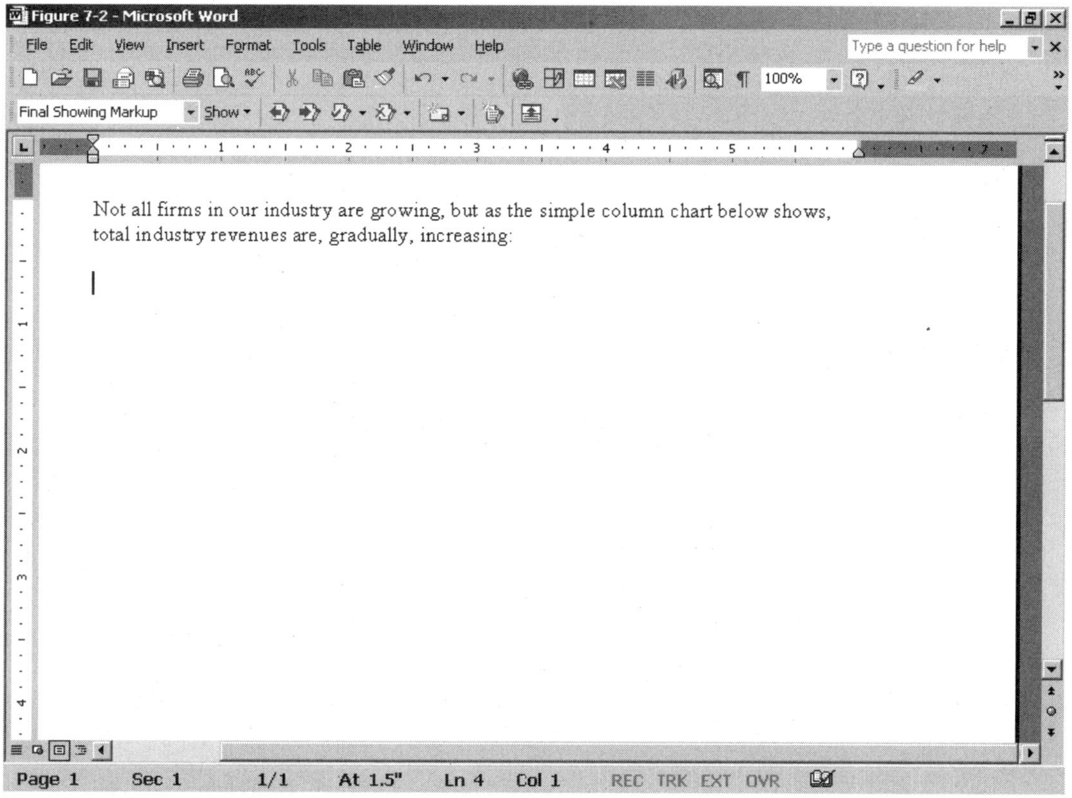

Figure 5-2 A Word document such as you might use for an OLE destination.

6. Paste the chart object into the client application's container document.

You can paste an object to the Clipboard by clicking the Paste toolbar button. You can also choose the Edit menu's Paste command. When you do, the client application (with Windows' help) creates an embedded object that looks as much like the source document object as the server application, Windows, and the client application allow. In other words, Windows and Windows programs use the richest format available for the pasted object. Figure 5-3 shows the Excel chart from Figure 5-1 embedded in the Word document from Figure 5-2.

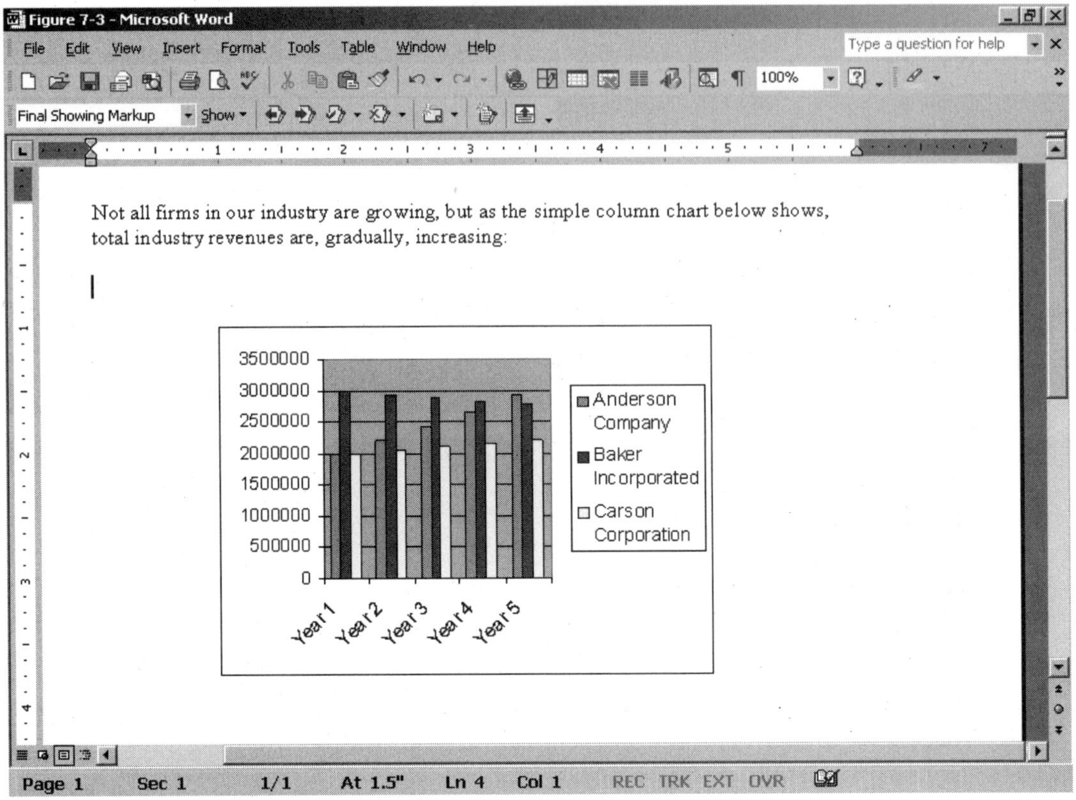

Figure 5-3 The Word document after adding the Excel chart object.

Creating a Linked OLE Object

You create a linked OLE object in almost the same way as you create an embedded OLE object. There's just one minor twist. You use the Edit menu's Paste Special command because it lets you indicate you want to create a linked object. For example, to create a linked OLE object using the same Excel chart shown in Figure 5-1 and the same Word document shown in Figure 5-2, follow these steps:

1. **Open both the source and container documents.**

   Again, to easily create embedded OLE objects, both the server application and the client application must be running and both the source document and container document should be open.

2. **Select the chart object.**

   As mentioned earlier, to select an object you simply click it.

3. **Copy the object to the Clipboard.**

   You can copy an object to the Clipboard by clicking the Copy toolbar button or by choosing the Edit menu's Copy command.

4. **Display the source document.**

   You could do this by clicking the document's button on the Taskbar.

5. **Position the insertion point at the location where you want to paste the object.**

   You can typically position the insertion point by clicking the point in the document where you want to place the object.

6. **Paste the chart object into the client application's container.**

   This is the only step that works differently from pasting an embedded object. When you paste a linked object, you need to use the Edit menu's Paste Special command. When you choose this command, the client program displays a Paste Special dialog box. (Figure 5-4 shows Microsoft Word's version of the Paste Special dialog box, but other programs' Paste Special dialog boxes look almost the same and work in the same basic way.) When the client program displays its Paste Special dialog box, click the Paste Link option button and click OK. Optionally, you can also select a format for the object from the As list box.

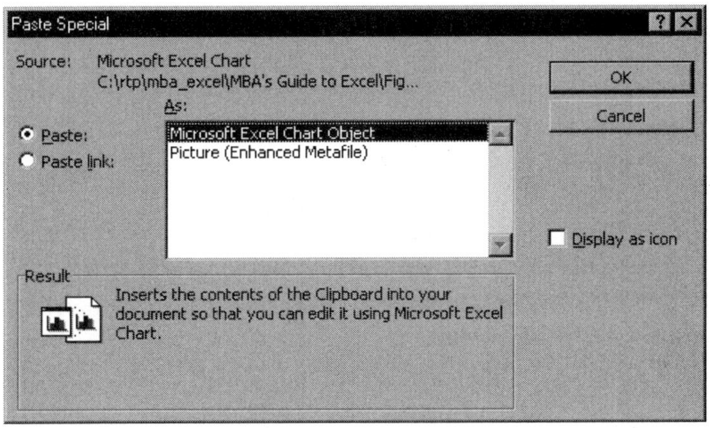

Figure 5-4 Microsoft Word's Paste Special dialog box.

When you open a document into which you've placed linked OLE objects, the program asks whether you want to update the links. If you do, click Yes, and the client application retrieves updated information from the source document.

NOTE *If you don't want the client application to automatically update links, you can tell it not to do so. To make this specification, in Excel, for example, choose the Tools menu's Options command, click the Calculation tab, and then clear the Update Remote References check box.*

By the way, it's possible to inadvertently break a link. For example, this may happen if the same source document is moved or renamed while the client application and container document are closed. In this case, you need to reestablish the link by repeating the steps you took to originally establish the link.

Editing OLE Objects

You can easily modify linked and embedded objects. To change an object, double-click it. The client application starts the server application and opens the appropriate source document. Once the server application is running and displaying the source, you can make your changes.

Inserting OLE Objects into Excel Workbooks

The object-sharing method described in the preceding paragraphs works well in situations in which you want to share data between programs and display that shared data in the container document. You should also know, however, that Excel's Insert menu provides an Object command, which you can use to place icons in a workbook that point to source documents.

To use the Insert menu's Object command to point to new OLE objects, choose the Insert menu's Object command. When Excel displays the Object dialog box, as shown in Figure 5-5, click the Create New tab, select the program necessary to create the object, and then click OK. Excel starts the server application, and you use it to create the new object. When you finish creating the object, click outside the object—such as on a worksheet cell—to return to Excel. Use the Display As Icon check box to indicate whether you want to see a picture of the object or simply a clickable icon you can use to access the object.

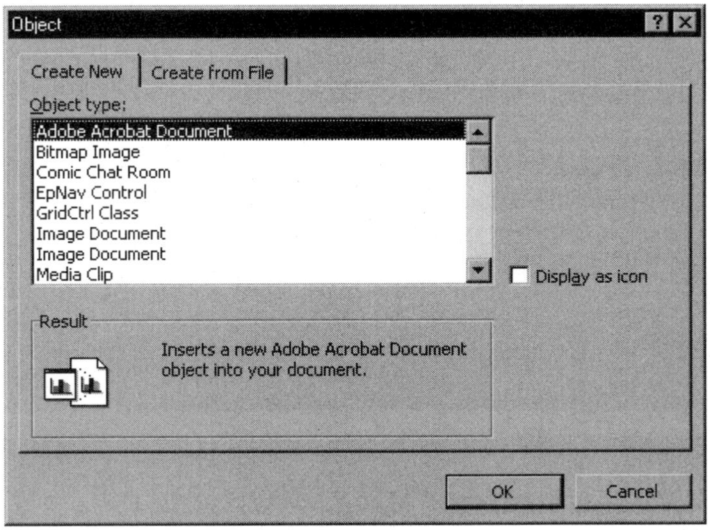

Figure 5-5 The Create New tab of the Object dialog box.

To use the Insert menu's Object command to point to an existing document, you also choose the Insert menu's Object command. When Excel displays the Object dialog box, however, you click the Create From File tab and then identify the file you want to use to create the object, as shown in Figure 5-6. To identify the file, enter the complete pathname in the File Name box or use the Browse button to display a dialog box you can use to search disks and folders for the file. Select the Link To File check box if you want to create a linked object. Select the Display As Icon check box to indicate whether you want to see a picture of the object or simply a clickable icon you can use to access the object.

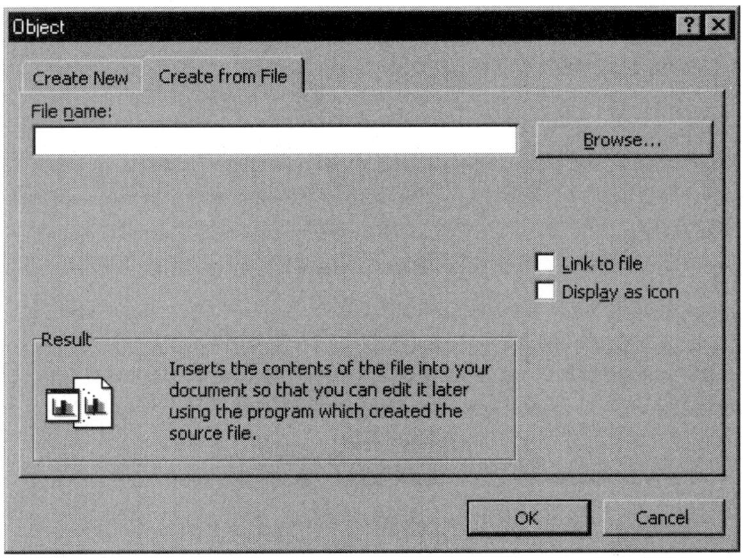

Figure 5-6 The Create From File tab of the Object dialog box.

Sharing Workbook Files

Excel provides several useful tools for sharing your actual workbooks, rather than just the information they contain. You can tell Excel to save or open workbooks in formats acceptable to other spreadsheet programs. You can direct Excel to save your workbooks on a network drive and then make the workbook simultaneously available to multiple users. And you can use electronic mail as a means of passing a workbook to other users.

NOTE *Excel also provides tools for publishing Excel workbooks to Web sites as Web pages, or HTML documents, and for placing interactive Excel objects into Web pages. At the end of this section, we'll discuss these tools and explain why you will probably never want to use them.*

Sharing Excel Workbooks with Other Programs

You can easily share an Excel workbook with other spreadsheet programs. You can, for example, export an Excel workbook so that someone using Lotus 1-2-3, another popular spreadsheet program, can open and work with the workbook. And you can also easily import spreadsheet documents created by other programs into Excel. For example, you can import a Quattro Pro workbook into Excel.

Exporting a Workbook

To export a workbook, you use the File menu's Save As command. When Excel displays the Save As dialog box, save the workbook file in the usual way—except use the Save As Type drop-down list to specify the file format as one acceptable to the other program, as shown in Figure 5-7. For example, if you want to export an Excel workbook to Lotus 1-2-3, choose the appropriate 1-2-3 file format.

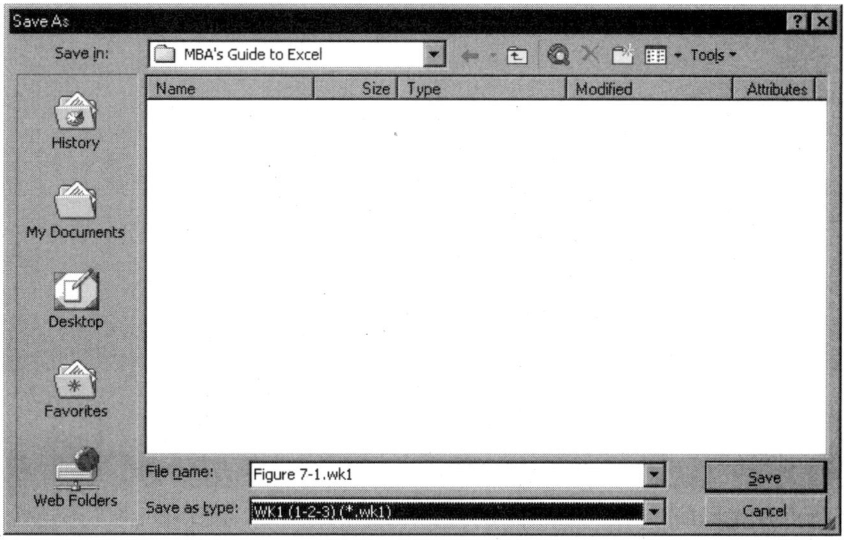

Figure 5-7 The Save As dialog box set to use the Lotus 1-2-3 format.

NOTE *You may need to determine the precise file format acceptable to the program that will later import the workbook you're exporting. Different versions of Lotus 1-2-3, for example, use different flavors of the standard 1-2-3 file format. Usually, if you know the file extension the spreadsheet program uses, you'll have enough information to select the appropriate format.*

If you can't determine the appropriate file format for the exported workbook file, you can try one of two tactics: You can use a simple standard spreadsheet format such as the tab-delimited format or the comma-separated value (CSV) format, which all spreadsheet programs understand. Or you can use a popular spreadsheet format, such as the Excel 95 file format or the Lotus 1-2-3 version 3 file format, which almost all spreadsheet programs understand.

NOTE *If you have questions about how to work with the other options on the Save As dialog box, refer to Chapter 1.*

Importing a Spreadsheet Document

To import a spreadsheet document, you use the File menu's Open command. When Excel displays the Open dialog box, you open the to-be-imported document in the usual way—except you use the Files Of Type drop-down list to specify the file format of the document you want to import, as shown in Figure 5-8. For example, to import a Lotus 1-2-3 spreadsheet document, select Lotus 1-2-3 Files from the list.

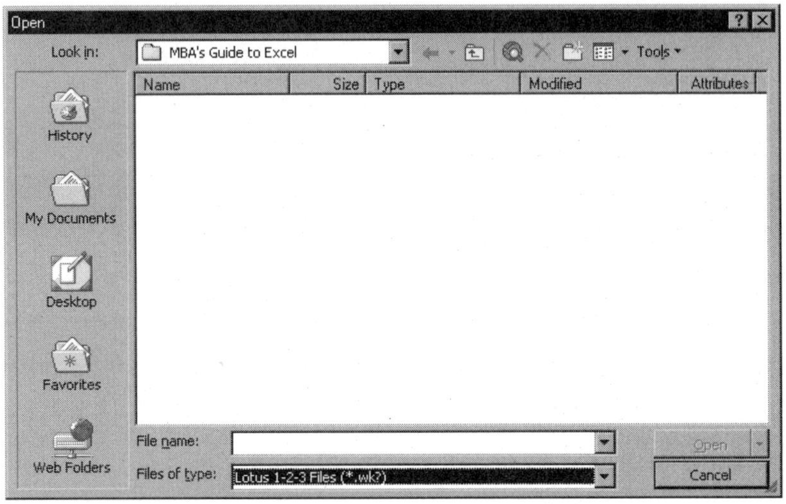

Figure 5-8 The Open dialog box with the Files Of Type list box indicating the Lotus 1-2-3 Files will be opened.

It's unlikely but not impossible that Excel won't recognize the other spreadsheet program's file format. In this case, before you save the spreadsheet document using this other spreadsheet program, you may need to choose a file format that Excel understands, such as any version of Excel, any version of Lotus 1-2-3, or a standard simple format such as CSV or tab-delimited.

NOTE *If you have questions about how to work with the other options in the Open dialog box, refer to Chapter 1.*

Sharing Excel Workbooks over a Network

You can share an Excel workbook with other Excel users over a network. In a nutshell, all you have to do is save the workbook in some accessible location, such as on a network drive or a shared local drive. With a workbook located on a network or shared local drive, network users with the appropriate level of authority and the requisite permissions can open, edit, and save the workbook.

NOTE *To view or open a network or shared local drive, you need to first map to the drive. You can map to a drive by clicking the Tools button in the Open or Save As dialog boxes, choosing the Map Network Drive command, and then entering the full pathname for the drive. If you have questions about the network pathname, ask your network administrator.*

If you do share a workbook over a network, you should be aware of a couple of points. First, and in general, if one user opens a workbook, other people can't open that same workbook except as a read-only document. What that means is that the person can't save the workbook using the same, original filename. The user can, however, save the workbook using a new filename or in a new location.

Excel tells you when you attempt to open a workbook that it's already being used, as shown in Figure 5-9. It then gives you the option of opening the workbook in read-only mode. You also have the option of asking Windows to notify you when the workbook document is fully available.

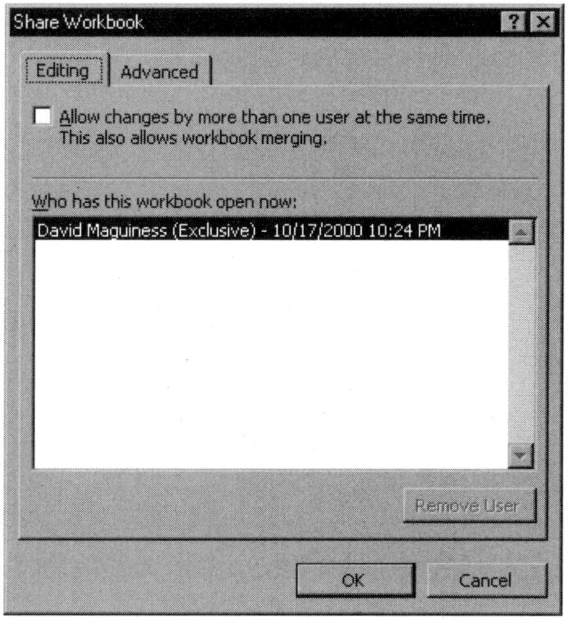

Figure 5-9 The Editing tab of the Share Workbook dialog box.

The second point you need to know about sharing a workbook over a network is that you have the option of telling Excel it's okay for multiple users to open and make changes to the same workbook. We can't emphasize enough that this option is extremely difficult to successfully use in a real-life work setting. You can just imagine all the trouble that can occur if people start making changes to the same parts of a workbook. If you want to do this, however, choose the Tools menu's Share Workbook command. When Excel displays the Share Workbook dialog box (see Figure 5-9), select the Allow Changes By More Than One User At The Same Time check box.

NOTE *The Share Workbook dialog box, as shown in Figure 5-9, also lists the names of the users who've opened a workbook.*

You can control many aspects of Excel's workbook sharing by using the Advanced tab of the Share Workbook dialog box, as shown in Figure 5-10. The Track Changes options, for example, let you tell Excel that it should keep a list of the changes made to a shared workbook and for how long this list should be kept. The Update Changes options let you specify when and how the shared workbook is updated for the changes that people make. Finally, the Conflicting Changes Between Users options let you specify what should happen when changes from different users are in conflict.

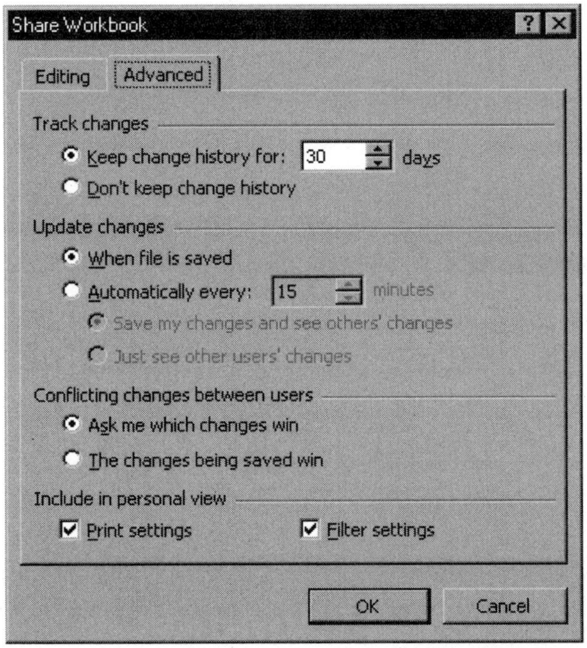

Figure 5-10 The Advanced tab of the Share Workbook dialog box.

Excel does attempt to resolve any conflicts that arise from workbook sharing. When a user saves a workbook, Excel looks for conflicts—such as the same cell being changed by different users. If Excel sees such a conflict, it displays the Resolve Conflicts dialog box, and asks how the conflict should be resolved. One important aspect of this conflict resolution, however, is that the person who saves the workbook and, therefore, sees the Resolve Conflicts dialog box, determines which changes should be saved and which should be discarded.

NOTE *If you choose to work with shared workbooks, you probably want to create a formal, perhaps written, policy to document how conflicts should be resolved. You may also want to plan for workbook sharing when you build the workbook. For example, you might build a workbook so different users would always be making changes to separate worksheets. This would prevent most conflicts.*

Sharing Excel Workbooks via E-Mail

Excel's File menu provides several commands, which you can use to share workbooks using electronic mail. When you share workbooks in this manner, you simply attach the workbook to an e-mail message and then send the message and its attachment, the workbook, to another person.

NOTE *If you can't e-mail someone a workbook, save the workbook to a floppy disk and deliver the disk.*

Sending a Workbook via E-Mail

If you regularly use e-mail, you'll find it very easy to share workbooks using mail. You simply send e-mail messages laden with Excel workbooks.

To e-mail the open Excel workbook, follow these steps:

1. **Choose the File menu's Send To command.**

   Excel displays the Send To submenu, which lists commands for sharing workbooks using electronic mail and, in some cases, other e-mail-like services, such as Microsoft's Exchange Server.

2. **Choose the Send To menu's Mail Recipient (As Attachment) command.**

   Excel opens your default e-mail client, opens a new message, and attaches the workbook. Figure 5-11 shows how the Microsoft Outlook Express e-mail client looks, but your e-mail client will probably look very similar even if you use one of the other popular e-mail programs.

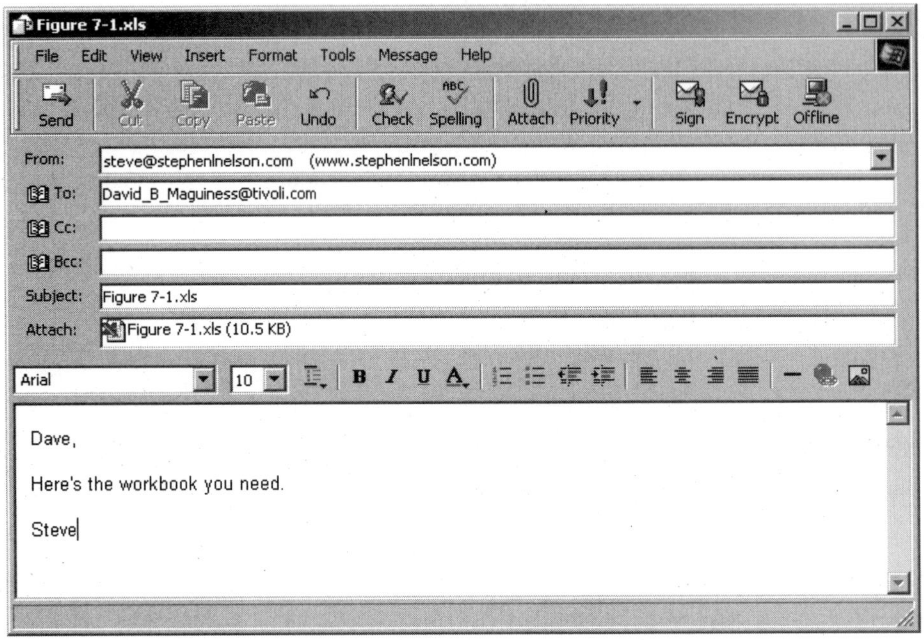

Figure 5-11 The Outlook Express message window with an Excel workbook attachment.

3. Complete and deliver the e-mail message in the usual way.

You complete your e-mail message in the usual way. For example, you need to provide the recipient's e-mail name or alias. And you probably want to provide a message subject and perhaps some message text to explain the message and your attachment. When you finish, send the message in the usual way.

NOTE *Some mail servers limit the size of the attachments they will accept. Some organizations discourage and even prohibit e-mail attachments because the attachments can contain viruses. Before you send an e-mail attachment, make sure that your recipient can accept an e-mail message with an attachment.*

Receiving a Workbook via E-Mail

You can also easily receive e-mail messages that contain Excel workbook attachments.

To receive and use an e-mailed Excel workbook, follow these steps:

1. **Start your e-mail program and retrieve your messages in the usual way.**

   Figure 5-12 shows the Outlook Express program window with the Inbox folder displayed. Other e-mail programs, however, typically show your incoming messages in a similar way. Notice that the first message includes a paperclip icon in front of it to indicate that a file is "attached."

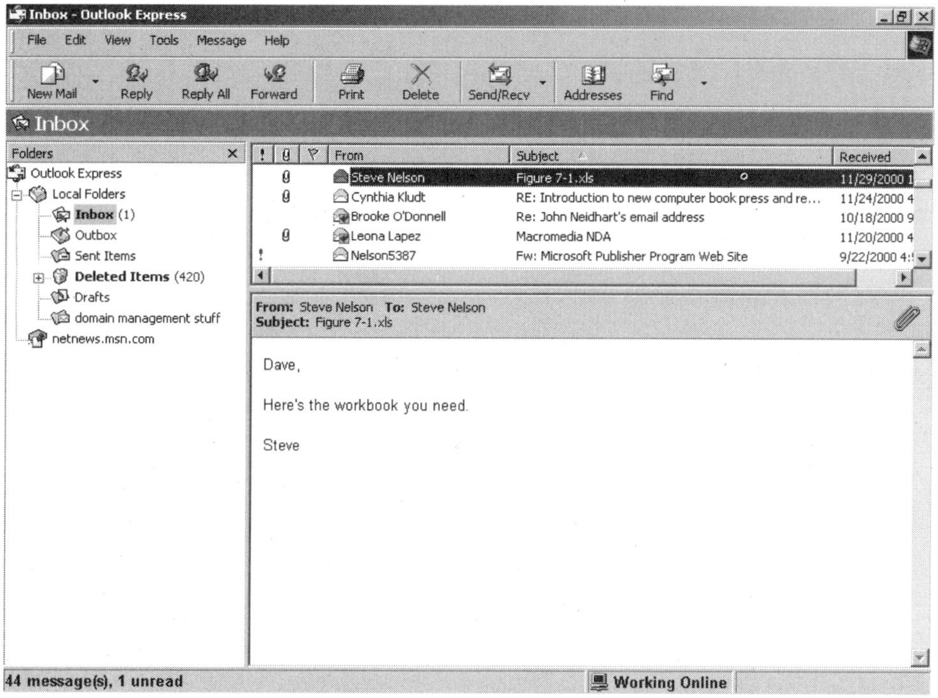

Figure 5-12 The Outlook Express Inbox folder showing incoming messages.

2. **Open the e-mail message with the attachment.**

   Figure 5-13 shows the Outlook Express message window displaying a sample message with an Excel workbook attachment. Again, your e-mail client will probably look very similar even if you use another program.

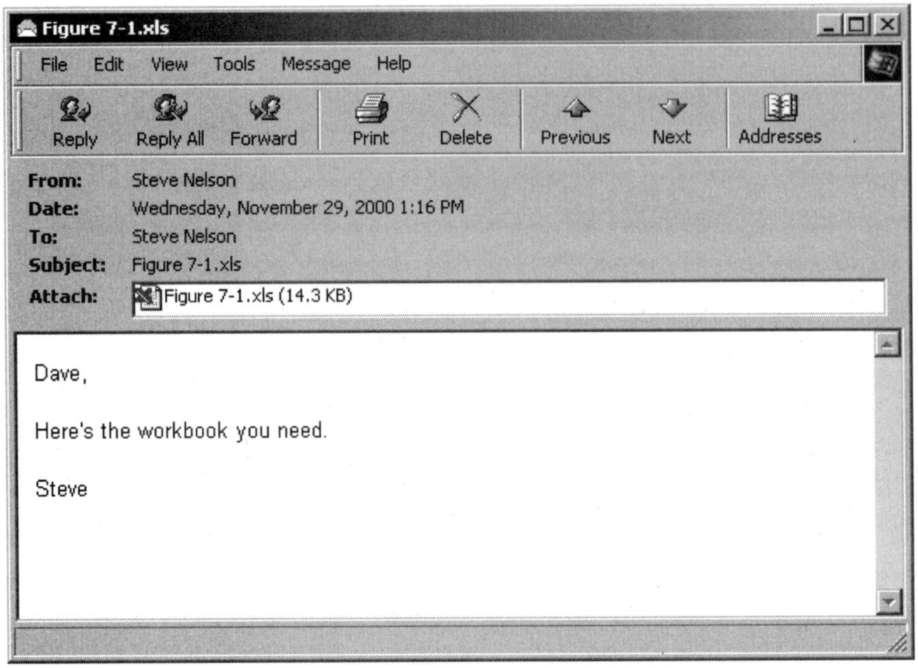

Figure 5-13 The Outlook Express message window with an Excel workbook attachment.

3. **Save the attachment.**

   You can typically do this by right-clicking the attachment icon and then choosing the shortcut menu's Save As command. The e-mail client then displays a Save As dialog box, and you use it to indicate where you want to save the workbook.

4. **Open the workbook.**

   You open the workbook in any of the usual ways. For example, you can start Excel and then choose the File menu's Open command.

Avoiding E-Mail Attachment Problems

E-mail attachment problems may be occurring more infrequently these days as the e-mail clients and the mail servers get smarter. Nevertheless, you should be aware that two problems are commonly encountered when sending attachments over the Internet: problems with attachment size and problems with attachment format.

Problems with attachment size stem from the fact that some mail servers limit attachment size. For example, a mail server may limit attachment size to less than one megabyte, and that may mean your largest Excel workbooks are too big to be attachments.

Problems with attachment format stem from the fact that an attachment can actually be included in a message in either of two formats: Uuencode or MIME. Some e-mail programs accept only one format or may by default assume that attachments use one of the formats. For example, an e-mail client may assume that attachments are Uuencode attachments and then become confused when trying to handle a MIME attachment.

While both problems are frustrating, fortunately neither problem is typically difficult to solve. If you encounter the first problem of attachment size, consult with the mail server administrators—and ask to have the attachment size limit changed. If you encounter the second problem of incompatible attachments, consult the e-mail client documentation to determine how to specify which format is used or assumed—and then make sure that both the sender's and recipient's e-mail clients use the same format.

Workbook Sharing with E-Mail

In the earlier chapter section "Sharing Excel Workbooks over a Network," we noted that if you enable workbook sharing, Excel will allow multiple users to simultaneously open a workbook. Then when these users attempt to save their changes, Excel looks for conflicts and attempts to help users resolve conflicting changes.

It turns out that you can have Excel also perform this same conflict resolution with workbooks you've shared, such as through e-mail or by physically delivering the workbook on a floppy disk. To use Excel's Workbook Sharing feature in these special cases, follow these steps:

1. **Turn on Workbook Sharing.**

   In order to merge workbooks, you need to first turn on Workbook Sharing in the workbook by using the Tools menu's Share Workbook command. This is described in the earlier chapter section "Sharing Excel Workbooks over a Network."

2. **Create identical copies of the same workbook.**

   You can create an identical copy by using the File menu's Save As command. Simply save the workbook using a new name.

3. **Distribute separate copies of the workbook you want to share.**

   You can do this by e-mailing the workbook, as described in the earlier chapter section "Sending a Workbook via E-Mail."

4. **Collect the workbooks after changes are made.**

   After people have made their changes, collect the workbooks. Save them in the same folder location.

5. **Open your master workbook.**

   The master workbook is the workbook in which you'll collect all the changes, and it's probably the same workbook you used to create the workbook copies you distributed.

6. **Choose the Tools menu's Compare And Merge Workbooks command.**

   Excel displays the Select Files To Merge Into Current Workbook dialog box shown in Figure 5-14.

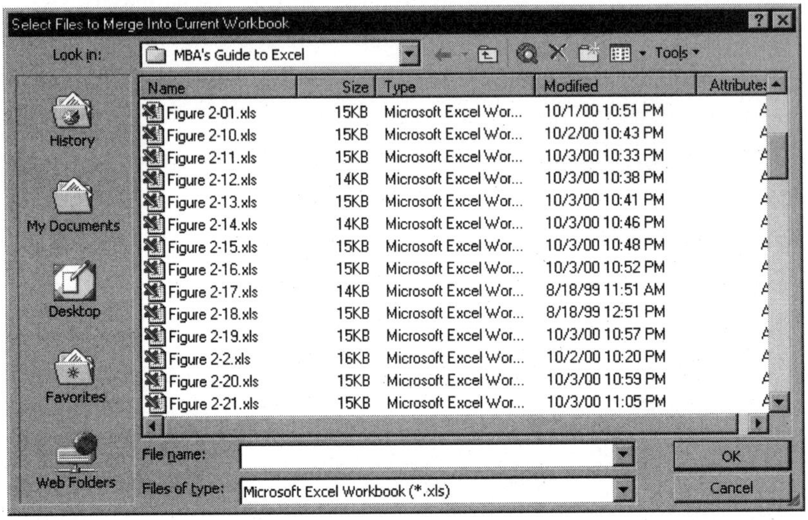

Figure 5-14 The Select Files To Merge Into Current Workbook dialog box.

7. **Select the workbooks you want to merge.**

   The Select Files To Merge Into Current Workbook dialog box works in the same basic way as the Save As and Open dialog boxes. You use the Look In drop-down list box to select the drive and folder you want to open. The main box of the dialog box lists the Excel workbooks in the open folder. To select a workbook, click it. To select multiple workbooks, hold down the Ctrl key and then click each workbook. Then click OK. Excel merges the changes from the selected workbooks into the master workbook.

Using E-Mail Routing Slips

If you choose the File menu's Send To command, you'll also notice a Routing Recipient command. The Routing Recipient command lets you build a list of e-mail addresses to which an Excel workbook can be sequentially routed, and then send the workbook to the first person on the list. When one recipient finishes with the workbook, Excel automatically routes, or sends, the workbook along to the next person on the list.

NOTE *The Routing Recipient command lets you have a group of people make workbook changes sequentially, which means that you avoid the sorts of conflicts described in the earlier discussions of workbook sharing and merging workbooks.*

Sending a Workbook Using Routing Slips

To use the Routing Recipient command, open the workbook you want to share and then follow these steps:

1. Choose the Routing Recipient command.

Excel displays the Routing Slip dialog box shown in Figure 5-15.

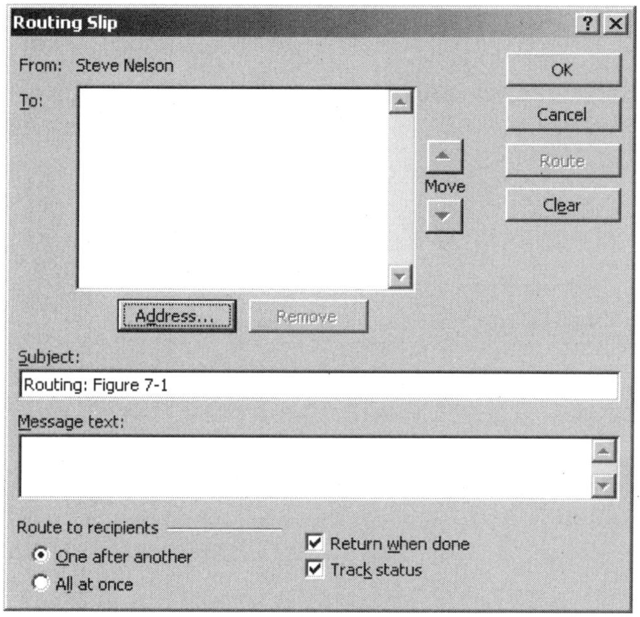

Figure 5-15 The Routing Slip dialog box you use to create a routing recipients list.

2. Build your list of recipients.

Click the Address button to display the Address Book. To add a name, click it and then click the To button. If you want to send the workbook to someone not yet in your Address Book, first add his or her name to your Address Book. You should add names in the same order as you want to route the workbook, but if you don't, note that you can use the Move buttons to move a selected name up or down on the routing list.

3. Optionally, provide a message subject and message text.

You can use the Subject and Message Text boxes to provide the e-mail message subject and message text. Each recipient sees this information.

4. Indicate you want to use sequential routing.

Click the One After Another option button to indicate that you want to use sequential routing. You don't have to use sequential routing, but sequential routing is often desirable. Sequential routing eliminates the need to resolve conflicting edits to a workbook. (What happens, of course, is that recipients will effectively resolve conflicts as they review the previous recipient's work and make further changes.)

NOTE *If you want the workbook returned after the last person on the list finishes, select the Return When Done check box. If you want to receive notification each time the workbook is routed to the next recipient, select the Track Status check box.*

5. Route the workbook to the first routing recipient.

You can begin routing the workbook in two ways: immediately or later. If you want to begin routing the workbook immediately, click the Route button; Excel sends the workbook to the first routing recipient on your list. If you want to make more changes or postpone routing, click the Add Slip button; Excel then saves your routing information. When you later want to send the workbook to the first routing recipient, choose the File menu's Send To command and then choose Next Routing.

NOTE *When a routing slip is attached to a workbook, Excel replaces the Send To submenu's Mail Recipient command with the Next Routing command.*

Receiving a Routed Workbook

You receive a routed workbook in the same manner as you receive other e-mail attachments, as described in the earlier section "Receiving a Workbook via E-Mail." When you finish with the workbook, however, choose the File menu's Send To command and then choose Next Routing to send the workbook to the next routing recipient.

NOTE *Excel provides these same instructions at the end of the e-mail message that goes along with your routed workbook.*

When you choose the Next Routing command, Excel displays the Routing Slip dialog box. Click the Route Document To option button, and then click OK to send the workbook to the next recipient.

NOTE *If you click the Send Copy Of Document Without Using The Routing Slip option button, Excel lets you send the workbook as an attachment to somebody besides the next person on the routing list and without a routing slip. This option is equivalent, then, to the Mail Recipient command, which appears on the Send To submenu when a workbook doesn't have a routing slip.*

Sharing Excel Data over the Web

Excel provides a special command—the File menu's Save As Web Page command—for creating a Web page version of an Excel workbook. You can also use the Save As Web Page command for creating interactive spreadsheet components for Web pages. The paragraphs that follow describe how you do both of these things—and also explain why you will rarely want to do either.

Creating a Web Page Version of an Excel Workbook

Excel lets you use hypertext markup language (HTML) as the format for your Excel workbooks. What this means is that you can create Excel workbooks that can both be opened and edited by Excel in almost the usual way and viewed using your Web browser. (If an Excel workbook is viewed with a Web browser, you can't edit the workbook data except in very limited circumstances, as described later in the section "Creating an Interactive Spreadsheet Component.")

Before we describe the steps for saving an Excel workbook using the Web page, HTML format, we need to emphasize that you don't want to use HTML as the default format for your workbooks. Much workbook information is lost and much workbook functionality is sacrificed when you use the HTML file format.

NOTE *You may be able to get a more complete list of the lost functionality that stems from using HTML as the Excel workbook file format from the Office Assistant. But know for starters that with HTML you lose the following items: the 1904 data system, arrays, cell comments, conditional formatting, custom views, data validation, external link references, formatting (including cell-level fonts, dashed and dotted borders, pattern fills, rotated and indented text), nested functions, password protection, precision-as-displayed options, range names, and scenarios.*

To create a Web page version of an Excel workbook, follow these steps:

1. **Choose the File menu's Save As Web Page command.**

   Excel displays the Save As dialog box shown in Figure 5-16.

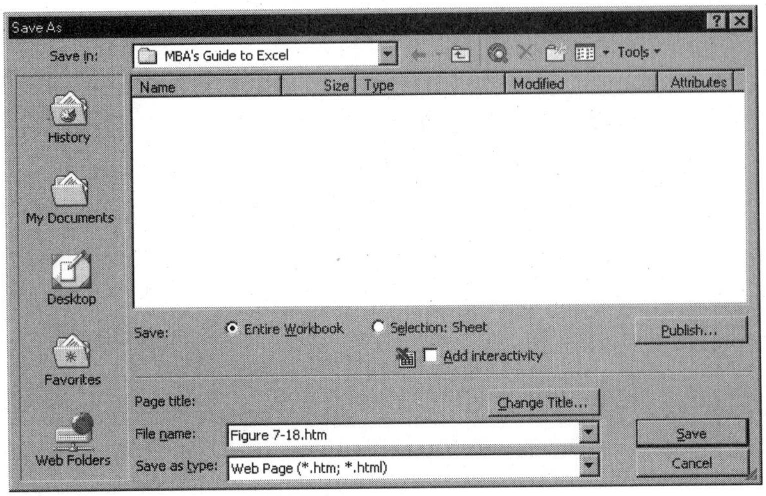

Figure 5-16 The Save As dialog box.

2. **Name the Web page.**

   Click the File Name box, and enter the filename you want to use for the Web page.

3. **Verify that the Save As Type box indicates the file format is Web Page, or HTML.**

   Excel lets you use either its standard binary file format, indicated by the .xls file extension, or its new Web page format, indicated by the .htm file extension. When you save a workbook as a Web page, predictably, you use the Web page format.

4. **Specify where you want the Web page saved.**

   Use the navigation bar's clickable icons to open the folder location where you want to save the Web page. Most often, you click the My Documents icon so that Excel opens your My Documents folder. You can also click the Web Folders icon so that Excel displays a list of Web folders to which you can add files.

NOTE *If you don't see any Web folders listed when you click the Web Folder icon, click Create New Folder. When Excel displays the Add Web Folder dialog box, type the Web folder URL in the box provided. Or, click the Browse button, and then use your Web browser to open the Web folder location.*

5. Click Publish to create the Web page.

When you click Publish, Excel creates an HTML, or Web page version, of the workbook in the specified location.

Once you create the Web page, you can view it using your Web browser. Or, you can open the Web page using Excel and then make the same general changes you make to any Excel workbook.

NOTE *If you do create Web page versions of Excel workbooks, you may want to develop proficiency in using the Insert menu's Hyperlink command. This command lets you add hyperlinks to a workbook—essentially by selecting the item you want to turn into a hyperlink, choosing the command, and then providing the Internet URL.*

Creating an Interactive Spreadsheet Component

Excel also lets you take Excel worksheets or worksheet ranges and convert them into miniature spreadsheet objects that can be placed in Web pages. These interactive spreadsheet components allow people to view the Web page with their Web browser. Figure 5-17, for example, shows a simple mortgage calculator workbook.

	A	B	C
1	Mortgage Payment Calculator		
2	Loan Balance	150000	
3	Repayment Term	360	
4	Annual Interest Rate	0.08	
5	Monthly Payment	($1,100.65)	
6			
7			

Figure 5-17 A simple workbook such as might be used to create an interactive spreadsheet component.

Figure 5-18 shows a Web page with a simple interactive spreadsheet component, which is actually the worksheet range A1:B5 from the workbook shown in Figure 5-17.

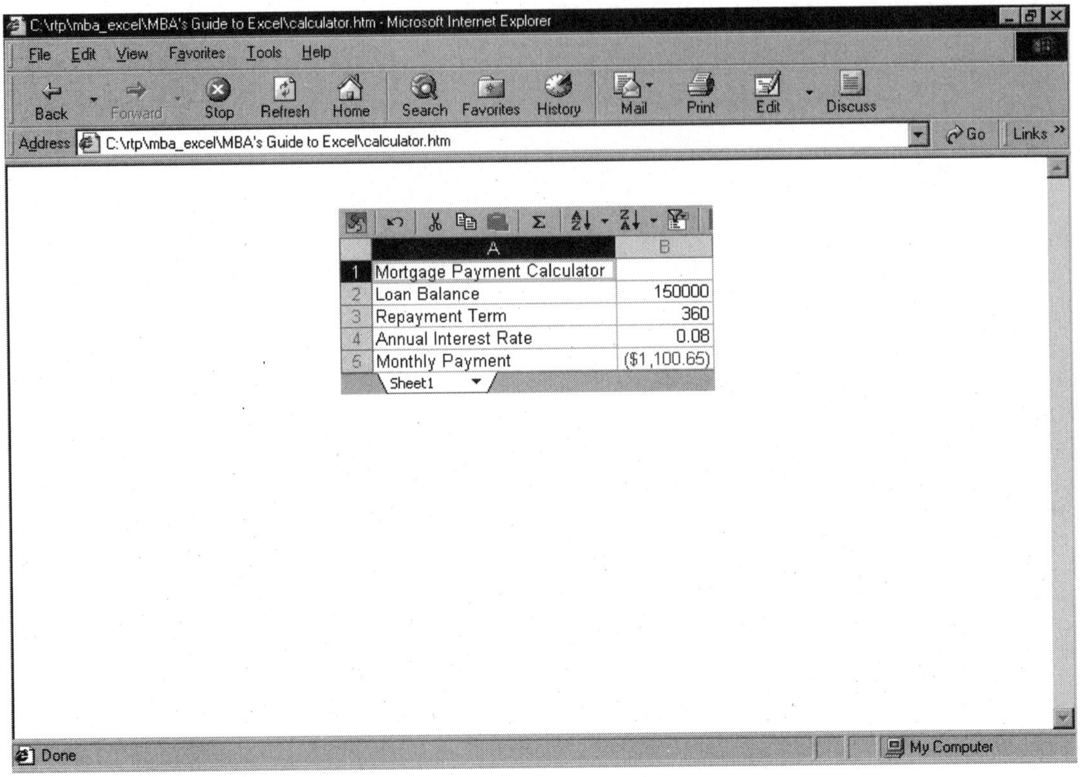

Figure 5-18 A Web page with a simple interactive spreadsheet component.

The unique feature of an interactive spreadsheet component is that when you view the component using Microsoft Internet Explorer version 4.1 (or a later version), you can make modest changes. In Figure 5-18, for example, if you enter a new interest rate, the interactive spreadsheet component calculates a new monthly mortgage payment.

In general, interactive spreadsheet components resemble Excel workbooks in their mechanics. Note, however, that even if you are familiar with Excel you will need to experiment a bit in order to become proficient with interactive spreadsheet components.

As with Excel Web pages, however, interactive spreadsheet components allow for only a subset of Excel's functionality. And, in fact, by using interactive spreadsheet components, you get only a very modest portion of Excel's functionality. What's more, to use interactive spreadsheet components, you must already have installed the Standard, Professional, or Premium version of Microsoft Office and the Office Web Components.

Accordingly, we wonder when interactive spreadsheet components would ever be the preferred method for sharing Excel data. Any time you can successfully share data using an interactive spreadsheet component, you've always got a superior solution that the recipient presumably already knows how to use: Excel.

Nevertheless, creating interactive spreadsheet components is easy. To create an interactive spreadsheet component, first select the worksheet range you want to use as an interactive spreadsheet component. Then follow these steps:

1. Choose the File menu's Save As Web Page command.

Excel displays the Save As dialog box shown in Figure 5-19.

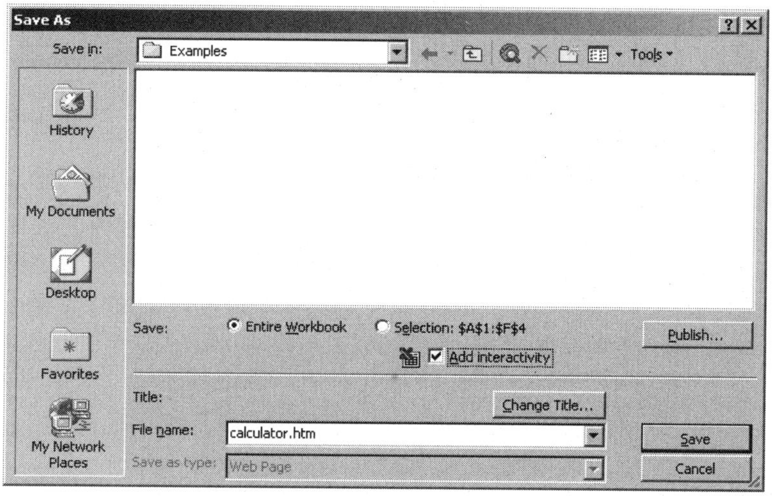

Figure 5-19 The Save As dialog box filled out to create an interactive spreadsheet component.

2. Click the Selection: Sheet option button.

This tells Excel you want to create a Web component for the selected portion of the workbook.

3. Select the Add Interactivity check box.

This tells Excel you want to create an interactive Web component for the selected portion of the workbook.

4. Name the Web page.

Click the File Name box, and enter the filename you want to use for the Web page.

5. **Specify where you want the Web page saved.**

   Use the navigation bar's clickable icons to open the folder location where you want to save the Web page. Most often, you click the My Documents icon so that Excel opens your My Documents folder. You can also click the Web Folders icon so that Excel displays a list of Web folders to which you can add files.

NOTE *If you don't see any Web folders listed when you click the Web Folder icon, click Create New Folder. When Excel displays the Add Web Folder dialog box, type the Web folder URL in the box provided. Or, click the Browse button, and then use your Web browser to open the Web folder location.*

6. **Optionally, give the Web page a name.**

   If you click the Change Title button, Excel displays a dialog box you can use to name the Web page. This Web page name appears on the title bar of the Web browser.

7. **Click Publish to create the Web page.**

   When you click Publish, Excel displays the Publish As Web Page dialog box shown in Figure 5-20.

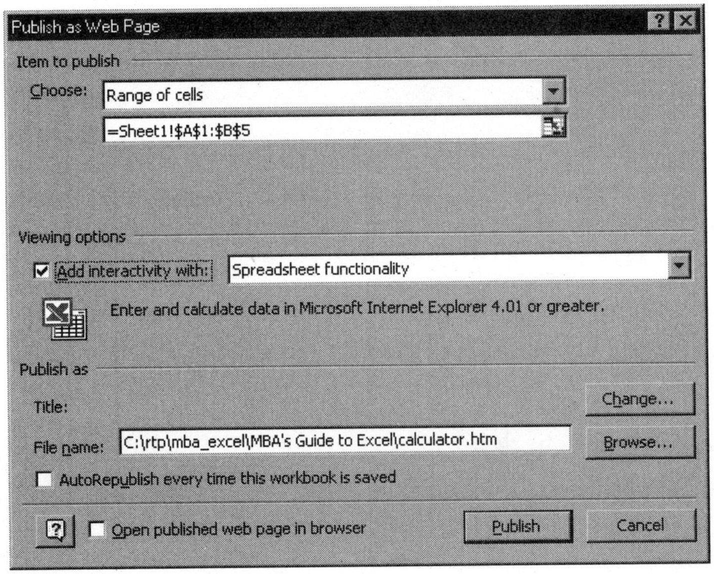

Figure 5-20 The Publish As Web Page dialog box.

8. **Verify the worksheet selection.**

   Review the Choose boxes to confirm that these correctly identify the worksheet selection you want to publish as an interactive spreadsheet component. Edit the contents if needed.

9. **Verify the form of interactivity.**

   Confirm that the Add Interactivity With check box shows the correct form of interactivity. For example, if you're creating an interactive spreadsheet component, the list box should show Spreadsheet Functionality.

10. **Verify the filename.**

    Confirm that the file pathname shows in the File Name box. If the correct file pathname doesn't show in the File Name box, edit the contents as needed.

11. **Publish the interactive spreadsheet component.**

    Click the Publish button.

Retrieving External Data with Excel

Most of the earlier sections of this chapter presuppose you use Excel to create data you then pass along to other programs and people. While many people are very likely to use Excel in this way, you may use Excel to retrieve data created or stored by some other program.

In the final pages of this chapter, then, we'll briefly explain how to use Excel to collect external data so you can exploit Excel's analytical power to examine the data. Specifically, the chapter discusses two tools: Excel's Import Wizard and its Get External Data commands.

Importing Textual Data into Excel

Excel lets you easily import textual data into an Excel workbook. This capacity may not sound interesting, but it means that anything you can get as a text file—such as a financial report generated by the mainframe accounting system—can be imported into Excel and then examined.

To import a text file into Excel, follow these steps:

1. **Open the text file.**

   Using the File menu's Open command, tell Excel that you want to open the text file. When Excel displays the Open dialog box, select the All Files item or the Text File items in the List Files Of Type box so that your text file is listed. Once you find the file, click it and then click the Open button. Excel displays the first Text Import Wizard dialog box, shown in Figure 5-21.

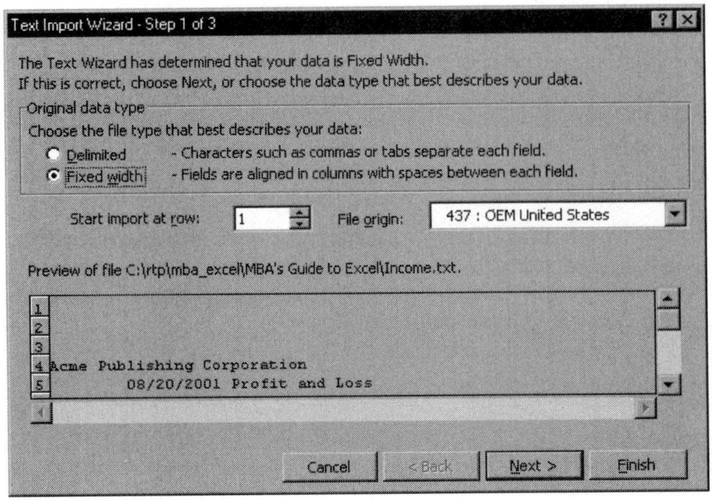

Figure 5-21 The first Text Import Wizard dialog box.

2. Indicate whether the file uses the fixed-width format or delimiting characters.

Use the Original Data Type option buttons—Fixed Width or Delimited—to indicate whether the file uses a fixed-width format, which is the same thing as a straight text file, or uses delimiting characters. Excel can usually guess correctly about which format your text file uses, by the way, so if you're not sure which option to select, accept Excel's default suggestion.

3. Indicate the first row that should be imported.

Use the Start Import At Row box to indicate which row of the text file is the first row you want to have imported. For example, you might not want to import reader header and title information, and might instead want only to begin importing the first row with the data.

4. Identify the file origin.

Use the File Origin box to identify the source of the file. If you're importing data created by another Windows program, select the Windows (ANSI) entry from the File Origin box. If you're importing data from a mainframe, select the MS-DOS (PC-8) entry from the File Origin box.

NOTE *You can use the Preview box to see how Excel interprets your to-be-imported data.*

5. Verify the fixed-width assumptions or delimited character assumptions made by Excel.

Once you finish with the first Text Import Wizard dialog box, you click Next. Excel then displays the second Text Import Wizard dialog box. If you're importing a fixed-width file, Excel displays the dialog box shown in Figure 5-22. You use this dialog box to verify how Excel breaks the text file into columns. You can create new break lines by clicking. You can remove an existing break line by double-clicking. You can also move an existing break line by dragging.

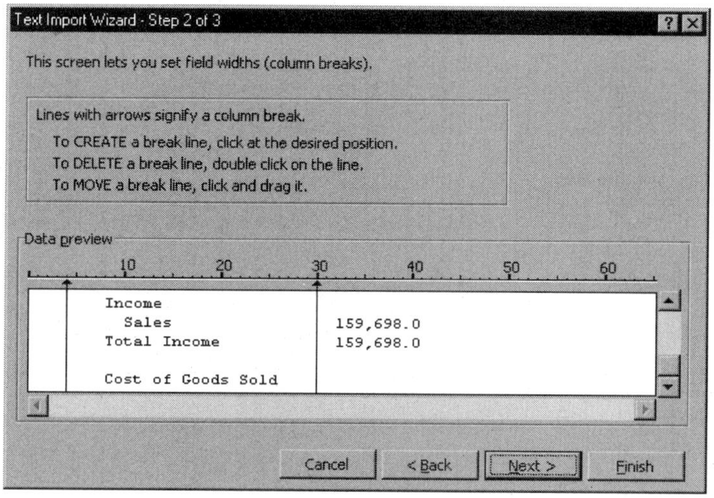

Figure 5-22 The second Text Import Wizard dialog box if you're importing a fixed-width file.

If you're importing a delimited character file, Excel displays the dialog box shown in Figure 5-23. You use this dialog box principally to verify that Excel has correctly identified the delimiter: The checked Delimiters box should identify the delimiter. You can also indicate if the text file uses a character (such as a quotation mark) to identify text. Note that you can tell whether Excel's delimiter assumptions correctly describe the text file because the preview box shows how your data look given the delimiter specifications.

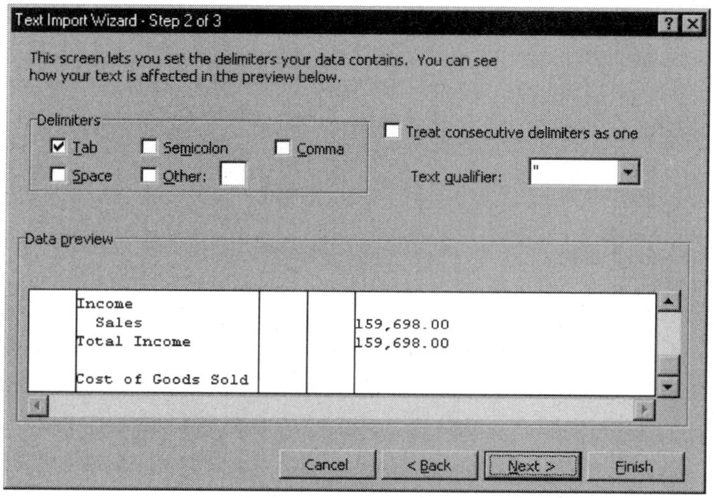

Figure 5-23 The second Text Import Wizard dialog box if you're importing a delimited character file.

6. **Select formatting for each column.**

   After you've verified the fixed-width or delimited character assumptions of Excel—and fixed any incorrect assumptions—click Next. Excel displays the third Text Import Wizard shown in Figure 5-24. You use this dialog box to specify the formatting assumptions Excel should make about the to-be-imported text file.

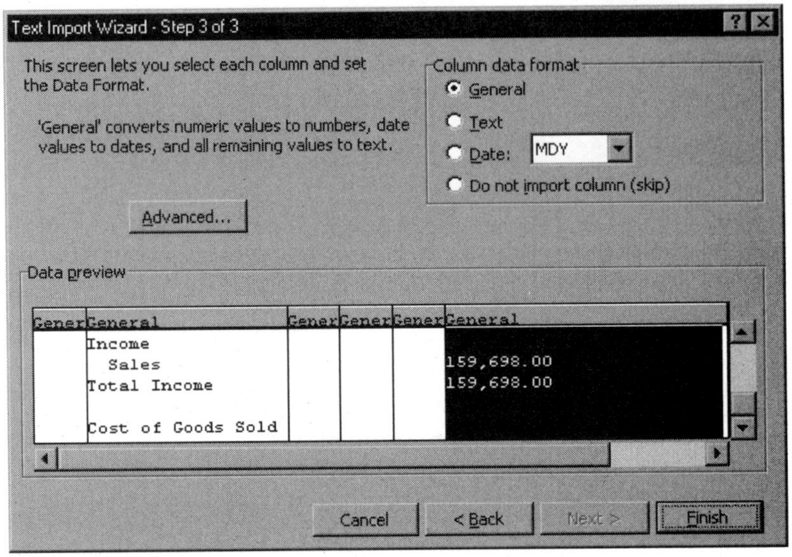

Figure 5-24 The third Text Import Wizard dialog box.

   Excel also guesses about the default formatting that it should use for each column of the text file you import. You should verify that each column uses the best default formatting. To change a column's format, click the column header and then the appropriate Column Data Format button. If you don't want to import a column, click it and then click the Do Not Import Column option button.

7. **Click Finish when you're finished.**

   Excel imports the text file into a new, blank, open workbook. At this point, you're ready to begin cleaning up the data so you can start working with it.

Using the Get External Data Commands

Excel, through the commands on the Get External Data submenu, provides tools that you can use to retrieve data from external data sources, such as from a database. Some of these tools are quite easy to use. And others require you to be proficient in the language and structure of databases. We're not going to describe how to use all of these tools in detail here. We will, however, describe how you use the most common of these tools, including the Query Wizard. And we'll also discuss each of the tools so you know just what Excel is capable of and about features you may want to explore in more detail.

Importing Text Files

If you choose the Data menu's Get External Data command and then choose the Get External Data submenu's Import Text File command, Excel lets you identify a text file you want to import. Once you've identified this text file, Excel starts the same Text Import Wizard described in the previous section, "Importing Textual Data into Excel."

When you use the Import Text File command, however, Excel does one thing differently from starting the Text Import Wizard from the File menu's Open command. When you use the Import Text File command, Excel maintains a link to the original text file by using external references. This means that if you want to re-import the text file—perhaps because the data has changed—you can easily do so. To re-import the data, click the Refresh All toolbar button on the External Data toolbar.

NOTE *If you don't see the External Data toolbar, right-click another toolbar and choose the shortcut menu's External Data command.*

Using the Query Wizard

Excel's Import External Data submenu provides access to the Query Wizard, which is the tool you'll most often use to retrieve external data. The Query Wizard, in effect, provides an interface you use from inside Excel to query an external database.

The Query Wizard works with most common databases. Excel provides database drivers for connecting to most (perhaps all) of the popular database engines, including the Microsoft Access, Excel, FoxPro, and SQL Server products and the third-party database products dBASE, Oracle and Paradox.

If you want to retrieve information from an external database that isn't on the list contained in the preceding paragraph, you can still retrieve data from the database. For example, almost surely, you can use the database program to create a text file that holds the information you want to query. And you may also be able to create database files, or tables, that use a format that mimics one of the databases listed.

NOTE *To import a text file, you use the Text Import Wizard. As noted in the preceding paragraphs, you can start the Text Import Wizard indirectly by choosing the File menu's Open command and then attempting to open the text file. Or you can start the Text Import Wizard directly by choosing the Data menu's Get External Data command and then choosing Import Text File.*

To use the Query Wizard, follow these steps:

1. **Open a blank workbook.**

   Excel places the external data you retrieve in the open workbook. This means you'll probably want to start with a blank, open workbook. If you want to place the data in an existing workbook, make sure you've got an empty worksheet on which to store the data.

2. **Start the Query Wizard.**

   To start the Query Wizard, choose the Data menu's Import External Data command and then choose New Database Query. Excel displays the Choose Data Source dialog box shown in Figure 5-25.

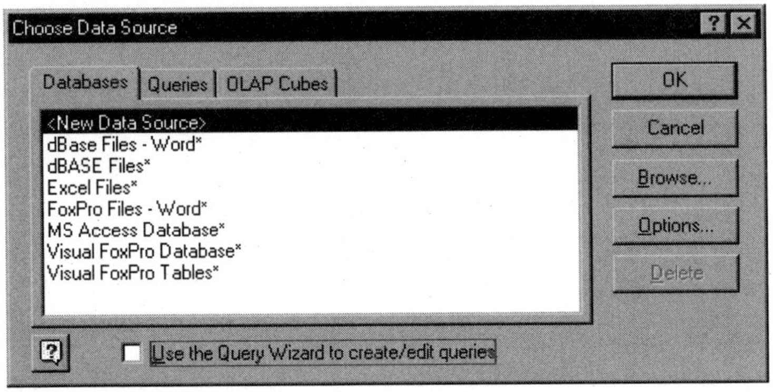

Figure 5-25 The Choose Data Source dialog box.

3. **Indicate you want to use the Query Wizard.**

   Check the Use The Query Wizard To Create/Edit Queries box to indicate you'll use the Query Wizard.

4. **Indicate the data source from which you'll retrieve the data.**

   To select the data source from which you want to retrieve data, first click the Databases tab. Then select the type of database from which you'll retrieve data. For example, if you're retrieving data from a dBASE database, click the dBASE Files entry in the list box. Click OK after you've selected your data source. The Query Wizard displays the Choose Columns dialog box shown in Figure 5-26.

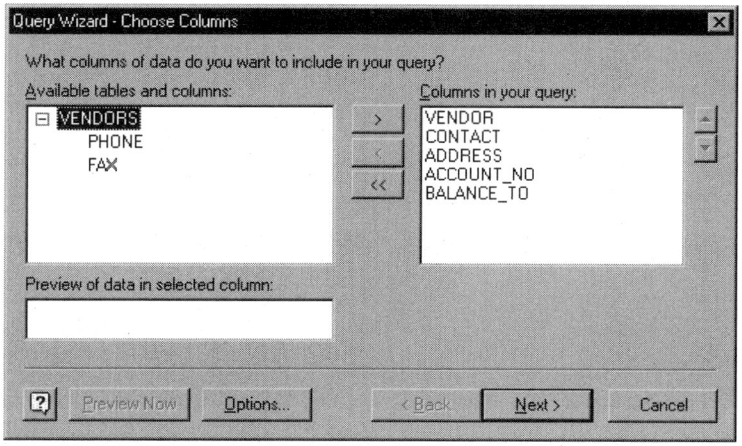

Figure 5-26 The Choose Columns dialog box.

NOTE *If you want to rerun an existing query, click the Queries tab to see a list of defined queries you can use to get external data. You can also click the OLAP Cubes tab to see a list of OLAP data sources that may be available.*

5. Select the table or tables that you want to query.

When Excel displays the Choose Columns dialog box, use the Available Tables And Columns list box to select the tables and columns, or fields, that you want to import. To see the columns that a table uses, click the plus symbol next to the table name.

6. Select the columns that you want to retrieve.

Select the columns you want to retrieve by clicking the column and then clicking the Add button. The Add button shows a single arrow pointing to the Columns In Your Query list box. To remove a column from the Columns In Your Query list box, click the column and then click the Remove button, which shows a single arrow pointing to the Available Tables And Columns List box. To start over, click the Remove All button, which shows a double arrow pointing to the Available Tables And Columns List box. When you finish selecting the columns you want to retrieve, click Next. The Query Wizard displays the Filter Data dialog box shown in Figure 5-27.

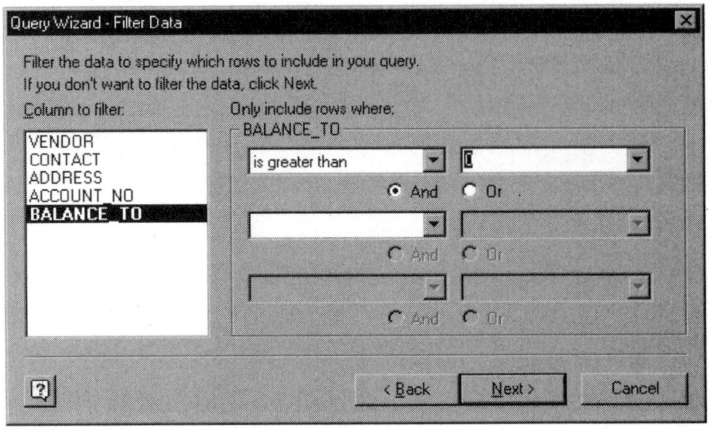

Figure 5-27 The Filter Data dialog box.

7. Describe the data the Query Wizard should retrieve.

To describe the data you want to retrieve, use filters based on the columns, or fields, that you're querying. To create a filter, select the column you want the query to examine. Then use the Only Include Rows Where boxes and buttons to indicate how this column is examined. Figure 5-27, for example, shows a filter that looks at the BALANCE_TO column to see whether this value is greater than or equal to zero. The first drop-down list box in the Only Include Rows Where area provides other logical operators you can also use. If you want to create a filter based on more than one comparison of the same column, use the And and Or option buttons and the next row of boxes. If you want to create a filter based on another column, select the column from the Columns To Filter list box and then repeat the preceding steps. When you finish specifying the filters you want to use, click Next. The Query Wizard displays the Sort Order dialog box shown in Figure 5-28.

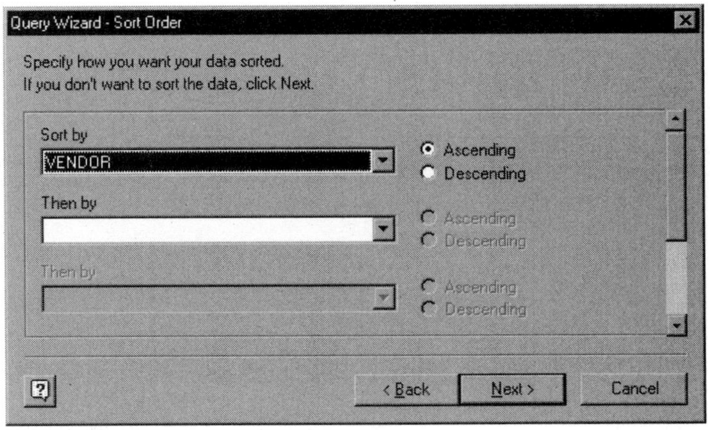

Figure 5-28 The Sort Order dialog box.

8. **Select a sort order for the retrieved data.**

When Excel displays the Sort Order dialog box, use the Sort By box and the Ascending and Descending option buttons to indicate how the retrieved data should be arranged in your worksheet. If some of the records, or rows, will use the same first sort key—this is what you specified using the Sort By box—you can provide a second sort key using the first Then By box and buttons. You can also provide additional sort keys using the other Then By box and buttons. When you finish specifying the sort order, click Next. The Query Wizard displays the Finish dialog box shown in Figure 5-29.

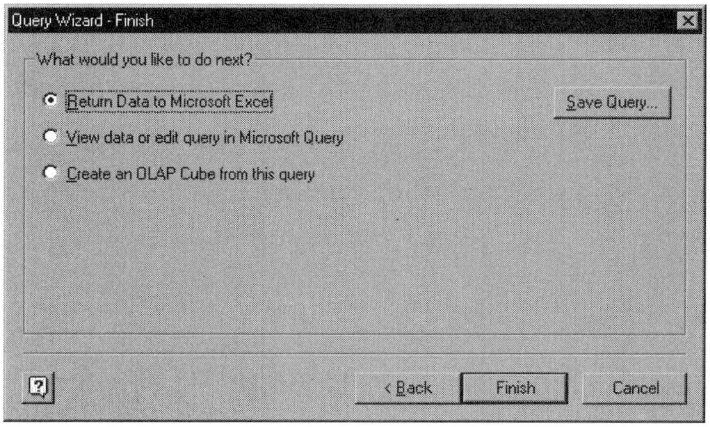

Figure 5-29 The Finish dialog box.

9. **Tell the Query Wizard where you want to place the data that the query returns.**

When the Query Wizard displays the Finish dialog box, use the What Would You Like To Do Next option buttons to select a location for the data. Presumably, you want to place the retrieved data in an Excel worksheet so you can use Excel's analytical tools to examine the data in ways that the database program doesn't allow. To do this, click the Return Data To Microsoft Excel button. Then click Finish. Excel runs the query and asks where the retrieved data should be stored using the Import Data dialog box shown in Figure 5-30.

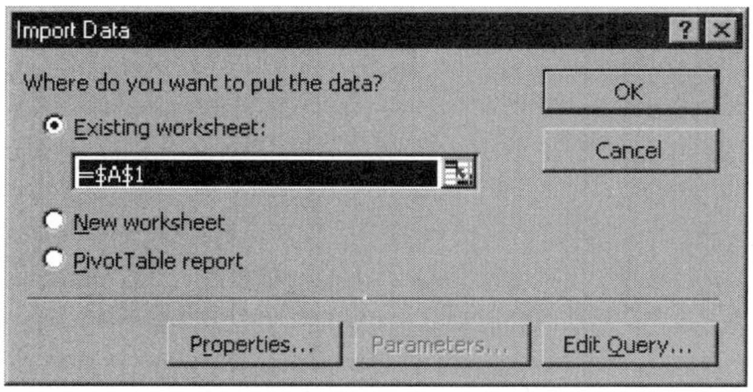

Figure 5-30 The Import Data dialog box.

NOTE *If you want to save the query so you can use it again, click the Finish dialog box's Save button. Then when Excel displays the Save As dialog box, use the File Name box to give the query a name. Once you've done this, click Save to save the query for future use.*

10. Select a location for the retrieved data.

When Excel asks where the retrieved data should be placed, use the Where Do You Want To Put The Data option buttons to select a location for the data: in the open workbook at the location of the cell selector, in a new workbook, or in a PivotTable report. Then click OK. Excel places the data in the indicated location.

After you place the retrieved data in an Excel workbook, you can begin to work with the data using Excel's features. You can use statistical functions to look closely at the data's characteristics, for example. And you can use charts to view and present the data visually.

The External Data toolbar, which Excel will probably display, provides several toolbar buttons you'll find useful, too. The Edit Query button, for example, restarts the Query Wizard so you can change the query. The Data Range Properties button displays the External Data Range Properties dialog box, which you can use to change the way that Excel handles the data it retrieves in the query. The Query Parameters button lets you describe how any query parameters are handled in the query. The Refresh Data button reruns the query to retrieve any new data. The Cancel Refresh button stops a refresh you might have started. The Refresh All button reruns all the queries in a workbook. Finally, the Refresh Status button displays a dialog box that reports information such as how long a refresh operation took.

NOTE *A query parameter is a value that you've said you will supply to the query before or as it runs. The Query Wizard doesn't let you create query parameters. If you create from-scratch queries using Microsoft Query, which is discussed briefly in the later section "Running Microsoft Query," you can use query parameters.*

Running a Web Query

The Get External Data submenu provides a Web Query tool that you can use to retrieve tabular data from a Web page. To run a simple Web query, open a blank workbook, choose the Data menu's Import External Data command, and then choose the Import External Data submenu's New Web Query command.

NOTE *Excel also comes with several Web queries already set up and saved, which you can run by choosing the Data menu's Import External Data command and then choosing Run Saved Query. When you do this, Excel displays the Run Query dialog box, which lists the saved queries. Excel places a small globe icon in front of the saved Web queries. To run one of the saved Web queries, click it and then click the Get Data button.*

If you choose the New Web Query command, Excel displays the New Web Query dialog box, as shown in Figure 5-31. To use the New Web Query dialog box, type or select the address in the Address box to open the Web page with the table from which you want to retrieve information. If you want to import more than one table, select the arrow next to the table. At this point, you can click Import and Excel will retrieve the table data. When Excel asks where the data should be placed using the Import Data dialog box (see Figure 5-30), indicate the appropriate location.

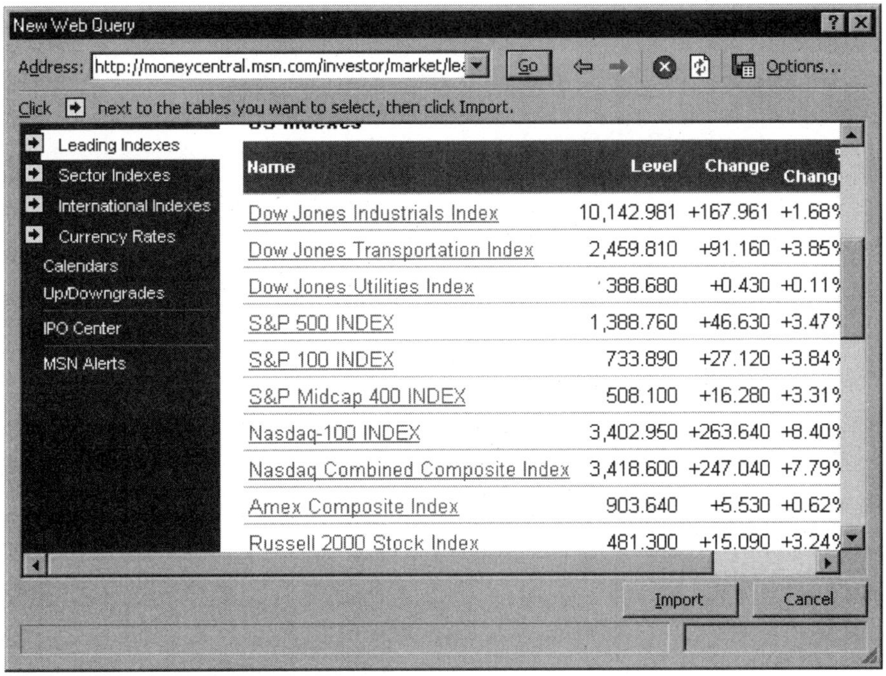

Figure 5-31 The New Web Query dialog box.

You can use the other option buttons in the New Web Query dialog box to control the Web query. In addition, the Options button enables you to choose how this data is formatted as it is imported into your workbook. Your best bet in working with these options is probably just to experiment and see which option settings produce the best results.

NOTE *The more you know about HTML, the more you can do with the Web Query tool. If you know HTML well, for example, you can use the New Web Query dialog box to specify that only specific tables should be retrieved from a Web page.*

Running Microsoft Query

The Query Wizard, described in the earlier chapter section "Using the Query Wizard," provides you with a simple way to access external data. You should know, however, that the Query Wizard is a tool you use to tell another program, Microsoft Query, how you want to query an external database. While the Query Wizard works well in most simple situations, you don't get access to all of Microsoft Query's power when you work through the wizard.

When you want more control over how a query operates, you can work directly with Microsoft Query. To work directly with Query, you also start by choosing the Data menu's Get External Data command and then choosing New Database Query. As with a query performed using the Query Wizard, when Excel displays the Choose Data Source dialog box (see Figure 5-25), you select the database source. To work directly with Query, however, you clear the Use The Query Wizard To Create/Edit Queries check box. When you click OK, Excel starts Microsoft Query.

NOTE *For more information on using the Choose Data Source dialog box, refer to the earlier section "Using the Query Wizard."*

To use Query, you follow a process similar to that used with the Query Wizard. For example, you start by identifying which tables you want to query, which columns, (or fields) you want to retrieve, how you want to filter, and how the data you retrieve should be sorted. Although Query provides less handholding than that of the Query Wizard, it offers you greater flexibility.

A more detailed discussion of Query is beyond the scope of this book, but here are two final observations: First, before you attempt to develop expertise or fluency with Query, make sure that you won't get farther, faster, simply by learning how to use the external data source's query capabilities. For example, Access is easier to learn (in part because it's better documented) and more useful than Query. It may not be a good use of your time to learn Query so that you can then query an Access database. Instead, you might be better off learning Access.

Second, the Excel help file provides detailed information about how to use Microsoft Query. To access this information, ask the Office Assistant a question such as, "How do I work with Microsoft Query?" Then explore the help topics that the Office Assistant provides.

Skill 6

PIVOTTABLES AND PIVOTCHARTS

Featuring:

- Using the PivotTable Wizard
- Editing PivotTables
- Creating PivotCharts

This chapter describes how you can use Excel's PivotTable features to work with data bases in Excel. If you use Excel to list records, you can use the PivotTables feature to sort, filter, and pivot fields so you can better focus on the information you want.

NOTE *Excel databases are simply worksheets that list information, as shown in Figure 6-1. The first row names the fields of the data. Subsequent rows hold the database. To sort a database, select the worksheet range holding the database and then choose the Data menu's Sort command. To filter a database, select the worksheet range holding the database and then choose the Data menu's AutoFilter command or its Filter command.*

Using the PivotTable Wizard

Figure 6-1 shows three years' worth of sales data for a microbrewery that sells six types of beer on the West Coast. The company recorded sales for each type of beer by state and by season. You can see that with the large amounts of information in the database, it's difficult to spot trends. Creating a PivotTable allows you to see which type of beer sells best in which region or during which season.

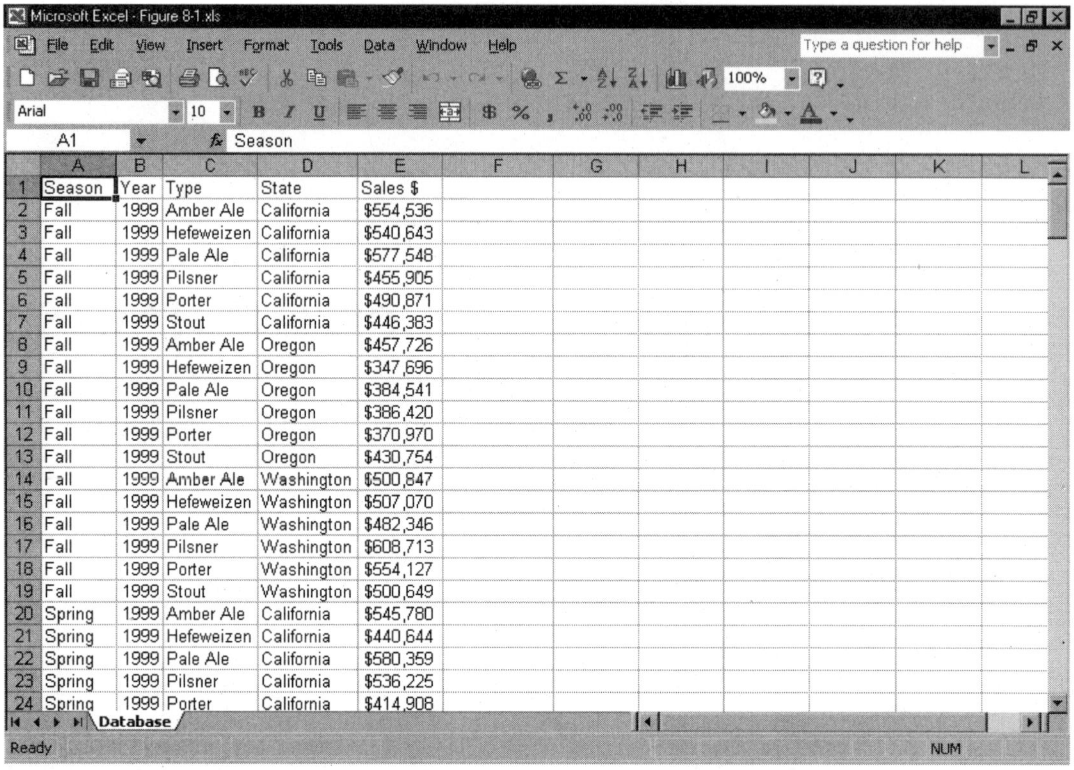

Season	Year	Type	State	Sales $
Fall	1999	Amber Ale	California	$554,536
Fall	1999	Hefeweizen	California	$540,643
Fall	1999	Pale Ale	California	$577,548
Fall	1999	Pilsner	California	$455,905
Fall	1999	Porter	California	$490,871
Fall	1999	Stout	California	$446,383
Fall	1999	Amber Ale	Oregon	$457,726
Fall	1999	Hefeweizen	Oregon	$347,696
Fall	1999	Pale Ale	Oregon	$384,541
Fall	1999	Pilsner	Oregon	$386,420
Fall	1999	Porter	Oregon	$370,970
Fall	1999	Stout	Oregon	$430,754
Fall	1999	Amber Ale	Washington	$500,847
Fall	1999	Hefeweizen	Washington	$507,070
Fall	1999	Pale Ale	Washington	$482,346
Fall	1999	Pilsner	Washington	$608,713
Fall	1999	Porter	Washington	$554,127
Fall	1999	Stout	Washington	$500,649
Spring	1999	Amber Ale	California	$545,780
Spring	1999	Hefeweizen	California	$440,644
Spring	1999	Pale Ale	California	$580,359
Spring	1999	Pilsner	California	$536,225
Spring	1999	Porter	California	$414,908

Figure 6-1 Database of beer sales.

To start the PivotTable Wizard, select any cell in the database and choose the Data menu's PivotTable And PivotChart Report command. Excel displays the dialog box shown in Figure 6-2.

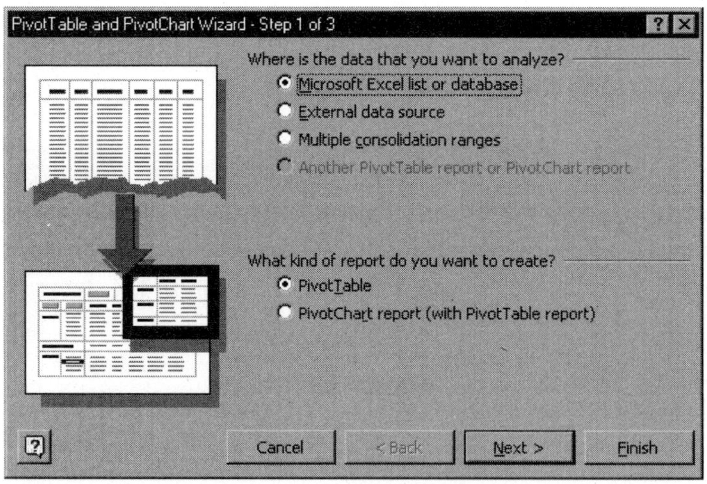

Figure 6-2 The first step of the PivotTable And PivotChart Wizard.

If your data is in a single range on a single worksheet in the current workbook, click the Microsoft Excel List Or Database option button. Then click the PivotTable option button, and click Next.

The second step of the PivotTable And PivotChart Wizard asks you to select the data you want to include in the PivotTable. Do so, and then click Next.

In the third and last step of the PivotTable And PivotChart Wizard, specify where you want Excel to put the PivotTable you're creating and click Finish. As shown in Figure 6-3, Excel displays the new, empty PivotTable in the location you specified. It also displays the PivotTable toolbar and PivotTable Field List dialog box, which you use to lay out and edit the PivotTable.

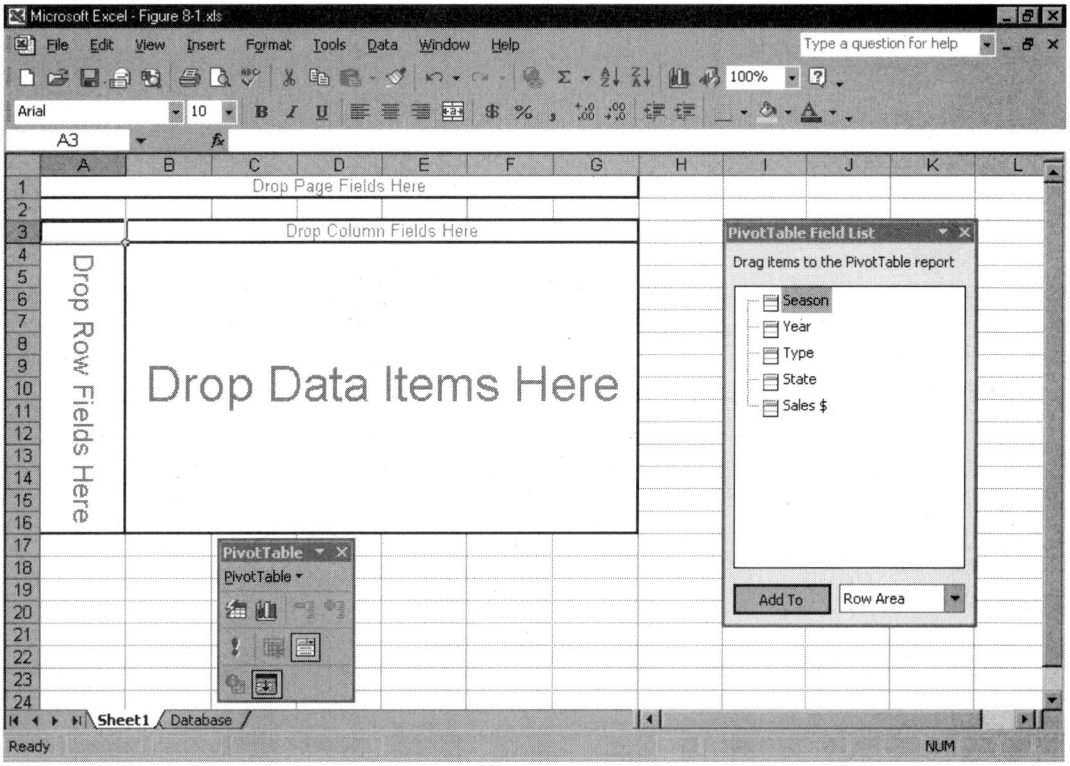

Figure 6-3 The new, empty PivotTable, the PivotTable toolbar, and the PivotTable Field List dialog box.

Specifying PivotTable Layout

To begin laying out your PivotTable, use the buttons on the PivotTable toolbar to drag fields to set up row and column headings. In the example shown in Figure 6-3, you could drag the Year field to the box labeled Drop Row Fields Here and the State field to the box labeled Drop Column Fields Here. You could then drag the Sales field to the Drop Data Items Here box. After you drag the Sales field to the Data area, Excel adds the data to the PivotTable. Figure 6-4 shows fields on a PivotTable filled with data.

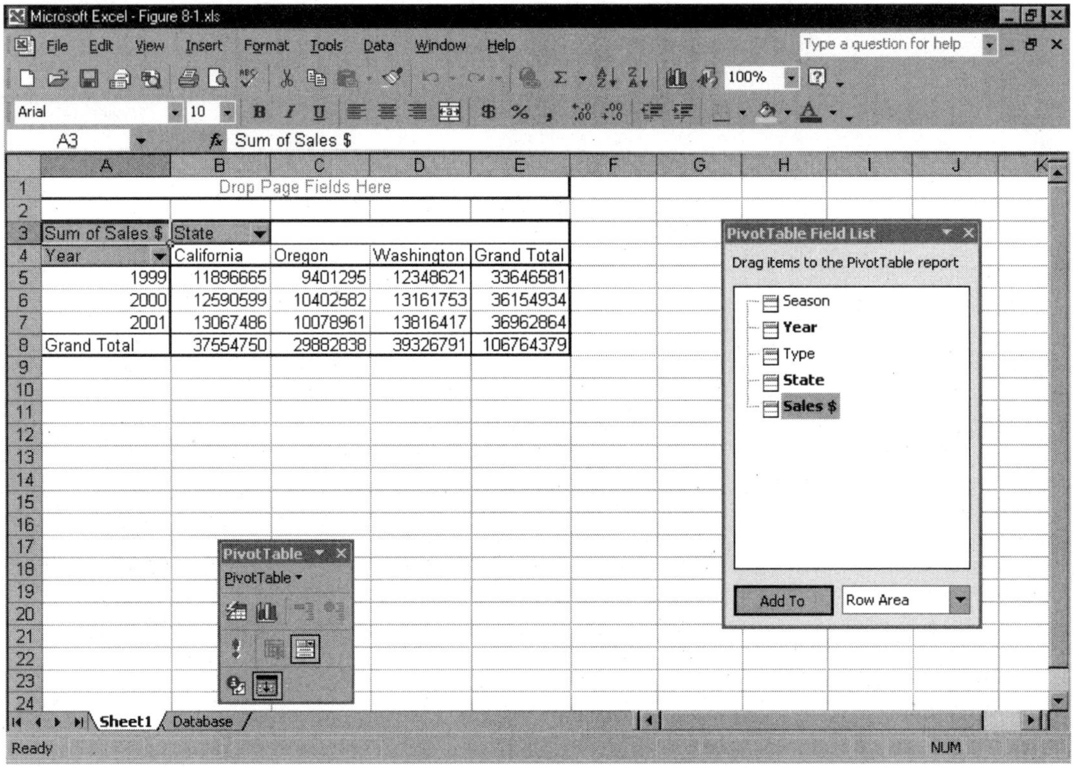

Figure 6-4 A PivotTable with data.

The box in the upper left corner reads Sum Of Sales $. This is because Excel assumes you want to subtotal and total sales figures. If you were to drag a label field instead of a value field into the Data area, Excel would by default count the occurrences of that label. You can change the operation performed on the data included in a PivotTable by selecting a cell in the part you want to change and clicking the PivotTable toolbar's Field Settings button. Excel displays the PivotTable Field dialog box shown in Figure 6-5. This dialog box's options differ slightly depending on the type of data presented in the part of the PivotTable you selected.

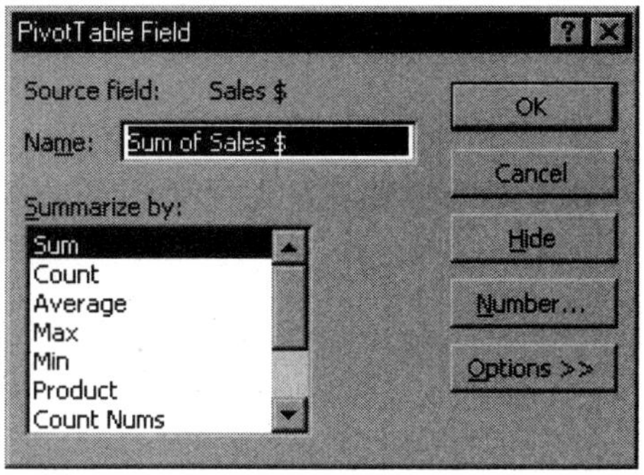

Figure 6-5 The PivotTable Field dialog box.

TIP *To rename a field, enter a new name in the Name text box in the PivotTable Field dialog box.*

To change the operation performed on items in the field, select an item from the Summarize By drop-down list box and click OK. For comparative operations, click the Options button. You can then list item data as a percentage of another item or as a difference from another item, for example.

You can drag multiple fields to a heading. To add another field to a PivotTable, just drag the field's button from the PivotTable Field List dialog box. For example, you could drag the Season field to the right of the Year column to sort by year and then by season. Figure 6-6 shows how the PivotTable looks when you do this. To remove a field from a table, just drag the field outside the table area.

NOTE *If you don't see the field buttons on the PivotTable toolbar, click the Display Fields button.*

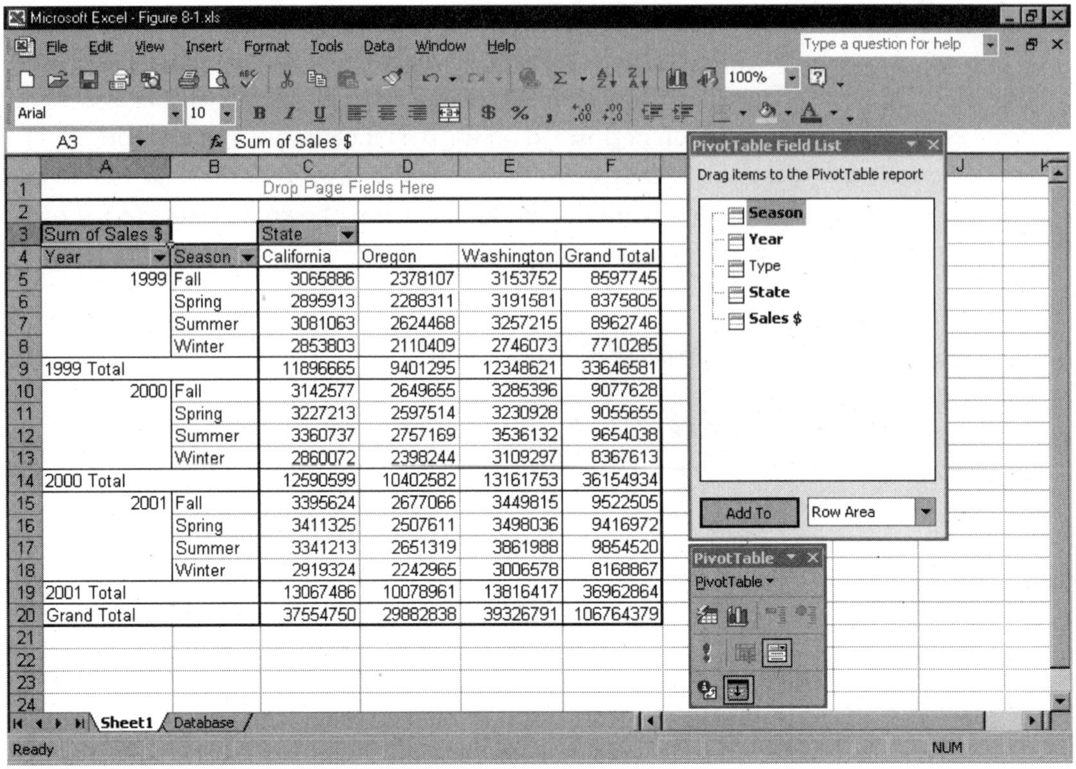

Figure 6-6 A PivotTable with multiple row fields.

NOTE *If you attempt to change the data summarized in a PivotTable (for example, the value in cell D7), Excel prevents you from doing so. This safeguard, of course, is because this cell sums the data for the various types of beer in the database, and you cannot change the sum without changing the values that make up the sum. If you want to change the values in the PivotTable, you must make the changes to the database upon which the PivotTable is based. Then return to the PivotTable and click the Refresh Data button on the PivotTable toolbar to update the PivotTable.*

Editing PivotTables

PivotTables got their name because you can easily rearrange, or "pivot," them. For example, you can move row headings to become column headings, or vice versa, or you can change the hierarchy of fields within a row or column heading. You can also separate PivotTable data among pages.

TIP *You can improve the visual appeal of a table by applying a style to it. To do so, click the Format Report button on the PivotTable toolbar, select a style from the AutoFormat dialog box, and click OK.*

Pivoting

To pivot a PivotTable, just drag a heading to a different axis. For example, you can drag the Season field to the column heading to create a long, narrow table, as shown in Figure 6-7. By doing this, each state has its own subtable within the table.

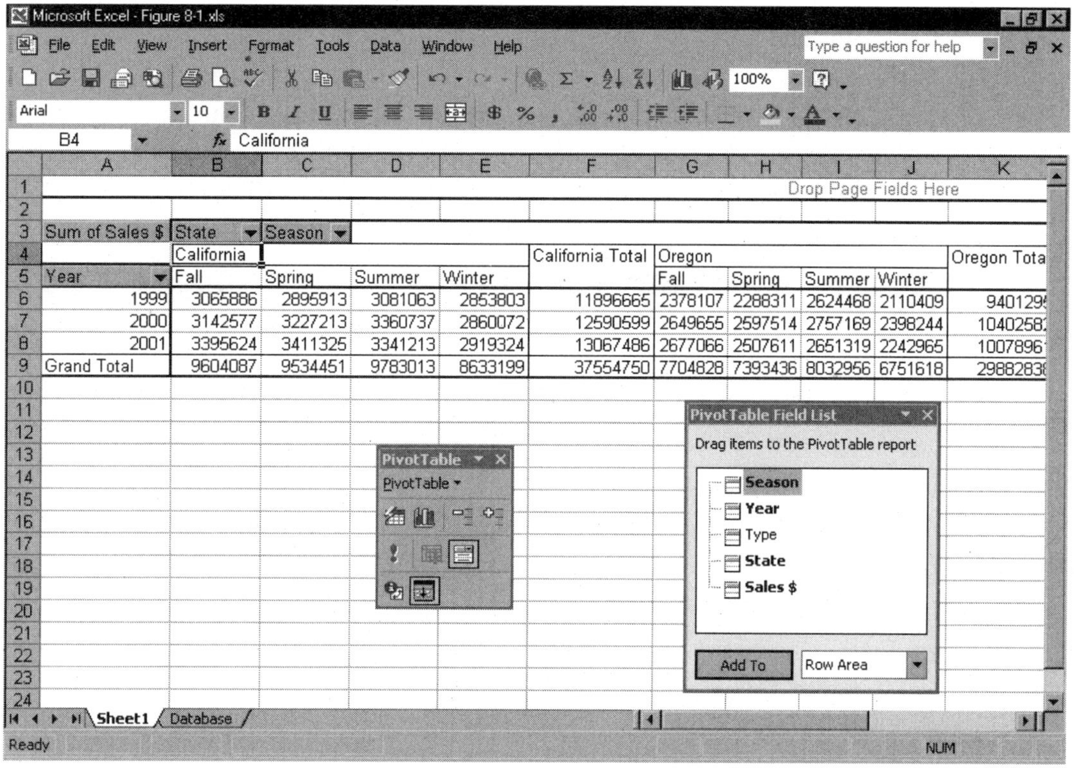

Figure 6-7 Pivoting a PivotTable.

You can also reorganize a PivotTable by changing the hierarchy of fields in a heading. For example, if you look back at the PivotTable in Figure 6-6, sales are grouped first by year and then by season within each year. However, if you drag the Season field to the left of the Year field, you can group first by season, and then within each season, by year.

Filtering Items in a Field

You can tell Excel which items you want to include in a PivotTable for each field. For example, if you don't want to worry about sales in California for the moment, you can exclude California from the table. To do so, click the down arrow on the right side of the State heading and clear the California check box. Then click OK.

Separating Data Between Pages

If your database is so large that your PivotTable is too long or wide to easily read without scrolling back and forth, you might want to view only certain parts of the data on a single worksheet page. For example, in the microbrewery database, you might want to put sales data for each year on a separate page. To do so, drag the Year field to the box labeled Drop Page Fields Here. You can view data for other years by clicking the down arrow on the right side of the Year heading and selecting a different year. You can also click the PivotTable button on the PivotTable toolbar and choose Show Pages from the pop-up menu to create new sheets in the workbook for each page field. Just select the page field from the list in the Show Pages dialog box, and click OK. Figure 6-8 shows how the PivotTable looks with Year as a page field, Type as a column heading, and Season and State as row headings.

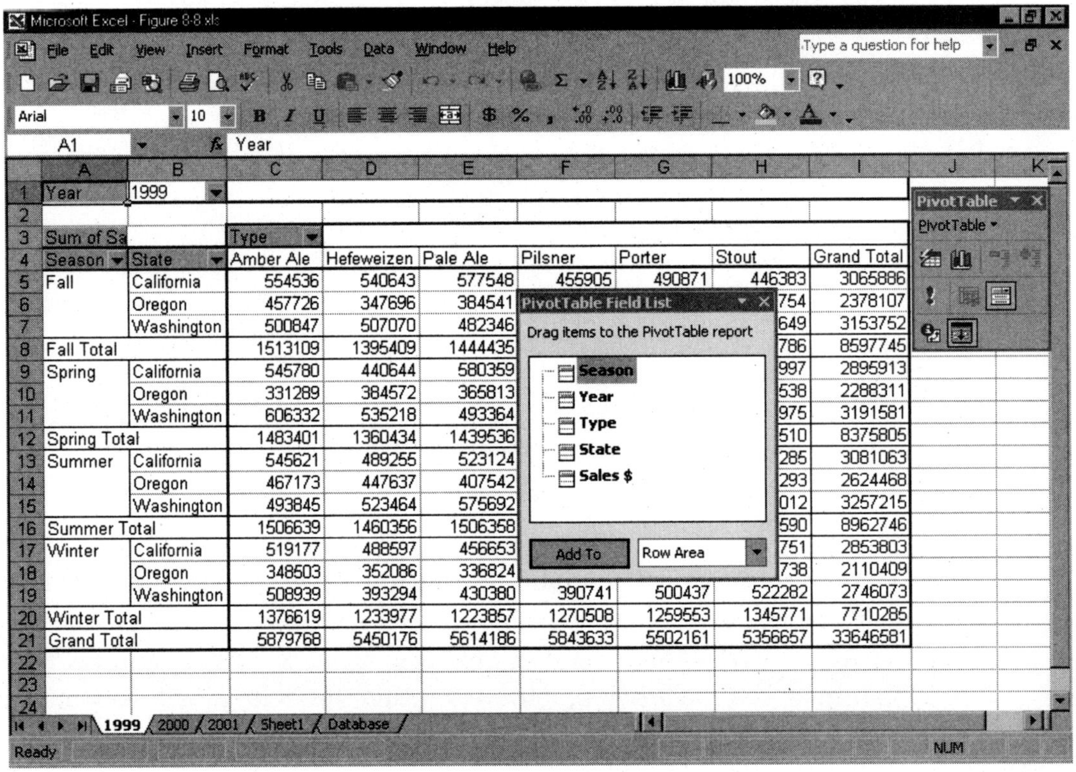

Figure 6-8 Pivoting a PivotTable once again.

Grouping PivotTable Data

With some fields, you can create subgroups. For example, you may want to group the Types shown in Figure 6-8 into ales and lagers or dark beers and light beers. To create a group for the ales and another for the lagers, select all the types you want to include in the group. (You can select nonadjacent items by holding down the Ctrl key as you click.) Choose the Data menu's Group And Outline command and then choose Group. Excel names the groups Group1, Group2, and so forth. You can rename the groups to something more descriptive by selecting the heading and typing a new name. Excel names the new field according to the field from which you're creating the Groups. In this example, Excel names the new groups of fields Type2 because the Type field was grouped. You can change the name of the group field by selecting a group name and clicking the Field Settings button on the PivotTable toolbar. Figure 6-9 shows how the PivotTable looks after grouping the types into Ales and Pilsners and naming the group field Fermentation.

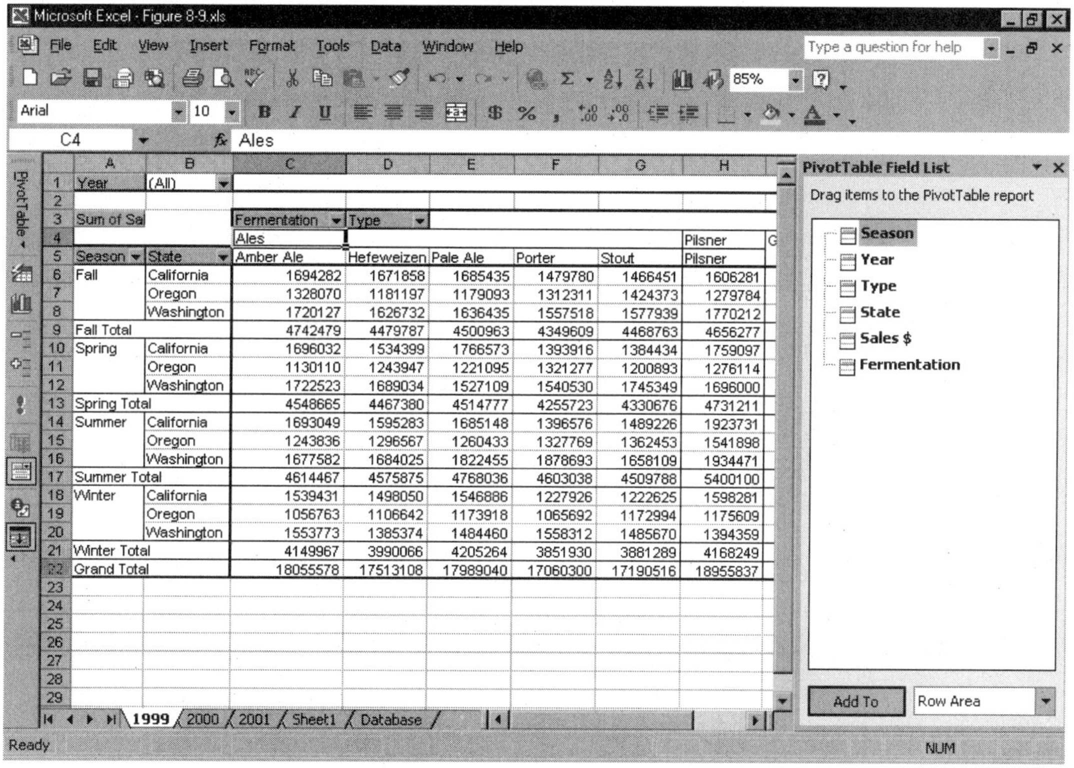

	A	B	C	D	E	F	G	H
1	Year	(All)						
2								
3	Sum of Sa		Fermentation	Type				
4			Ales					Pilsner
5	Season	State	Amber Ale	Hefeweizen	Pale Ale	Porter	Stout	Pilsner
6	Fall	California	1694282	1671858	1685435	1479780	1466451	1606281
7		Oregon	1328070	1181197	1179093	1312311	1424373	1279784
8		Washington	1720127	1626732	1636435	1557518	1577939	1770212
9	Fall Total		4742479	4479787	4500963	4349609	4468763	4656277
10	Spring	California	1696032	1534399	1766573	1393916	1384434	1759097
11		Oregon	1130110	1243947	1221095	1321277	1200893	1276114
12		Washington	1722523	1689034	1527109	1540530	1745349	1696000
13	Spring Total		4548665	4467380	4514777	4255723	4330676	4731211
14	Summer	California	1693049	1595283	1685148	1396576	1489226	1923731
15		Oregon	1243836	1296567	1260433	1327769	1362453	1541898
16		Washington	1677582	1684025	1822455	1878693	1658109	1934471
17	Summer Total		4614467	4575875	4768036	4603038	4509788	5400100
18	Winter	California	1539431	1498050	1546886	1227926	1222625	1598281
19		Oregon	1056763	1106642	1173918	1065692	1172994	1175609
20		Washington	1553773	1385374	1484460	1558312	1485670	1394359
21	Winter Total		4149967	3990066	4205264	3851930	3881289	4168249
22	Grand Total		18055578	17513108	17989040	17060300	17190516	18955837

Figure 6-9 A PivotTable with grouped fields as headings.

Creating PivotCharts

Excel provides two ways of creating PivotCharts. If you've already created a PivotTable and want to chart the information on which it focuses, you can save time and space by creating a PivotChart directly from the PivotTable. If you haven't created a PivotTable and are instead more interested in creating a PivotChart, you can create the PivotChart using the PivotTable and PivotChart Wizard without specifying the layout of a PivotTable.

Creating a PivotChart from an Existing PivotTable

To create a PivotChart from an existing PivotTable, select a cell in the PivotTable and click the Chart Wizard button on the PivotTable toolbar. Figure 6-10 shows a PivotChart based on the PivotTable in Figure 6-8.

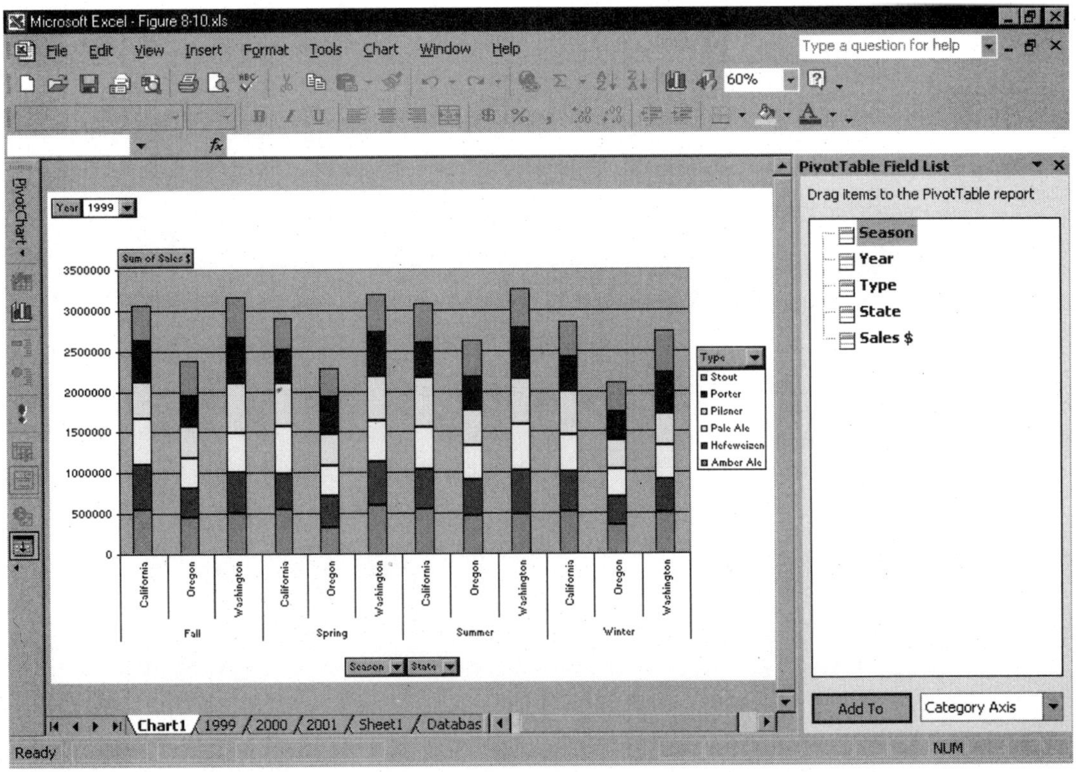

Figure 6-10 A PivotChart.

You manipulate PivotCharts in much the same way as you manipulate PivotTables—by dragging field buttons to different axes. You can also filter a PivotChart's data to include only certain items in a field. To do this, click the down arrow on the right side of the field button and select or clear the check boxes to include or omit items from the PivotChart. Click OK to redraw the chart.

After you've created the PivotChart, you can click the Chart Wizard button on the PivotTable toolbar again to start the Chart Wizard and customize the PivotChart. Using the Chart Wizard, you can specify such items as chart type, axis titles, and legend placement.

NOTE *For more information about chart types and customizing charts in Excel, see Chapter 3.*

Creating a PivotChart Directly from a Database

To create a PivotChart directly from a database, open the database and choose the Data menu's PivotTable And PivotChart Report command. In step one of the wizard, click the PivotChart (With PivotTable Report) option button. In the second step, select the data you want to include in the PivotChart. In the last step, specify where you want Excel to put the new PivotChart. When you click Finish, Excel displays a new, blank PivotChart, as shown in Figure 6-11.

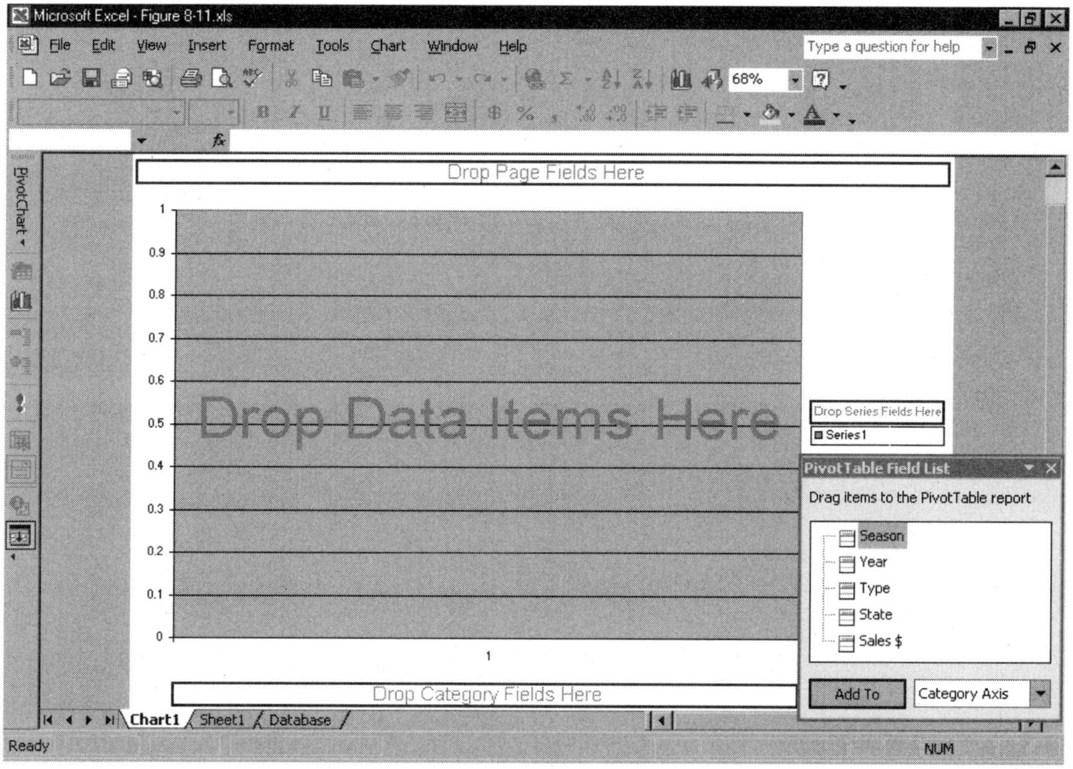

Figure 6-11 A new PivotChart.

To add data to the PivotChart, drag the field buttons from the PivotTable toolbar to the various parts of the PivotChart until it displays the information you want. You can move fields to other axes by dragging them as well. To remove a field from a chart, drag its button off the chart area.

After you've created the PivotChart, you can click the Chart Wizard button on the PivotTable toolbar again to start the Chart Wizard and customize the PivotChart. Using the Chart Wizard, you can specify such items as chart type, axis titles, and legend placement.

Skill 7

SMALL BUSINESS FINANCIAL MANAGER

Featuring:

- Installing and Starting the Small Business Financial Manager
- Importing Financial Data
- Working with the Report Wizard
- Working with the Financial Analysis Tools
- Refreshing Imported Data
- Rearranging and Modifying Imported Data

This chapter describes how you can use the Small Business Financial Manager that comes with the Small Business, Professional, and Premium versions of Microsoft Office. The Small Business Financial Manager lets you retrieve financial data from popular small business accounting programs, including QuickBooks and Peachtree Accounting, and then analyze this data using Excel.

Unfortunately, the Small Business Financial Manager was not available at the time of publication. The information presented in this chapter was based on an earlier version of the Small Business Financial Manager but should apply very closely to the version in the future update.

NOTE *As soon as a new version of the Small Business Finance Manager is available, we will post an updated version of this chapter at the Redmond Technology Press web site, www.redtechpress.com.*

Installing and Starting the Small Business Financial Manager

The Small Business Tools, which include Small Business Financial Manager, aren't automatically installed when you install Office applications. These extra programs come on Disk 2 of the Office CD set. You may therefore need to install these tools.

To install the Small Business Tools, insert Disk 2 in your CD-ROM drive and then follow the onscreen instructions.

NOTE *The Small Business Tools include four distinct tools: Business Planner, Direct Mail Manager, Small Business Customer Manager (which works with Microsoft Outlook), and Small Business Financial Manager.*

After you install the Small Business Tools, you can start the Small Business Financial Manager directly by clicking the Start button, choosing Programs, choosing Small Business Tools, and then choosing the Small Business Financial Manager. Or, you can start the Small Business Financial Manager by starting Excel and then choosing one of the Financial Manager menu commands.

NOTE *When you install Small Business Financial Manager, you add the Financial Manager menu of commands to the Excel menu bar.*

Importing Financial Data

Before you can begin using the Small Business Financial Manager, you import the financial data stored in your accounting system and store it in a database. You may also need to reorganize the data slightly once it's in this database. And, of course, as your accounting records change, you'll want to update the database used by Excel and the Small Business Financial Manager.

NOTE *Excel doesn't change your accounting; it only creates a copy of the data that can be used by the Small Business Financial Manager.*

Importing Data for the First Time

To import your data for the first time, follow these steps:

1. **Choose the Financial Manager menu's Import Wizard command, or click the Import button on the Startup Screen.**

   Excel displays the New Database Wizard dialog box, as shown in Figure 7-1. Click Next to begin the process of importing your accounting data.

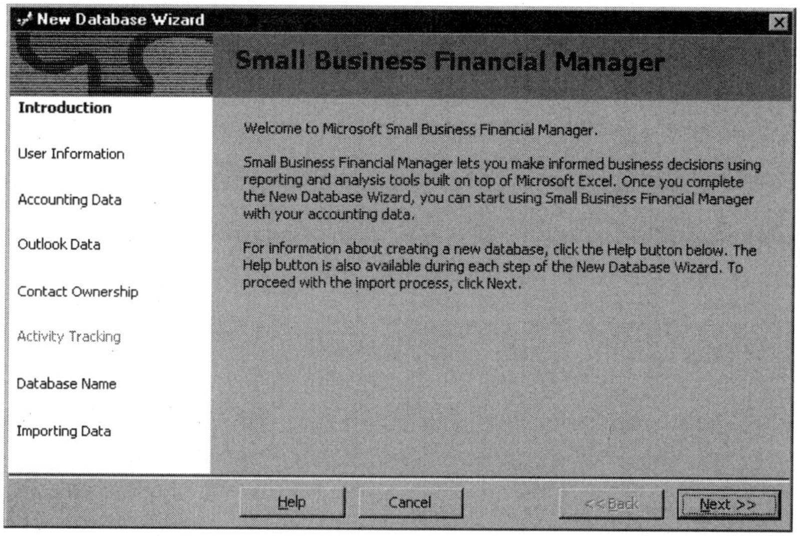

Figure 7-1 The first New Database Wizard dialog box.

2. **Provide a user name and password.**

   Excel asks for a password and then asks you to type the password again to confirm what you typed the first time. Excel uses this password to limit access to the financial data you're creating using the Financial Manager. Click Next to continue.

3. **Select the correct accounting data.**

   After you provide a password, the Small Business Financial Manager reviews your local hard disk drive for any accounting data files and then displays a list of the accounting data files it finds, as shown in Figure 7-2. Typically, the Small Business Financial Manager finds at least two files: your actual accounting data files and the sample data files that come with the accounting software. To select the accounting data files that you want to import, click the data files and then click Next.

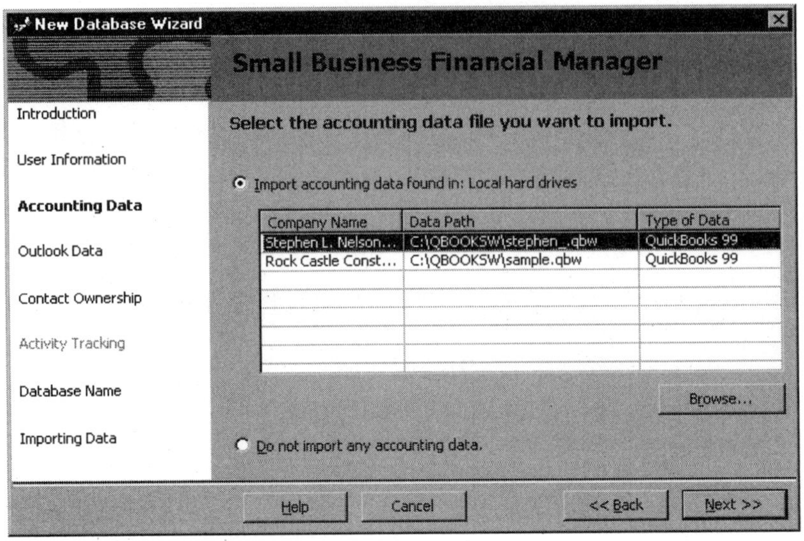

Figure 7-2 The third New Database Wizard dialog box.

4. **Initiate the importation of the accounting data.**

   After you identify the accounting data you want to import, Small Business Financial Manager displays a message box that tells you that it is building a database of your accounting and customer information for use with the Small Business Financial Manager and the Small Business Customer Manager. Click OK to close this message box, and then click Finish to begin the importation of accounting data into this database.

NOTE *If you restrict access to your accounting data using a password, the Small Business Financial Manager asks for this password before it begins importing data.*

Depending on the size of your accounting database, the importation will probably take several minutes—and perhaps longer. When the New Database Wizard finishes importing your data, it displays another message box. Click OK to close the message box and begin working with the data.

Working with the Report Wizard

After you've imported your accounting data, you use the Report Wizard to produce a financial report based on the imported accounting data.

Reviewing the Report Wizard Reports

The Report Wizard produces reports that fall into one of seven categories: balance sheets, cash flow statements, change in stockholders' equity, income statements, ratio reports, sales analysis reports, and trial balance reports. Table 7-1 briefly summarizes the types of reports that the Report Wizard produces in each of these categories.

CATEGORY	REPORT OPTIONS AVAILABLE
Balance Sheet	Simple balance sheets, balance sheets with prior-year comparisons, and balance sheets with scenarios you've created using the what-if analysis tools.
Cash Flow	Simple one-period cash flow statements with year-to-date and prior-period comparisons, rolling 12-period cash flow reports, and one-period cash flow reports and year-to-date cash flow reports with scenarios created using the what-if analysis tools.
Change in Stockholders' Equity	One-period reports and year-to-date reports of the changes in stockholders' equity.
Income Statement	Simple income statements with one-period and year-to-date comparisons, income statements with 12-period and four-quarter trends, income statements for a fiscal year and periods, income statements for a fiscal year and quarters, and income statements with scenarios created using the what-if analysis tools.
Ratios	A rolling 12-period report showing trends in financial ratios.
Sales Analysis	Sales reports from a variety of perspectives, including by customers and by types of services.
Trial Balance	Simple trial balance reports with one-period and year-to-date comparisons and trial balance with scenarios created using what-if analysis tools.

Table 7-1 The Report Wizard report categories and report options.

Using the Report Wizard

To use the Report Wizard to create one of its reports, follow these steps:

1. Start the Report Wizard.

You can do this either by choosing the Financial Manager menu's Report Wizard command or by clicking the Report button on the Startup Screen, as shown in Figure 7-3.

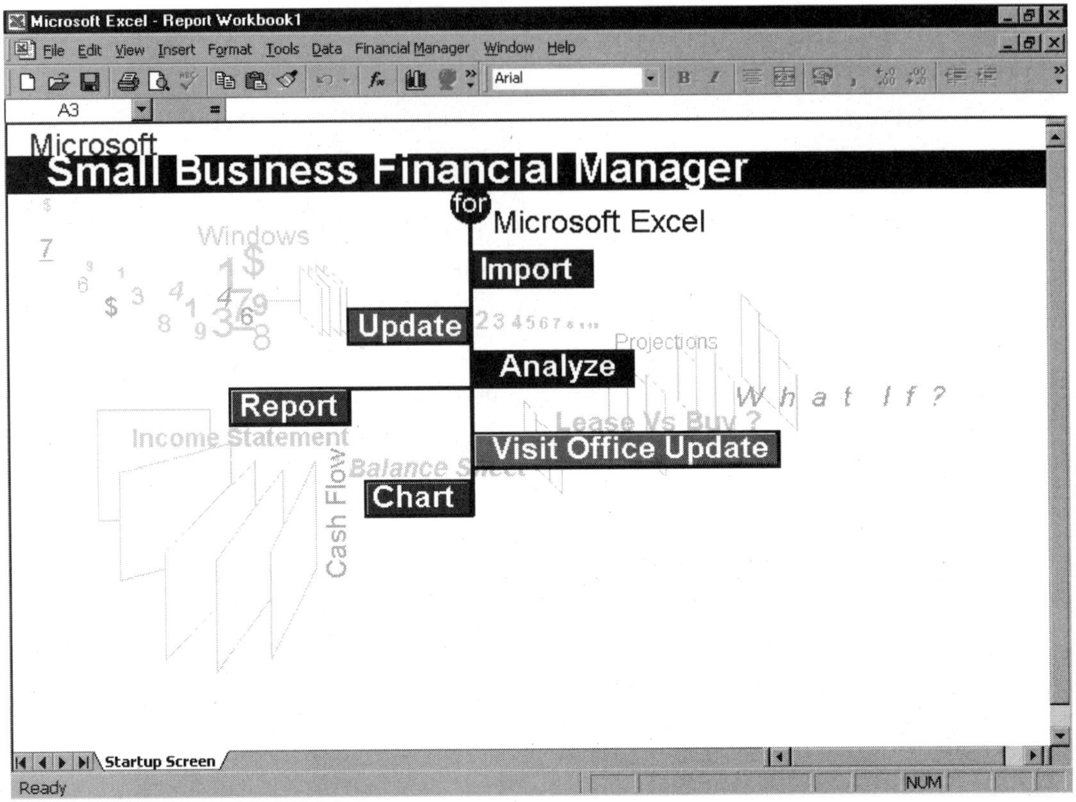

Figure 7-3 The Small Business Financial Manager Startup Screen.

2. **Select the category of financial reports you want to create.**

   To select a financial report category, click an entry in the Financial Reports list box, as shown in Figure 7-4. After you select a financial report category, click Next.

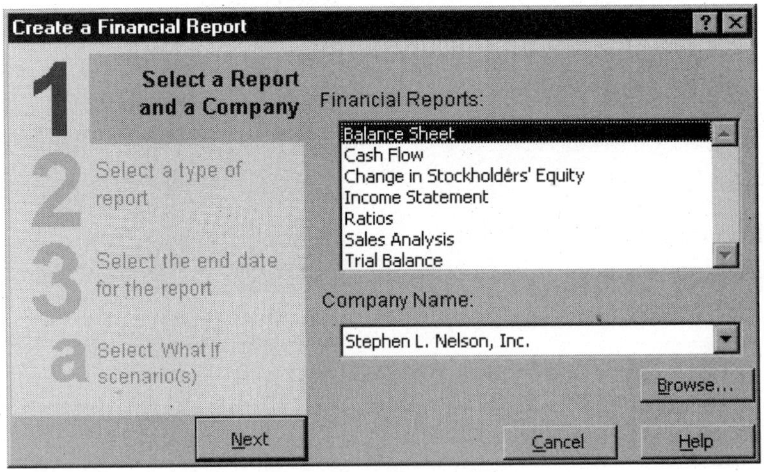

Figure 7-4 The first Report Wizard dialog box.

3. **Provide the user name and database password.**

   If Small Business Financial Manager requests it, provide the user name and database password you created during the importation of your accounting data.

4. **Select the type of report you want.**

   When Excel asks what type of report you want, select an entry from the Report Types list box. Then click Next.

NOTE *You can't select a report type that relies on a scenario unless you've already created the scenario using the what-if analysis tools.*

5. **Select an end date for the report.**

   When Excel asks for the report end date, select an entry from the End Date For This Report list box. Then click Finish.

The Report Wizard creates a financial report based on your parameters and places the report on a new worksheet in the open workbook. Figure 7-5 shows an example of one such financial report, an income statement for December 1998 with year-to-date and prior-period comparisons.

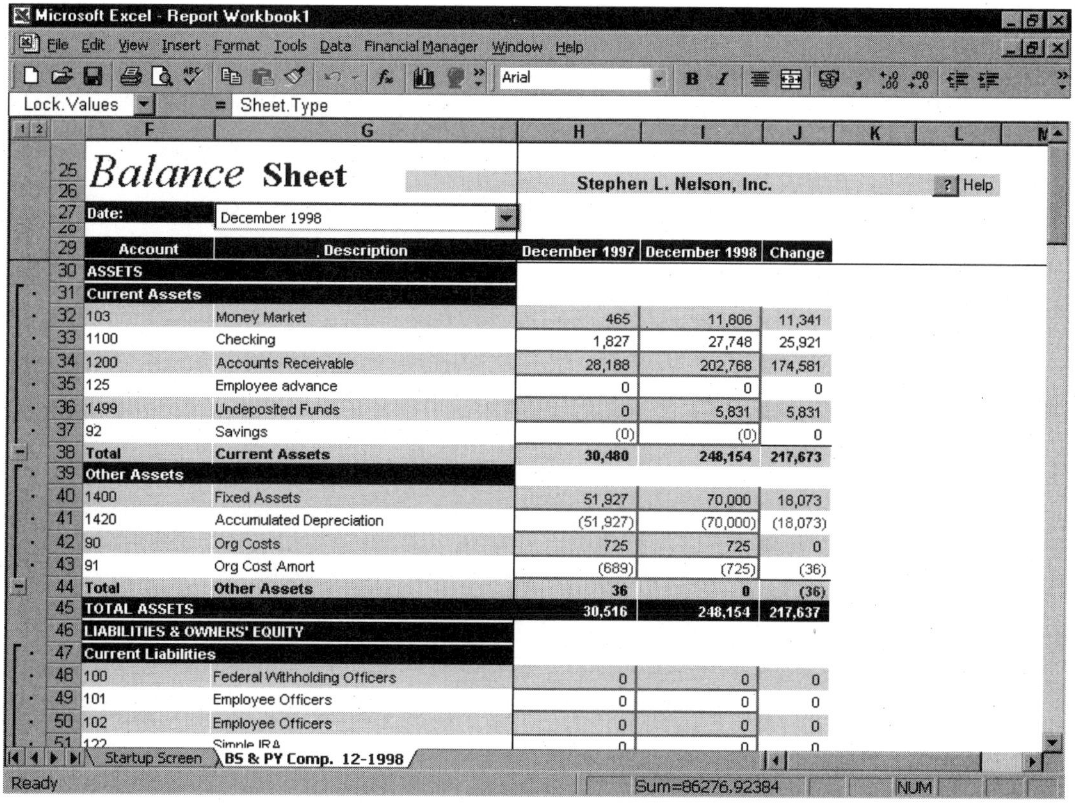

Figure 7-5 An example financial report created by the first Report Wizard.

Using the Report Wizard's Reports

The principal reason for using the Report Wizard is to generate a report so that you can analyze the report using Excel. This may mean simply viewing the report, perhaps onscreen or in a printed copy. If you're using Small Business Financial Manager in this way, however, you may be doing so only because the reporting capabilities of your accounting software are very limited or restricting.

The other way you can use the Report Wizard reports, of course, is to use the now-in-a-workbook financial data for making your own calculations. This work is something you can't do with your accounting program's reports. Once you've got a report stored in an Excel workbook, it's relatively easy to create formulas that manipulate the data, extract information so it can be analyzed, and chart information so it can be visually analyzed or shared. This type of work requires the basic Excel skills discussed in Chapters 1 and 2.

NOTE *If the information on which a report is based changes, choose the Financial Manager menu's Recalculate Reports command.*

Working with the Financial Analysis Tools

The Small Business Financial Manager provides you with four financial analysis tools: Business Comparison Report, Buy Vs. Lease, a Create Projection Wizard, and What-If Analysis.

NOTE *You can move backward and forward within a wizard's dialog boxes by clicking the Back and Next buttons. You can also return to a wizard to change the analysis you've performed by clicking the Change Wizard hyperlink, which appears in the upper left corner of the workbook that the tool creates.*

Using the Business Comparison Report Tool

The Business Comparison Report tool creates a report that lets you compare one business's financial profile with industry averages of other businesses of a similar size in the same industry. The first page compares well-known financial ratios of the company to the industry averages. The second page of the business comparison report, an Income Statement, compares key income statement data—such as sales, gross margin, and profit—to the industry averages. The third page of the business comparison report, a Balance Sheet, compares key balance sheet data, including current assets and current liabilities—to industry averages.

To use the Business Comparison Report tool, follow these steps:

1. **Start the Business Comparison Wizard.**

   Click the Analyze button on the Startup Screen, and then select a Business Comparison item from the list box in the Select A Financial Manager Analysis Tool dialog box and click Next. Excel displays the first Business Comparison Wizard dialog box, as shown in Figure 7-6.

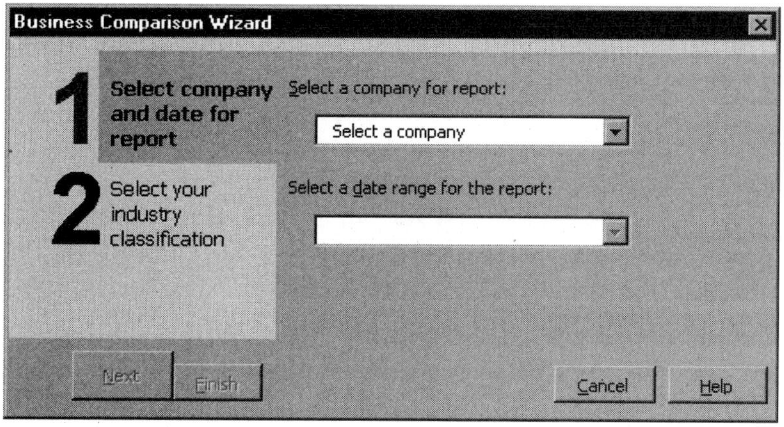

Figure 7-6 The first Business Comparison Wizard dialog box.

2. **Select the company and the period you want to compare.**

   Select the company you want to compare, if necessary, from the Select A Company For Report box. Select an accounting period you want to compare from the Select A Date Range For The Report box, and then click Next. Excel displays the second Business Comparison Wizard dialog box, as shown in Figure 7-7.

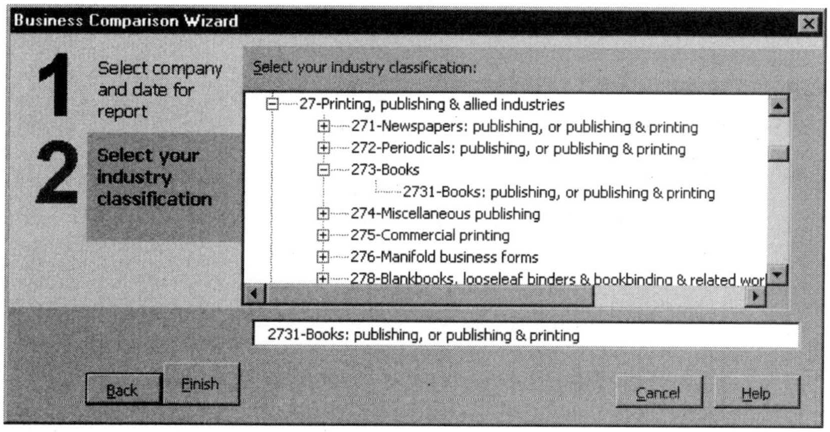

Figure 7-7 The second Business Comparison Wizard dialog box.

3. **Select the industry in which the company operates.**

The Business Comparison Wizard organizes industries into a tree diagram. To expand a tree branch, click its plus sign. To collapse a tree branch, click its minus sign. When you find the industry that most closely matches your company, click it and then click the Finish button. The Business Comparison Wizard compares your company to the industry averages, producing a report similar to the one shown in Figure 7-8.

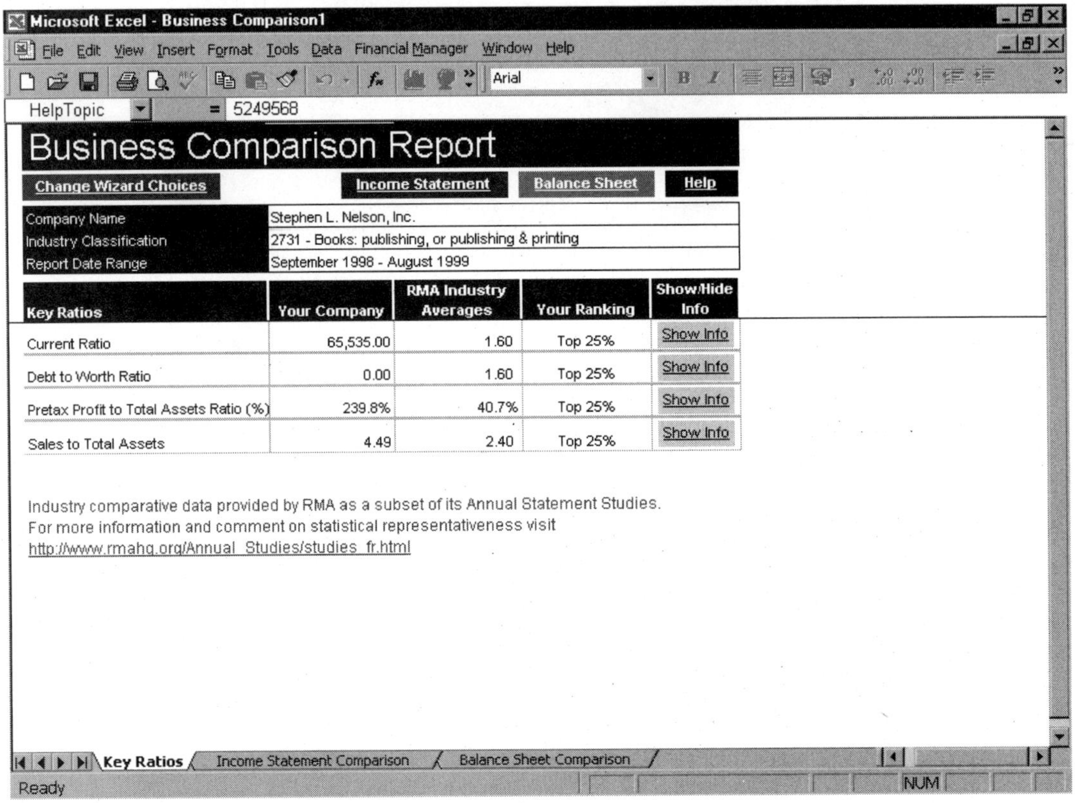

Figure 7-8 The first page of a Business Comparison report.

Although the Business Comparison tool produces thought-provoking data, unfortunately, many business users will find its information of very limited value. For one thing, the effectiveness of the comparison depends to a great extent on how closely a business matches the selected industry classification. If a company truly resembles the industry into which it's placed, the comparison may be very useful. If a company doesn't resemble the industry, however, the comparison may be meaningless.

Another issue concerns the accounting policies and conventions used both by the company and the industry. Even large companies show considerable variety and creativity in the accounting policies they adopt and the conventions they follow. And we can only assume that small companies show even more variety and creativity. Differences in accounting treatment, of course, also make comparisons more difficult.

Using the Buy Vs. Lease Tool

The Buy Vs. Lease tool helps you choose between buying or leasing some asset. The Buy Vs. Lease Wizard is perhaps most useful for forecasting the cash flows that stem from an asset purchase. Predictably, the wizard suggests that you borrow to buy an asset when the cost of borrowing is less than the cost of capital. For this reason, you don't really need to use the wizard to determine which financing option works best: the cheapest financing option is the cheapest financing option.

The Buy Vs. Lease Wizard is more useful, however, when you want to explore the effects of a purchase on your cash flows. In small companies, perhaps especially those that are growing, the cash flow effect of an asset purchase becomes a major issue—sometimes one that's more important than net present value measures.

To use the Buy Vs. Lease tool, follow these steps:

1. **Start the Buy Vs. Lease Wizard.**

   Click the Analyze button on the Startup Screen, and then select a Buy Vs. Lease item from the list box in the Select A Financial Manager Analysis Tool dialog box. Excel displays the first Buy Vs. Lease Wizard dialog box, as shown in Figure 7-9.

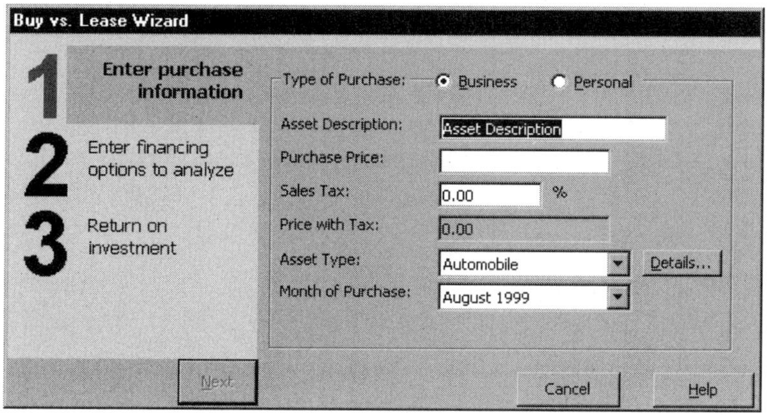

Figure 7-9 The first Buy Vs. Lease Wizard dialog box.

2. **Describe the asset.**

   Use the first Buy Vs. Lease Wizard dialog box to describe the asset you may buy or lease. Use the Type Of Purchase buttons to indicate whether the asset is a business or personal asset. Use the Asset Description box to name the asset. Use the Purchase Price box to provide the asset's purchase price. Use the Sales Tax box to provide the sales tax percentage that will be charged in addition to the purchase price. Use the Asset Type drop-down list box to identify the asset category. Finally, use the Month Of Purchase box to indicate when you'll purchase the asset. When you've provided this information, click Next. Excel displays the second Buy Vs. Lease Wizard dialog box, as shown in Figure 7-10.

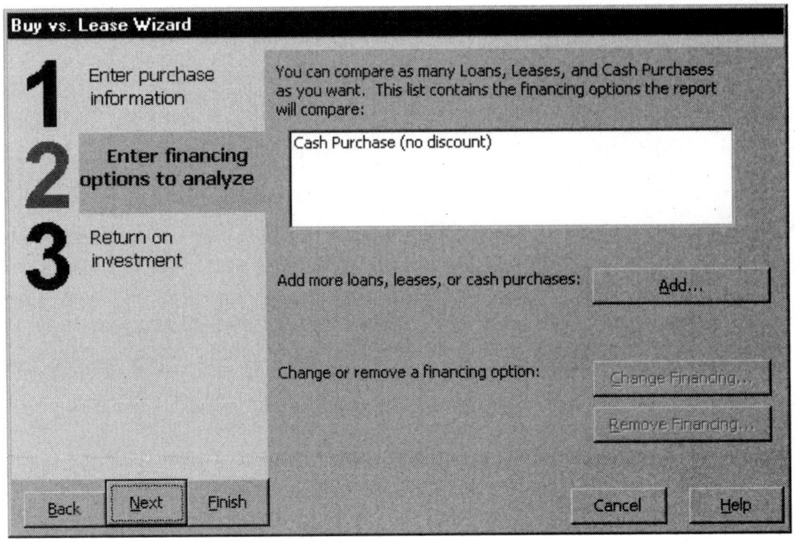

Figure 7-10 The second Buy Vs. Lease Wizard dialog box.

NOTE *The Asset Type and Month Of Purchase information lets the wizard correctly calculate the tax effects of your purchase.*

3. Describe each of the financing alternatives.

Initially the second Buy Vs. Lease Wizard dialog box lists a single financing alternative—that of buying the asset for cash. You can add more financial alternatives by clicking the Add button and then providing a description of the alternative by clicking buttons and filling in boxes. To add a loan-financing alternative, for example, click Add. When the wizard asks what kind of financing option you're adding, click Loan Purchase and then click OK. When the wizard displays the Loan Purchase Information dialog box, enter the loan down payment, interest rate, and repayment term information. To describe other financial alternatives, repeat this process. When you've provided information on each of your financing alternatives, click Next. Excel displays the third Buy Vs. Lease Wizard dialog box, as shown in Figure 7-11.

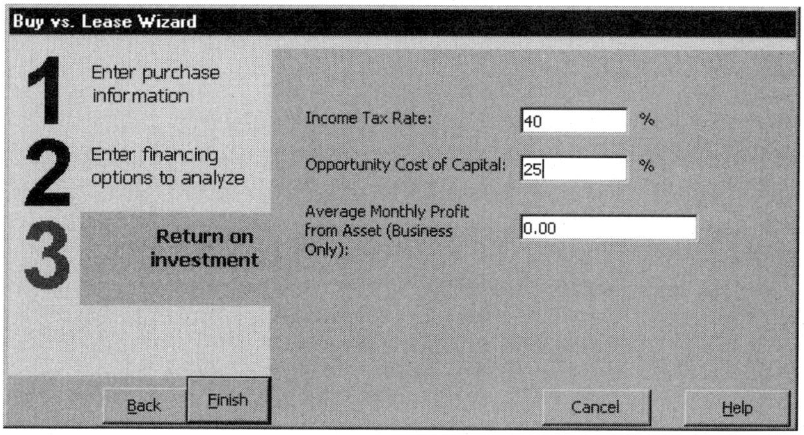

Figure 7-11 The third Buy Vs. Lease Wizard dialog box.

The Buy Vs. Lease Wizard provides a multipage report that summarizes the financial effects of the asset purchase under each of your financing alternatives. In addition, the wizard creates a depreciation schedule for a purchased asset and an amortization schedule for any loans.

4. **Describe each of the financing alternatives.**

   Use the third Buy Vs. Lease Wizard dialog box to describe your income tax rate, the cost of capital that the wizard should use in its discounted cash flow calculations, and the average monthly profit of an asset if the asset is one you'll use for business. Then click Finish.

Using the Create Projection Wizard Tool

The Create Projection Wizard tool helps you create a financial projection by inflating or deflating historical accounting data.

NOTE *After you create a financial projection, you view it by using the Projection Reports tool, which is described in the next section, "Using the Projection Reports Tool."*

To use the Create Projection Wizard tool, follow these steps:

1. **Start the Create Projection Wizard tool.**

   Click the Analyze button on the Startup Screen, select the Create Projection Wizard item from the list box in the Select A Financial Manager Analysis Tool dialog box, and then click Next. Excel displays the first Financial Manager Projection Wizard dialog box, as shown in Figure 7-12.

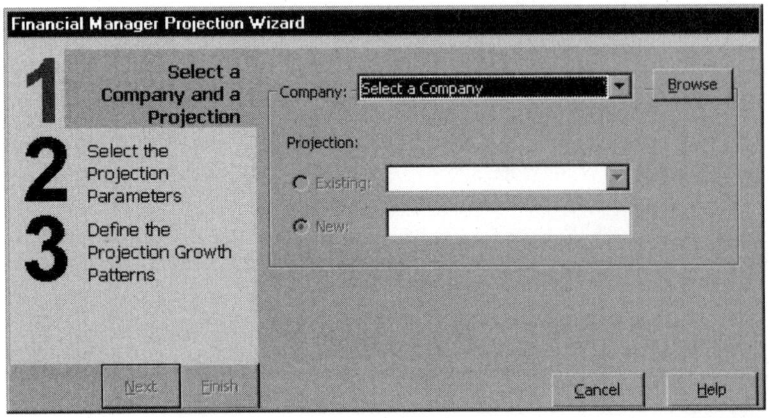

Figure 7-12 The first Financial Manager Projection Wizard dialog box.

2. **Select the company, and indicate that you want to create a new projection.**

   Select the company you want to compare, if necessary, from the Company box, and then click the New button. Name your projection using the Name box, and then click Next. Excel displays the second Financial Manager Projection Wizard dialog box, as shown in Figure 7-13.

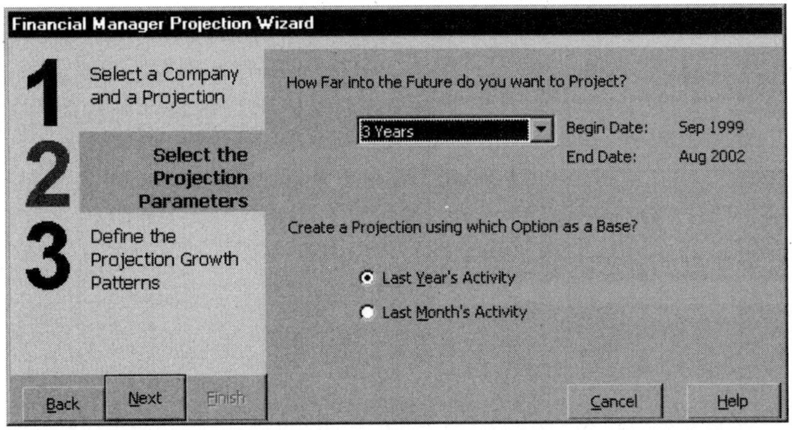

Figure 7-13 The second Financial Manager Projection Wizard dialog box.

3. **Describe the forecasting horizon.**

   Use the How Far Into The Future Do You Want To Project box to indicate how many months or years into the future you want to project.

4. **Tell the wizard what the projection should be based on.**

   Use the Last Year's Activity and Last Month's Activity option buttons to indicate what data you want to base your projection on. Then click Next. Excel displays the third Financial Manager Projection Wizard dialog box, as shown in Figure 7-14.

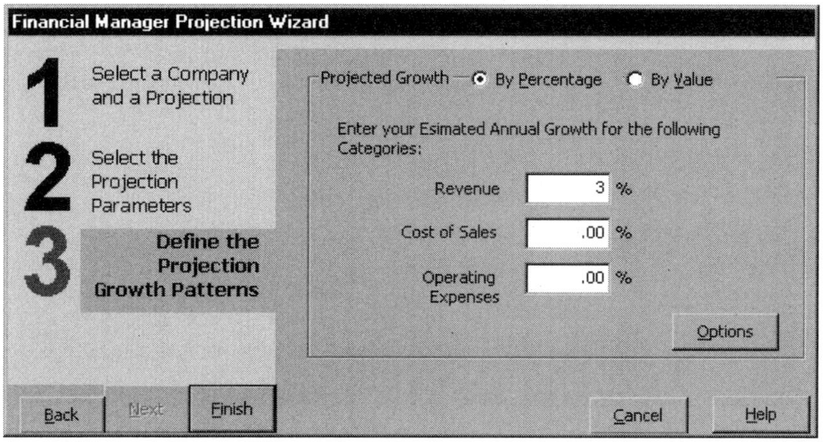

Figure 7-14 The third Financial Manager Projection Wizard dialog box.

5. **Tell the wizard how to change the base values.**

   Click the By Percentage option button if you want the wizard to inflate or deflate base values by a set percentage. Alternatively, click the By Value option button if you want the wizard to inflate or deflate base values by some stated value. Once you indicate whether you want to change the base values based by a percentage or value, use the Revenue, Cost Of Sales, and Operating Expenses boxes to provide the percentage or value. Click the Finish button to direct the wizard to create the projection based on your directions.

NOTE *You can click the Options button, which appears on the third Financial Manager Projection Wizard dialog box, to display still another dialog box which gives you far finer control over the way that base values are adjusted.*

When the wizard finishes creating your projection, click OK. You can use the Projection Reports tool, which is described in the next section, to view the projection.

Using the Projection Reports Tool

After you create a projection—which is actually just a set of numbers created by the Create Projection Wizard—you can produce a report based on the projection. To produce such a report, follow these steps:

1. **Start the Projection Reports tool.**

   Click the Analyze button on the Startup Screen, and then select the Projection Reports item from the list box in the Select A Financial Manager Analysis Tool dialog box. Excel displays the first Create A Projection Report dialog box, as shown in Figure 7-15.

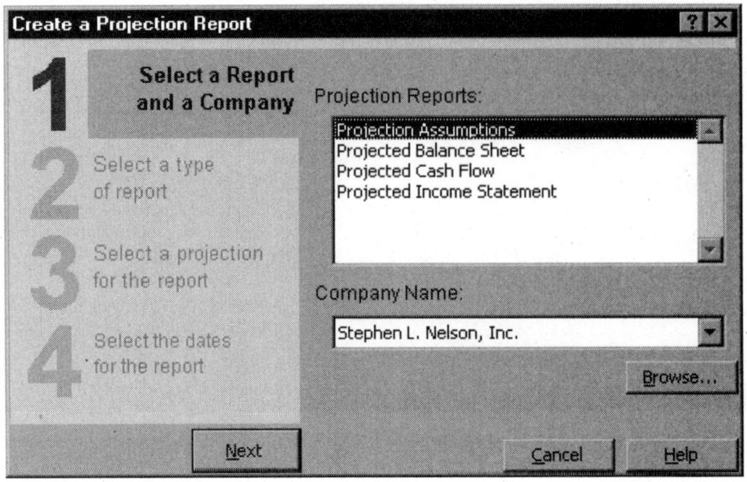

Figure 7-15 The first Create A Projection Report dialog box.

2. **Select a report category.**

   Select a report category by clicking one of the entries in the Projection Reports list box.

3. **Select the company.**

   If necessary, select the company you want to compare from the Company box. Then click Next. Excel displays the second Create A Projection Report dialog box, as shown in Figure 7-16.

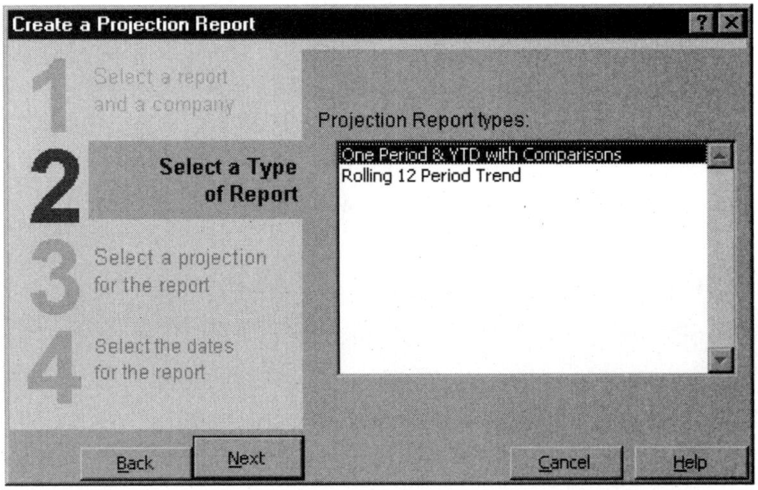

Figure 7-16 The second Create A Projection Report dialog box.

4. **Select the specific report.**

   Select the specific type of report you want to prepare by clicking one of the reports listed in the Projection Report Types list box. Then click Next. Excel displays the third Create A Financial Report dialog box, as shown in Figure 7-17.

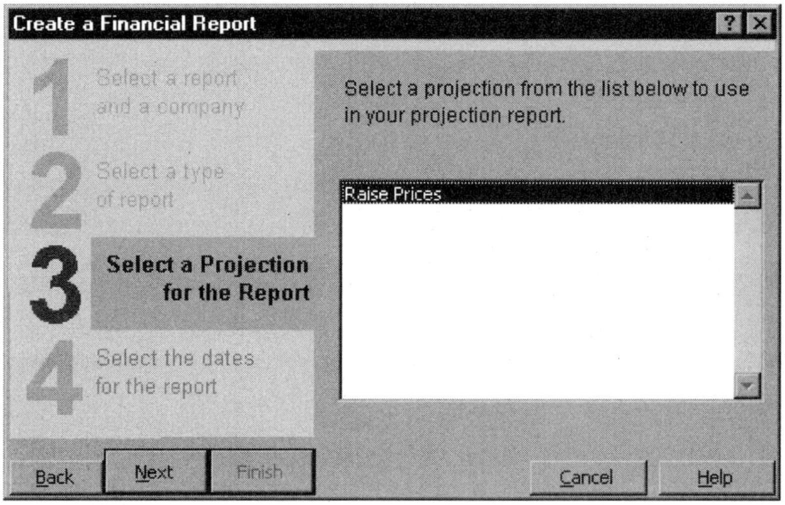

Figure 7-17 The third Create A Financial Report dialog box.

5. **Select the projection to use.**

   Select the projection you want to use to create the report by clicking it in the only list box provided by the third Create A Financial Report dialog box. Then click Next. Excel displays the fourth Create A Financial Report dialog box, as shown in Figure 7-18.

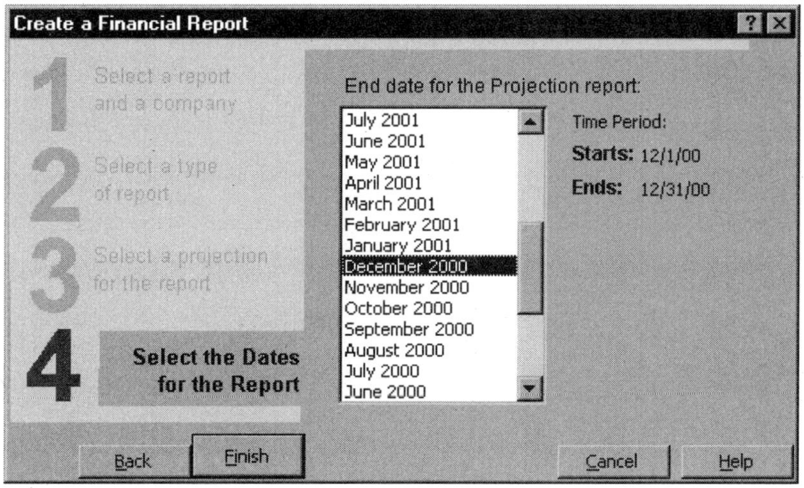

Figure 7-18 The fourth Create A Financial Report dialog box.

6. **Select an end date for the projection report.**

   Select an end date for the projection report by clicking one of the end dates listed in the fourth Create A Financial Report dialog box. Click the Finish button to direct the wizard to create the projection report using the specified projection.

Excel adds new worksheets to the workbook showing pro forma financial statements based on your projections.

Using the What-If Analysis Tool

The What-If Analysis tool creates a workbook you can use to perform what-if analysis. For example, you can experiment with changing sales or expenses, vendor payment terms and customer financing terms, and bank financing agreements.

Creating a What-If Workbook

To create the what-if analysis workbook, which you'll use to perform your what-if modeling, follow these steps:

1. **Start the What-If Analysis tool.**

   Click the Analyze button on the Startup Screen, and then select the What-If Analysis item from the list box in the Select A Financial Manager Analysis Tool dialog box. Excel displays the first Perform A What-If Analysis dialog box, as shown in Figure 7-19.

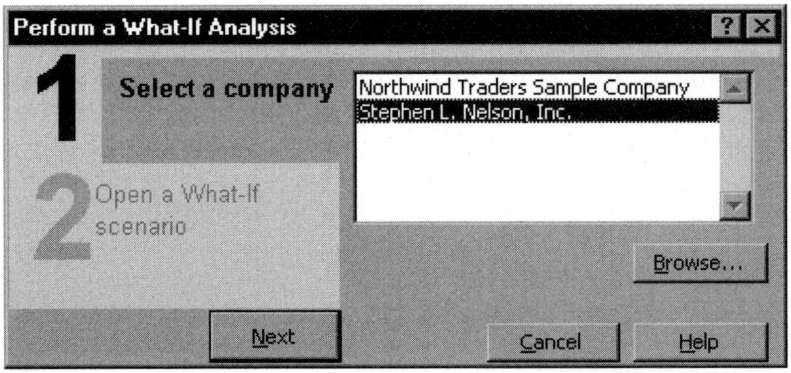

Figure 7-19 The first Perform A What-If Analysis dialog box.

2. **Select the company.**

   Select the company you want to analyze, and click Next. Excel displays the second Perform A What-If Analysis dialog box, as shown in Figure 7-20.

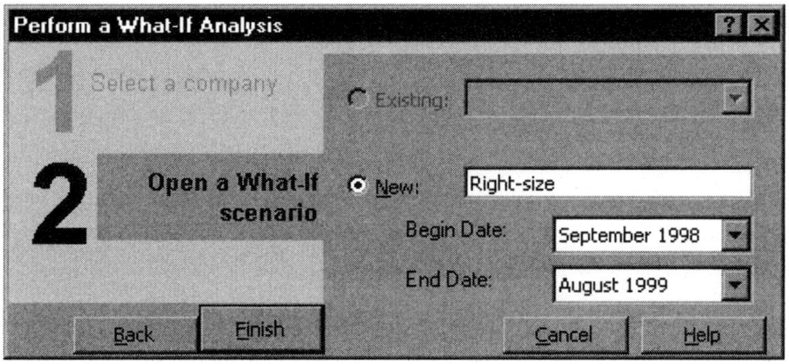

Figure 7-20 The second Perform A What-If Analysis dialog box.

3. Indicate that you want to create a new what-if analysis.

Click the New option button, and then give a name to your what-if analysis. Provide begin and end dates for the analysis using the Begin Date and End Date boxes, and then click Next. Excel displays the Save As dialog box.

NOTE *After you create a what-if projection, you can also use the second Perform A What-If Analysis dialog box to select a what-if analysis from the Existing box.*

4. Save the what-if analysis.

Use the Save As dialog box to save your what-if analysis. Use the File Name box to name the new what-if analysis workbook. And use the Save In box to choose a folder location. After you specify the name and location of the what-if analysis, click the Save button. Excel creates and saves the what-if analysis workbook and displays its overview worksheet, as shown in Figure 7-21.

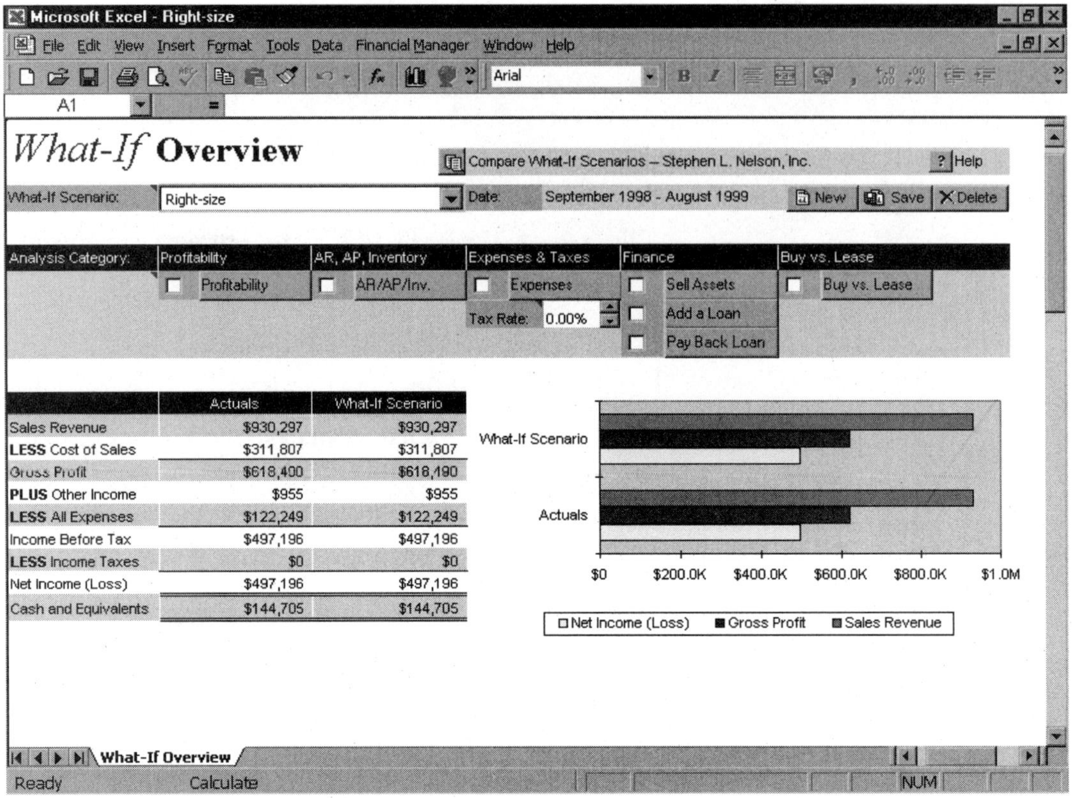

Figure 7-21 The what-if analysis overview worksheet.

Using a What-If Workbook

Once you create the what-if analysis workbook, you use the analysis boxes and buttons to ask your what-if questions.

To ask what-if questions about how sales affect your profitability, for example, click the Profitability button. When Excel displays a dialog box listing the ways that your accounting data reports sales, select a sales category and click OK. Excel next displays a new worksheet, as shown in Figure 7-22, that lets you see sales by the selected category. To change some number, click the cell and then type your new number. To return to the overview worksheet, click the What-If Overview button.

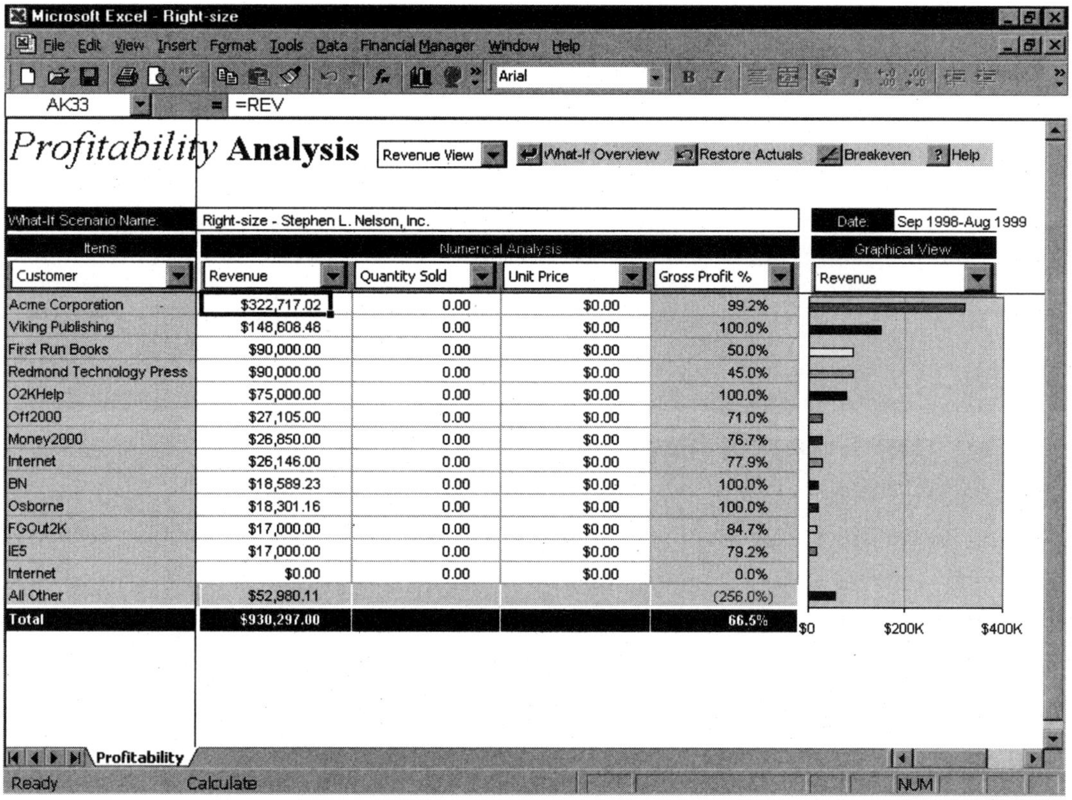

Figure 7-22 The what-if analysis profitability worksheet.

NOTE *You can change the information displayed in the what-if profitability worksheet by clicking the column heading drop-down list boxes and selecting an entry.*

To ask what-if questions about how accounts payable and accounts receivable payment terms and inventory balances affect your cash flow, click the AR/AP/Inv. button. When Excel displays a new worksheet that lets you see accounts receivable, accounts payable, and inventory detail, change these asset or liability values by clicking cells and then typing your new numbers. Or, adjust the slider button that corresponds to the item you want to experiment with.

To ask what-if questions about how expenses affect your profitability, click the Expenses button. When Excel displays a new worksheet that lets you see expenses by account, change expense values by clicking cells and then typing your new numbers. Or, adjust the slider button that corresponds to an expense.

To create asset purchase and financing what-if scenarios, click one of the Finance buttons or the Buy Vs. Lease button. When Excel displays a dialog box, describe the scenario and click OK.

The what-if analysis overview worksheet provides several other buttons worth mentioning. You can create a new what-if scenario by clicking the New button and then providing a name when prompted. Excel creates the new scenario by using the existing scenarios values, but as you make changes your new scenario evolves. You can display another scenario by choosing it from the drop-down list box in the top-left corner of the overview worksheet. Finally, you can save the workbook by clicking the Save button or delete the workbook by clicking the Delete button.

Using the Chart Wizard

You use the Small Business Financial Manager's Chart Wizard to create financial charts of your imported accounting data. To use the Chart Wizard, follow these steps:

NOTE *The Small Business Financial Manager's Chart Wizard is not the same as Excel's regular Chart Wizard. Chapter 2 describes how to use that feature.*

1. **Start the Chart Wizard.**

   You can do this either by choosing the Financial Manager menu's Chart Wizard command or by clicking the Chart button on the Startup Screen.

2. **Select the category of financial chart you want to create.**

   To select a financial chart category, click an entry in the Financial Charts list box, as shown in Figure 7-23. After you select a financial chart category and select the company name, if necessary, click Next.

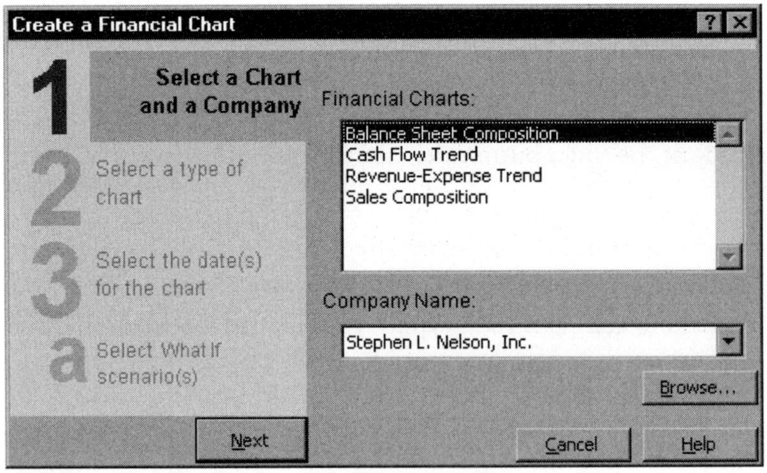

Figure 7-23 The first Create A Financial Chart dialog box.

NOTE *If Small Business Financial Manager requests it, provide the user name and database password you created during the importation of your accounting data.*

3. Select the type of report you want.

When Excel asks what type of chart you want, use the boxes and buttons provided to describe it. Then click Next.

NOTE *Different financial chart categories provide you with different reporting options.*

4. Select an end date for the report.

When Excel asks for the chart end or as-of date, select an entry from the list box. Then click the Finish button.

The Chart Wizard creates a financial chart according to your instructions and places the chart on a new sheet in the open workbook. Figure 7-24 shows an example of a financial chart, a cash flow trend chart for January 1998 through August 1999.

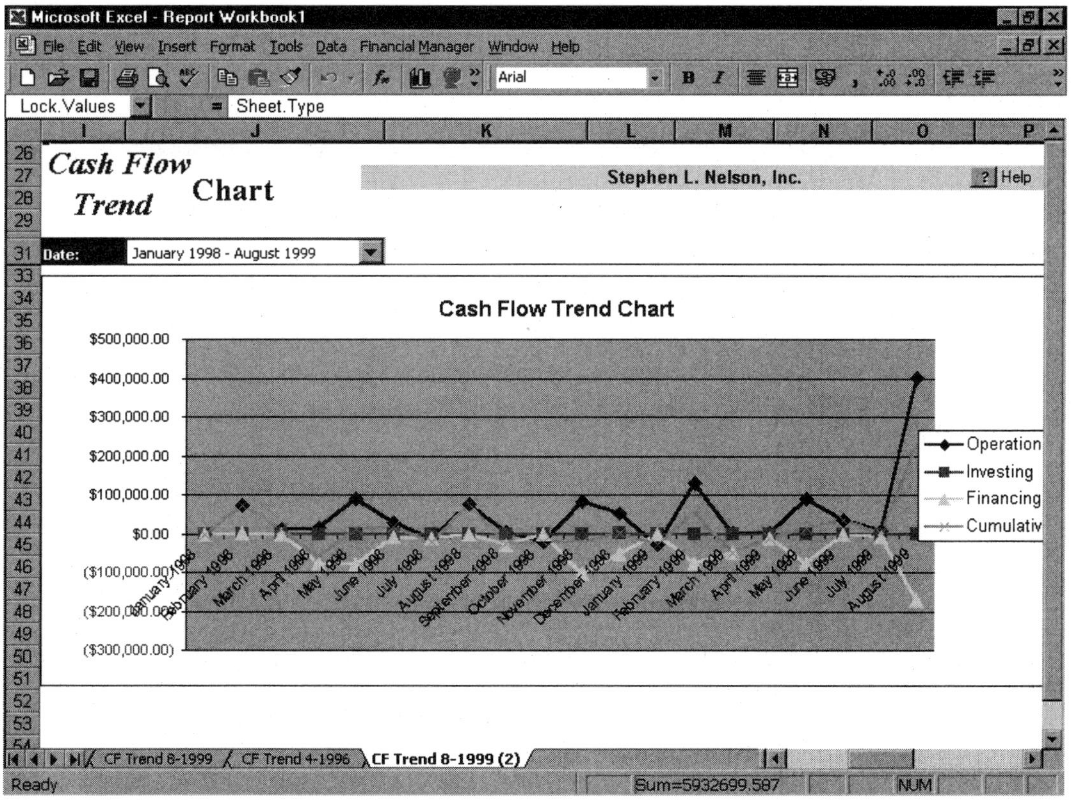

Figure 7-24 An example financial chart created by the Chart Wizard.

Refreshing the Imported Data

Over time, of course, your accounting database changes as it's updated to reflect new activity. To refresh the imported data for these changes, simply click the Update button, which appears on the Startup Screen of the Small Business Financial Manager workbook. The Small Business Financial Manager prompts you for your password, and then it imports any new data needed to refresh the database used by the Small Business Financial Manager.

Rearranging and Modifying Imported Data

One problem of working with the Small Business Financial Manager is that it expects your chart of accounts—the list of accounts you use—to be organized in a very conventional way. If you haven't organized your chart of accounts this way, you may need to rearrange, or remap, the data.

To remap the data, choose the Financial Manager menu's Remap Data command. When Excel displays the Map Your Accounts dialog box, as shown in Figure 7-25, review the organization of the accounts as shown in the tree diagram. If you see an account grouped incorrectly, drag it to its correct location.

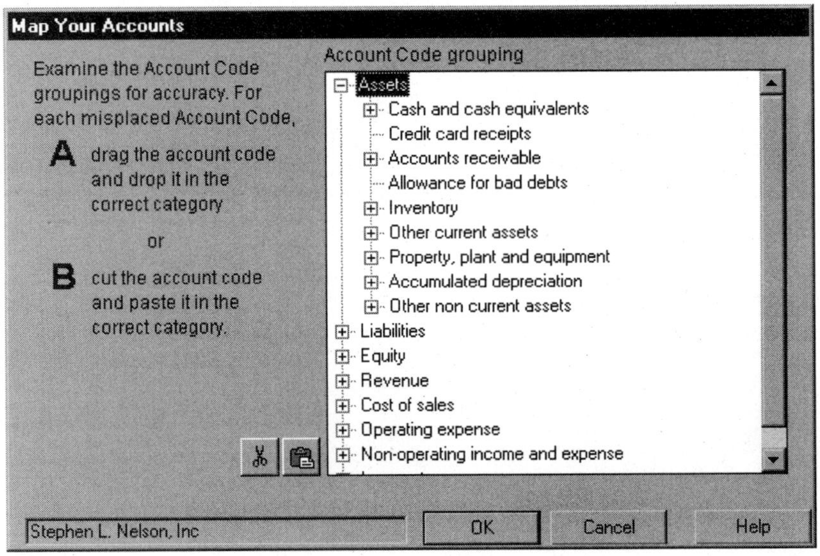

Figure 7-25 The Map Your Accounts dialog box.

NOTE *The Financial Manager menu also provides an Insert Balance command, which you can use to place a specific account balance or full account information in the active cell.*

GLOSSARY

absolute cell reference

A **cell reference** that isn't adjusted by Excel as it's copied.

active cell

The currently selected **cell** on an Excel **worksheet.**

active sheet

The currently selected (and usually visible) sheet in an Excel **worksheet.**

alignment

How Excel positions **labels** and **values** in **cells.** Typically, labels are left-aligned and values are right-aligned.

area chart

An area **chart** plots **data point** values using lines. Optimally, they stack the lines so they show cumulative **data point values** and color the areas between the lines.

argument

The input value supplied to an Excel **function.** Functions can use **values, formulas,** and even other functions as arguments.

array

A set of numbers stored in a row or column.

array formula

An array formula uses one **formula** to calculate an **array** of numbers.

bar chart

A bar **chart** plots **data point** values in individual bars but arranges the bars so you calibrate them using a horizontal **values** axis.

Boolean formulas

Boolean formulas make logical comparisons using operators such as equal to, greater than, and less than. If the comparison is true, the Boolean formula returns one. If the comparison isn't true, the formula returns zero.

bubble chart

A bubble **chart** treats the horizontal axis as a second values axis, thereby plotting pairs of **data points** just as XY charts do. Bubble charts differ from XY charts, however, in that Excel sizes the bubbles using the values of a third data point.

cell

The intersection of a row and column, a cell is the place on the Excel **worksheet** where you enter or edit **labels, values, functions,** or **formulas.**

cell protection

Cell formatting that prevents a user from entering information into a cell or changing the contents of a cell.

cell reference

Each **cell** has an address, called a *reference,* consisting of the column letter and row number. For example, the cell in the top left corner of the **worksheet** is cell A1.

cell selector

A dark outline that identifies the **active cell.** The reference of the active cell also appears on the left side of the **formula bar** in the Name box. If you type a number and press the Enter key, Excel places the number in the active cell.

chart

A graphical representation of the data in an Excel **worksheet.**

chart area

The area in an Excel **chart** that includes plot area, any **chart text,** and a **legend.**

chart text

A description of a **chart** or some part of a chart.

chart type

Excel supplies 14 different types of charts: Column, Bar, Line, Pie, XY (Scatter), Area, Doughnut, Radar, Surface, Bubble, Stock, Cylinder, Cone, and Pyramid. Each chart type uses unique **data markers.**

Chart Wizard

The Excel tool used to quickly and easily create professional, presentation-quality **charts** based on **worksheet** data.

Clip art

Pictures you can paste into a **workbook.**

Clipboard

A temporary storage area that Windows programs like Excel use to hold items you copy.

Column chart

A column **chart** plots **data point** values in individual bars but arranges the bars so you calibrate them using a vertical values axis.

conditional formatting

Cell formatting that shows only if the contents of a cell meet certain criteria.

cone chart

A cone **chart** plots **data point** values in individual three-dimensional cones. Cone charts use either horizontal or vertical category axes.

criteria

Conditions you specify for **filtering** and **sorting** a **database.**

cylinder chart

A cylinder **chart** plots **data point** values in individual three-dimensional cylinders. Cylinder charts use either horizontal or vertical category axes.

database

A **range** of common information, arranged in consecutive rows and columns. Each **cell** in a row in a database contains unique data, while each cell in a column contains similar data.

data category

A set of related **data points** in an Excel **chart.**

data map

A **chart** that maps geographic data. Excel doesn't create data maps, but the MapPoint program, which comes with Excel, will.

data marker

Graphical elements used to represent individual **data point values** in a **chart,** such as a symbol or point in a line chart.

data marker description

An explanation of **data markers,** such as axis scales and data **labels.**

data point

Individual **values** of a **chart** created from an Excel **worksheet.**

data series

Values that are related in an Excel **chart.**

data table

A table of data that calculates results based on changing one input variable of one or more **formulas** or changing two input variables in a formula.

date values

Values that represent dates. Typically, date values are formatted so they look like recognizable dates and not values. By convention, the number 1 represents January 1, 1900.

dependent cell

A **cell** that depends on, or references, another cell's **formula** results.

doughnut chart

A doughnut **chart** works similar to pie charts, plotting **data series** in concentric rings and showing each **data point value** as a segment, or "bite," of the ring.

drag and drop

A technique for copying and moving information by using the mouse. You *drag* your selection to the desired new location and when you release the mouse, it *drops* into place.

field

A column of similar data in a **database.**

filter

A process where only the **records** based on a criteria you specify are displayed in a **database.**

form

A dialog box you use to enter database **records** into a **database.**

formula

An equation you create and enter into Excel. Formulas begin with an equal sign (=) and include standard mathematical operators and parentheses as appropriate.

formula bar

The bar directly above the **worksheet** window that displays the **label, value, function,** or **formula** in the selected worksheet **cell.**

formula errors

It's possible to build an illogical or unsolvable **formula.** When you do, Excel displays an error message in the **cell** rather than calculating the result. The error message, which begins with the # symbol, describes the formula error.

formula

Excel lets you enter formulas into worksheet **cells.** Excel doesn't display the formula, however, in the **worksheet.** It calculates and then displays the formula result. (You can see the formula in the **formula bar.**) A formula begins with the = symbol and then uses other operators (+, -, *, and /) and numbers.

function

A predefined **formula** in Excel, such as SUM.

Goal Seek

The Goal Seek command determines which input **value** for a **formula** produces a specified formula result.

HTML

An abbreviation for Hypertext Markup Language, the language used to create documents that display in a Web browser program.

label

A text entry in an Excel **worksheet** that describes quantitative data.

legend

A legend names and identifies the **data series** in an Excel **chart.**

line chart

A line chart plots individual **data points** in a line, using either different **data marker** symbols or different colored lines to distinguish the **data series,** and using a horizontal data category axis.

Microsoft Office User Specialist (MOUS)

A person who has passed the Microsoft Office User Specialist (MOUS) certification test at either the proficient user level or the expert user level.

OLE

A Microsoft Windows tool for sharing data. With OLE, or Object Linking and Embedding, you can transfer data between Excel and other Windows programs by copying and pasting.

operator precedence

The set of mathematical rules that specify in which order mathematical operations should occur in a **formula.** Excel follows standard rules of operator precedence and first performs exponential operations, then multiplication and division operations, and finally, addition and subtraction. (To override these rules, you must use parentheses.)

pie chart

A pie chart shows a single **data series** and depicts individual **data points** as segments of the circle, or slices of the pie.

PivotChart

A **chart** based on **PivotTable** data. You manipulate PivotCharts in much the same way as you manipulate PivotTables—by dragging field buttons to different axes.

PivotTable

An Excel feature that enables you to **sort, filter,** and pivot data in a manner that displays important information more clearly.

plot area

The area in an Excel **chart** that includes **data markers** and **data marker descriptions.**

precedent cell

A **cell** that supplies its **formula** result to another cell for its formula.

Query Wizard

An Excel tool that retrieves data from an external **database** for analysis inside Excel.

radar chart

A radar **chart** plots each data category's **data point values** on separate value axes and connects the data point values of each **data series** with a line.

range

A rectangular area of the **worksheet,** such as a two-cell by two-cell square, a five-cell by nine-cell rectangle, or even an entire worksheet. Excel uses opposite corner **cell references** and a colon to define ranges.

range name

A single **cell** or group of cells you designate with a name. **Range** names simplify the process of creating **formulas.**

record

A row of data in a **database.**

relational database

A more complex **database** with multiple tables linked together. You can't build a relational database using Excel. You need to use a relational database program such as Microsoft Access.

relative cell reference

A **cell reference** that, if copied, gets adjusted by Excel.

Scenario Manager

An Excel tool that lets you change several **cell values** at a time and explore the effect on large numbers of **formulas.**

scientific notation

A method used to express very large or very small numbers in an abbreviated form. For example, if a **value** is too large to fit into a single **cell,** Excel either increases the cell width or displays the cell contents using scientific notation. The number 123456789, for example, may appear as something like 1.2E+08 or 1.235E+08, depending on the width of the cell. Likewise, the number .0000001 may appear as something like 1E-07.

Small Business Finance Manager

An Excel tool that extracts financial information from an accounting program's **database** and then helps you analyze this information.

Solver

Excel's Solver tool lets you solve optimization-modeling problems, also commonly known as linear programming problems. With an optimization-modeling problem, you optimize an objective function while at the same time recognizing that there are constraints, or limits.

sort

Arranging data in a **database** in ascending or descending order.

status bar

The bar directly above the Windows taskbar that displays information about a command or an Excel process that is running. CAPS, SCROLL, or NUM are displayed on the right side of the status bar when the corresponding key is active.

stock chart

A stock **chart** plots security prices in a common open-high-low-close format.

surface chart

A surface **chart** plots **data series** in a three-dimensional grid, generally using color not to identify data series but rather to indicate value axis **ranges.**

Task pane

The window on the right side of the **workbook** window that provides easy access to Workbook, **Clipboard,** and Search capabilities.

title bar

The Microsoft Excel title bar presents the title of the program and appears at the top of the program window, just above the menu bar.

toolbar

The toolbar or toolbars, located just below the menu bar, provide a series of buttons that allow for faster selection of frequently used menu commands.

value

A number in a **worksheet** that can be used in formulas to calculate a result.

Web Query

An Excel tool you can use to retrieve tabular data from a Web page.

what-if analysis

The process of changing one or more input variables to determine the effect on a calculated result.

workbook

An Excel file that contains at least one **worksheet.** The standard Excel workbook contains three worksheets. An Excel workbook file extension is .xls.

workgroup

A group of individuals who use the same Excel **workbook.**

worksheet

A grid of **cells** that you enter **labels, values,** and **formulas** in Excel. One or more worksheets comprise an Excel **workbook.**

XY (scatter) chart

An XY (scatter) **chart** lets you visually explore the relationships between **data series** by treating the horizontal axis as a second values axis. To accomplish this, XY charts actually plot pairs of **data points.**

Index

C

D

E

F

G

N

O

P

Q

R

S

T

U

V

W

X

The manuscript for this book was prepared and submitted to Redmond Technology Press in electronic form. Text files were prepared using Microsoft Word 2000. Pages were composed using PageMaker 6.5 for Windows, with text in Frutiger and Caslon. Composed files were delivered to the printer as electronic prepress files.

Project Editor

Paula Thurman

Layout

Minh-Tam S. Le

Indexer

Julie Kawabata

Need a fast overview of PowerPoint 2002 so you can get back to your business or job?

Written specifically for busy executives, managers, and other professionals, ***Effective Executive's Guide to PowerPoint 2002*** walks you through the seven steps of creating high-value, high-impact presentations:

> **Step 1: Learn the Logic.** Start here with an overview of what PowerPoint is and how it helps you make better presentations.
> **Step 2: Outline Your Content.** Create a textual list, or *outline,* of the messages and points you want to share.
> **Step 3: Add Objects.** Use tables, charts, and pictures to augment the information in your outline.
> **Step 4: Design Your Look.** Move past the substance of your presentation and address its appearance and "look" to create a professional presentation.
> **Step 5: Add Special Effects.** Use transitions, animation, sound, and video to enhance your presentation's impact.
> **Step 6: Prepare Your Presentation.** Prepare by creating speaker's notes, rehearsing, producing any handouts, and tailoring your presentation's slides for the presentation method.
> **Step 7: Deliver Your Presentation.** Deliver a successful, memorable presentation to your audience by comfortably using the appropriate PowerPoint tools.

Appendixes then suggest how to use Microsoft Graph and WordArt more effectively and explain how to customize PowerPoint. More than just a book about PowerPoint, ***Effective Executive's Guide to PowerPoint 2002*** explains how to make effective, compelling presentations that audiences understand and remember.

ABOUT THE AUTHORS

With more than 3 million books sold in English, **Stephen L. Nelson** is arguably the best-selling author writing about using computers in business. Formerly a senior consultant with Arthur Andersen & Co., he is also the co-author of ***MBA's Guide to the Internet*** (Redmond Technology Press, 2000).

The President of APPLAUSE! Associates, **Michael Buschmohle** has more than 40 years' experience delivering presentations to Fortune 500 companies and government agencies. He coaches CEOs, executives of high-tech firms, attorneys, U.S. mayors, and government officials on presentation and media skills. His clients have appeared on *Oprah, Good Morning America,* and the *Today* show.

256 pages, paperback, $24.95 — Available at bookstores everywhere and at all online bookstores

ISBN: 1-931150-00-1

Need a fast overview of Outlook 2002 so you can get back to your business or job?

Written specifically for busy executives, managers, and other professionals, ***Effective Executive's Guide to Outlook 2002*** provides a fast-paced summary of the seven core skills you need to know to use Microsoft® Outlook 2002 at work, on the road, or at home:

> **Skill 1: Getting Started with Outlook.** Skill 1 shows you how to set up Outlook and explains its interface.
>
> **Skill 2: Reading E-Mail.** Skill 2 explains how to check for new messages, read messages, work with attachments, and protect yourself from viruses and virus hoaxes.
>
> **Skill 3: Sending E-Mail.** Skill 3 shows you how to send and deliver messages and provides useful related information on addressing, composing, and delivering e-mail messages.
>
> **Skill 4: Managing Your E-Mail.** Skill 4 covers topics such as finding and organizing messages, creating message templates, and setting up Outlook to automatically process your e-mail and filter out junk e-mail (spam).
>
> **Skill 5: Using a Contacts List.** Skill 5 discusses how to create, edit, and use Outlook contact items and distribution lists, how to share contact information, and how to manage multiple contacts lists.
>
> **Skill 6: Managing Your Time.** Skill 6 shows you how to use the Outlook Calendar to make appointments, schedule meetings, and track tasks that you need to accomplish.
>
> **Skill 7: Maintaining Outlook.** Skill 7 explains how to keep Outlook running smoothly by managing your data files and e-mail accounts, backing up your data files and settings, and customizing Outlook.

Effective Executive's Guide to Outlook 2002 also includes appendixes that show you how to use the Outlook Notes feature, how to use Outlook with Exchange Server, and how to automatically process form data (such as may be sent from a Web site).

ABOUT THE AUTHORS

Jason Gerend, a Microsoft Certified Systems Engineer, has co-authored a series of acclaimed and bestselling computer books, including ***New Webmaster's Guide to FrontPage 2002*** (Redmond Technology Press, 2001).

Charles Bermant writes the popular Inbox column for the *Seattle Times,* a weekly discussion of e-mail behavior.

272 pages, paperback, $24.95
ISBN: 1-931150-04-4

Available at bookstores everywhere and at all online bookstores

Need a fast overview of Office XP so you can get back to your business or job?

Written specifically for busy executives, managers, and other professionals, ***Effective Executive's Guide to Office XP*** provides a fast-paced summary of the seven core skills you need to know to use Microsoft® Office XP at work, on the road, or at home:

Skill 1: Use Common Office Tools. One of the great advantages of the Office suite is that the applications look, and to a certain extent, act alike. Skill 1 discusses these common tools, including the toolbars, the Clipboard, and Office Help.

Skill 2: Manage Files. Skill 2 shows you how to create new document files and save, close, and reopen them. You also learn how to print from any of the Office programs.

Skill 3: Use Outlook for Easy Organization. Skill 3 explains how to use Outlook for e-mail, scheduling appointments, tracking contacts, and managing your task lists.

Skill 4: Use Word for Document Generation. Skill 4 covers entering and editing text (including the new Speech Recognition feature), formatting documents, and using editing tools (like the spelling and grammar checkers).

Skill 5: Use Excel for Spreadsheet Functions. From writing formulas and using functions to formatting data and creating charts—everything you need to know about Excel spreadsheets is discussed in Skill 5.

Skill 6: Use PowerPoint for Professional Presentations. For detailed information on creating effective PowerPoint presentations, turn to Skill 6.

Skill 7: Use Access for Data Management. Skill 7 explains the four basic elements of Access and then describes how to use wizards to create database solutions.

ABOUT THE AUTHORS

Carolyn M. Connally, a writer and editor, has more than five years of experience teaching business professionals and executives how to use Microsoft Access. Connally also contributed to the ***MBA's Guide to Microsoft Office XP*** (Redmond Technology Press, 2001).

With more than 3 million books sold in English, **Stephen L. Nelson** is arguably the bestselling author writing about using computers in business. Formerly a senior consultant with Arthur Andersen & Co., he is also the co-author of ***MBA's Guide to Microsoft Excel 2002*** (Redmond Technology Press, 2001).

288 pages, paperback, $24.95
ISBN: 1-931150-07-9

Available at bookstores everywhere and at all online bookstores

Need a fast overview of Internet so you can get back to your business or job?

Written specifically for busy executives, managers, and other professionals, ***Effective Executive's Guide to the Internet*** provides a fast-paced, executive summary of the seven core skills you need to know to use the Internet at work, on the road, or at home:

Skill 1: Understanding the Environment. This skill gives you an overview of the Internet: what it is, how it works, and how it came to be.

Skill 2: Making Internet Connections. This skill provides step-by-step instructions for connecting your computer or network to the Internet.

Skill 3: Browsing the Web. This skill focuses on the Internet Explorer Web browser included with all the latest versions of Windows. We explain how a Web browser works and how to customize Internet Explorer.

Skill 4: Communicating with Electronic Mail. In this skill, we describe how to use Outlook Express, the mail and news reader included with Windows.

Skill 5: Using Search Services. This skill describes in detail how search services work and how you can best use them. A special topic at the end of this skill gives you some ways to get started gathering business information.

Skill 6: Understanding Other Internet Services. In this skill, we look at FTP, Telnet, Mailing lists, and using your computer as a fax machine and telephone.

Skill 7: Publishing on the Web. Learn how Web pages work, how to develop a Web strategy, how to set up your domain and your server, how to collect and create digital content, and how to create your Web pages.

ABOUT THE AUTHORS:

Pat Coleman writes about intranets, the Internet, and Microsoft Windows 2000. Formerly the editorial director of Microsoft Press, Coleman is also the co-author of the best-selling ***Effective Executive's Guide to Project 2000*** and ***Effective Executive's Guide to Windows 2000,*** both published by Redmond Technology Press.

Stephen L. Nelson: With more than 3 million books sold in English, Nelson is arguably the best-selling author writing about using computers in business. Formerly a senior consultant with Arthur Andersen & Co., he is also the co-author of ***Effective Executive's Guide to Project 2000*** and ***Effective Executive's Guide to PowerPoint 2000.***

288 pages, paperback, $24.95
ISBN 0-9672981-7-2

Available at bookstores everywhere and at all online bookstores.

Need a fast overview of Windows 2000 so you can get back to your business or job?

Written specifically for busy executives, managers, and other professionals, ***Effective Executive's Guide to Windows 2000*** provides a fast-paced, filtered executive summary of the seven core skills you need to know to use Microsoft Windows 2000 Professional at work, on the road, or even at home:

Skill 1: Understanding the Desktop. This skill explains logging on, using the Start menu, using the Taskbar, working with the desktop icons, and creating shortcuts.

Skill 2: Managing Files and Folders. This skill explains the Windows 2000 Professional file systems, including how to organize and protect your documents.

Skill 3: Printing. This skill shows you how to install and manage a local printer, how to print documents, how to customize the printing process, and how to install and use fonts.

Skill 4: Working on a Network. This skill gives you step-by-step instructions for setting up a small network, installing a network printer, setting up users and groups, and installing network applications.

Skill 5: Customizing Windows 2000 Professional. This skill suggests ways to customize everything from the display to the hardware.

Skill 6: Using the Internet. This skill tells you how to connect to the Internet and how to use Internet Explorer and Outlook Express.

Skill 7: Preventive Maintenance and Troubleshooting. This skill gives you guidelines for protecting the health of your computer, maintaining the system, and troubleshooting when a problem arises.

In addition, ***Effective Executive's Guide to Windows 2000*** also includes two appendixes that review the Windows 2000 Professional Accessories (including Address Book, NetMeeting, Notepad, WordPad, Fax Service, and Calculator) and explain how to use Windows 2000 Professional on a portable computer.

ABOUT THE AUTHOR:

Pat Coleman is a technical editor and author who writes about intranets, the Internet, and Microsoft Windows 2000. Coleman is also the co-author of the best-selling ***Effective Executive's Guide to Project 2000*** and ***Effective Executive's Guide to the Internet,*** both published by Redmond Technology Press.

288 pages, paperback, $24.95 Available at bookstores everywhere and at all online bookstores
ISBN: 0-9672981-8-0

Need a fast overview of Project 2000 so you can get back to your business or job?

Written specifically for busy executives and project managers, ***Effective Executives—Guide to Project 2000*** walks you through the eight steps of organizing, managing and finishing your project using Microsoft® Project 2000:

Step 1: Learn the Language. Start here with a refresher on the language of project management, and Project 2000.

Step 2: Describe the Project. Describe your project in general terms, including start date, end date, and calendar of workdays.

Step 3: Schedule Project Tasks. Break your project down into component tasks, specifying task order and relationships.

Step 4: Identify and Assign Project Resources. Identify and then allocate project resources, such as people and equipment.

Step 5: Review Project Organization. Review your project for structural soundness and reasonableness.

Step 6: Present Project to Stakeholders. Present your plan to project team members and management.

Step 7:Manage Project Progress. Monitor progress and costs, assuring your project stays on course.

Step 8: Communicate Project Status. As the project progresses, keep project team members and other stakeholders apprised of the project's status and communicate important project information and changes.

ABOUT THE AUTHORS:

With more than 3,000,000 books sold in English, **Stephen L. Nelson** is arguably the best-selling author writing about using computers in business. Nelson's project management experience includes work in software development, commercial real estate development, and book publishing.

Pat Coleman is a technical editor and author who writes about intranets, the Internet, Windows, and Windows applications. The co-author of *Mastering Intranets, Mastering Internet Explorer 4,* and *Windows 2000 Professional: In Record Time* (all published by SYBEX), Coleman has worked as the editorial director of Microsoft Press, deputy editor at World Almanac and as a project analyst at Encyclopaedia Britannica.

Kaarin Dolliver is the managing editor of Redmond Technology Press and has been a contributing editor to a series of bestselling books.

304 pages, paperback, $24.95
ISBN: 0-9672981-1-3

Available at bookstores everywhere and at all online bookstores

Looking for a thorough business reference to the Internet?

The ***MBA's Guide to the Internet: The Essential Internet Reference for Business Professionals*** is the only book that specifically describes how you can more easily, more productively, and more powerfully use the Internet as a business tool:

- The first part of the book provides QuickPrimers™ that move you to professional proficiency in all Internet skill categories, including how to connect to the Internet and how to use popular tools like the Web, e-mail, newsgroups, mailing lists, and even other more esoteric Internet tools like FTP, chat, streaming video and audio, and Telnet.
- The second part of the book—and a distinguishing feature—provides deep, rich coverage of those Internet services that are essential tools for business users: Internet search engines, fee-based services (such as Lexis-Nexis and Dun & Bradstreet), directories of business and government Internet resources, and wireless Web and e-mail services.
- The last part of the book provides thorough, step-by-step plans for accomplishing common Internet business projects, including setting up a Web site, setting up a Web store, publishing an e-mail newsletter, using the Internet for publicity and promotion, publishing PowerPoint presentations to the Web, using the Internet for recruiting and employment, setting up and using an personal or small business online banking system, and setting up and managing an online investment portfolio.
- Because the main chapters of the book describe how to use the Windows versions of Microsoft's Internet Explorer and Outlook Express programs, appendixes explain how to use Netscape Navigator and Messenger and the Macintosh versions of Internet Explorer and Outlook Express.

Written for business people who want to use the Internet, the ***MBA's Guide to the Internet*** works
for business users with graduate degrees and undergraduate degrees in business or a related field—and for anyone else who's serious about turning the Internet into a tool for making better business decisions.

ABOUT THE AUTHORS:

With more than 3 million books sold in English, **Stephen L. Nelson** is arguably the best-selling author writing about using computers in business. Nelson is also the author of the ***MBA's Guide to Microsoft Excel 2000*** (Redmond Technology Press), the best-selling Excel book for business users.

Pat Coleman is a technical editor and author who writes about intranets, the Internet, Windows, and Windows applications. Coleman is the co-author of the best-selling ***Effective Executive's Guide to Project 2000*** and the author of the ***Effective Executive's Guide to Windows 2000*** (both from Redmond Technology Press).

720 pages, paperback, $39.95 Available at bookstores everywhere and at all online bookstores

ISBN: 0-9672981-6-4

Looking for a thorough business reference to Excel 2002?

MBA's Guide to Microsoft Excel 2002: The essential Excel reference for business professionals is the only book that specifically describes how the business professional can more easily, more productively, and more powerfully use Microsoft® Excel 2002.

- **Part 1** provides friendly help on all the basics, including building simple worksheets, working with databases, and creating charts you can use for both analysis and presentation.
- **Part 2** provides rich detailed coverage of Excel business tools and features: statistical functions, financial functions, shared workbooks, PivotTables and PivotCharts, Solver, BackSolver, and Small Business Finance Manager.
- **Part 3** explains and illustrates how to use Excel for common business projects, including business planning, profit-volume-cost analysis, breakeven calculations, capital budgeting analysis, asset depreciation, and debt amortization. The companion CD supplies copies of starter workbooks for these projects (and samples of all the workbooks shown or discussed throughout the book).

Written for anyone who wants to use Excel as a business tool, ***MBA's Guide to Microsoft Excel 2002*** works for MBA students, MBA graduates, Excel users with undergraduate degrees in business or a related field—and for anyone else who's serious about using Excel as a tool for making better business decisions.

ABOUT THE AUTHORS

With more than 3 million books sold in English, **Stephen L. Nelson,** an MBA and certified public accountant, is arguably the best-selling author writing about using computers in business. Formerly a senior consultant with Arthur Andersen & Co. as well as the finance columnist for *Inc.* magazine, his recent bestsellers include *Quicken 2001 for Dummies* and *QuickBooks 2001 for Dummies* (Hungry Minds, 2001) and *MBA's Guide to the Internet* (Redmond Technology Press, 2000).

David B. Maguiness, an MBA, is a senior technical writer with Tivoli Systems and the author of *Excel Expert Solutions* (Que, 1996) as well as many other computer books and articles. Maguiness, who has held financial analyst positions with several Fortune 500 companies, is an active member of the Society for Technical Communication.

512 pages, paperback, $39.95
ISBN: 1-931150-01-X

Available at bookstores everywhere and at all online bookstores